CULTURE and
PERSONALITY

Studies in Anthropology

consulting editors

MORTON H. FRIED and
MARVIN HARRIS
columbia university

CULTURE and PERSONALITY

second edition

ANTHONY F. C. WALLACE

university of pennsylvania

random house  new york

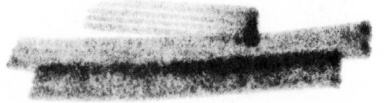

PREFACE to the second edition

Much has happened in anthropology since the publication of the first edition of *Culture and Personality* in 1961: the reporting of L. S. B. Leakey's discoveries, which affect the evolutionary time-scale discussed in Chapter II; the proliferation of formal analyses of the cognitive systems implicit in such cultural domains as folk taxonomies and mythology; the increased study of animal behavior as a source of insight into basic dimensions of human nature; and efforts from many directions to apply anthropological understandings to current social problems such as war, poverty, and the consequences of racial antagonisms. Nonetheless, I feel that the main theses of the earlier edition remain fundamental. The present edition differs from the former principally by the addition of a chapter entitled "Culture and Cognition" and by the addition or deletion of various brief sections of the original chapters, including the addition of a discussion of the concept of human nature in Chapter IV and of an outline of paradigm development processes in evolutionary culture change in Chapter V. The discussion of cyclical models of time in Chapter III is drawn from a paper entitled "Some Formal Properties of Three-Place Free Transformation Systems," which was read at a meeting of the American Association for the Advancement of Science on December 30, 1962. The section on the terminology of emotions is taken from an unpublished manuscript by Margaret Carson and myself summarizing the results of some research at the Eastern Pennsylvania Psychiatric Institute. A number of items have been added to the bibliography. But the basic design of the book remains the same.

A. F. C. W.

179595

PREFACE to the first edition

This study in culture-and-personality expresses the writer's belief that the main business of science is to describe, in sufficiently general language for the descriptions to be valid beyond the individual case, how classes of systems work. In order to carry on this business successfully, the scientist must be constantly skeptical; he must use concepts and techniques of observation which will make possible a demonstration of the predictive value, and not merely the plausibility, of his general assertions. Hence, in this study we shall not attempt to summarize empirical studies of particular peoples, nor to present a comprehensive bibliography of such studies. The emphasis will fall on such logical and methodological foundations as culture-and-personality, as science, may possess; and the bibliography is intended only to refer the reader to representative papers and books useful in discussing these foundations. The student and the instructor should use this brief study in conjunction with a collection of descriptive papers and monographs which will flesh out the skeleton of concepts and generalizations.

Many persons have directly or indirectly contributed to the forming of the writer's approach to culture-and-personality. To Dr. A. Irving Hallowell and Dr. Loren C. Eiseley in particular, acknowledgement is due for encouraging him as a student to work in this area and to extend his methodological and theoretical interests beyond the conventional boundaries of the subject. Other colleagues and friends will recognize, and hopefully will not be distressed by, the uses to which their encouragement and suggestions have been put. To all of them, named and unnamed, the writer is grateful.

Portions of several chapters have been presented in the form of papers read to scientific audiences. The discussion of equivalence structures in Chapter I incorporates much of a paper entitled, "Equivalence Structures and the Cultural Articulation of

Private Cognitive Worlds," read at the Cognitive Structures Symposium at the 1959 meetings of the American Anthropological Association in Mexico City. Most of Chapter II is drawn from a paper on evolution and the brain read to the 1958 seminar on the biological foundations of behavior at the Albert Einstein College of Medicine, Yeshiva University, New York.

A. F. C. W.

CONTENTS

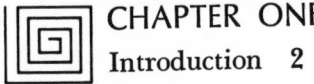

CULTURE and
PERSONALITY

chapter one
INTRODUCTION

In this short study of culture-and-personality, we shall be guided by two assumptions about the field of anthropology itself: first, it is the business of anthropology to develop a scientific theory of culture; and second, any theory that pretends to explain or to predict cultural phenomena must include noncultural phenomena in its formulations. Many of these noncultural phenomena can be subsumed under the general rubric of "personality."

THE PURPOSE OF THIS STUDY

In order to form a critical synopsis of any special branch of knowledge, the student must summarize certain major laws, principles, theories, or substantive discoveries that have current significance in that field of knowledge and must evaluate the internal logical and methodological structure of the field of knowledge itself. In the former task, the locus of reference is the "real world," the primary reality "out there," of observable phenomena that the scientist is attempting to describe, predict, and understand. In the latter task, the locus of reference is the scientific process itself by which these primary phenomena are being studied. It is one of the conspicuous features of modern science that major advances in substantive knowledge depend upon major advances in the self-awareness of the scientist. Only as the scientist comes to recognize the limitations imposed on his vision by the concepts he chooses to consider important and by the assumptions he makes about the logic of inference and the technique of observation, can he achieve the flexibility of approach required to solve new problems.

In anthropology, more than in any of the other social sciences, the need for self-evaluation is now especially acute. Anthropolo-

gists have only lately begun to realize that new ethnographic
description, like daily weather reporting, is an endless task. There
is not a finite number of cultures, which, once described, will
stay fixed forever on some *scala culturae*. Culture change is constant, ubiquitous, and only moderately predictable; the ethnographic inventory will never be complete and will always have
to be supplemented by ethnographic monitoring. Thus the problem for the theoretical anthropologist has shifted from the Lin-
naean classification of cultures and their aspects on a temporal or
geographic continuum to the discovery and analysis of the laws
of cultural process. These laws, furthermore, are recognized by
most investigators to involve the dynamics not merely of cultural
entities, but of ecological, demographic, physiological, and psychological entities as well. It is about as meaningful to claim that
"culture must be explained in terms of culture," leaving out
biological and psychological levels of explanation, as to assert
that "life must be explained in terms of life," without reference
to chemistry and physics.

Culture-and-personality is thus significant in the field of cultural anthropology because it is concerned with certain aspects
of the theory of culture process, including the intergenerational
transfer of culture ("enculturation" or socialization), culture
change, and the institutionalization of modes of coping with
individual diversity. Culture-and-personality is least significant
in the monitoring of specific cultures, since a good ethnography
permits far more accurate prediction of specific behavior than
does any national character study. Its raison d'etre resides in the
fact that it systematically takes account of noncultural data in
explaining and predicting cultural phenomena.

But while the strategic importance of culture-and-personality
is great, it has not inspired universal confidence among anthropologists. To many people (including the writer), it has often
seemed "soft" in logical structure and in research method. This
failure to gain acceptance commensurate with its pretensions is
partly owing to the insularity of the brand of psychology that
it has chiefly used: namely, psychoanalytic theory. Despite the
claim of Sigmund Freud, its creator, that psychoanalysis is based
on biological knowledge, his disciples have so heavily emphasized

the autonomy of psychological process that two-way bridges between dynamic psychology and physiology have been few. This has tended to reduce the natural affinity between culture-and-personality and the relatively "hard" sciences of neurology, general physiology, biochemistry, and experimental psychology. Personality theory, which emphasizes the emotions, has been somewhat insulated from the academic psychological core-tradition and its concern with perceptual, cognitive, and learning processes. A complementary difficulty has been the slowness with which physical anthropology itself (to which anthropologists in search of physiological knowledge might reasonably turn) has taken up the vast resources of the modern sciences of neurology, general physiology, biochemistry, psychopharmacology, and so on. A final obstacle has been the fact that most of those who have worked in culture-and-personality were trained, as graduate students, to be descriptive ethnographers, with only peripheral acquaintance with the other substantive fields to which we have referred, or with formal logic, mathematics, descriptive statistics, and the like. Thus, even with the best will in the world, culture-and-personality workers have been hampered in their efforts to advance the theoretical understanding of cultural processes because of a relative unfamiliarity with some of the necessary tools.

There is evidence that this unsatisfactory situation is now improving. The continuing popularity of interdisciplinary research, despite the common disillusionment that afflicts some of its overly enthusiastic practitioners, attests to the awareness of the need Much of such research has become institutionalized beyond the to approach theoretical problems on many levels simultaneously. project level in various institutes, research centers, seminars, and combined departmental programs. Participation in such activities has led many anthropologists to extend their training and interest to other fields and to incorporate into their own thinking the data and concepts of other disciplines. Eventually this process of ideological expansion hopefully will result in culture-and-personality training programs that require the student to take formal instruction in subjects such as physiology, symbolic logic and mathematics, and cognitive theory, as well as in descriptive statistics, dynamic psychology, and projective testing.

The present chapter is concerned with evaluating certain features of culture-and-personality as an intellectual system; the other five chapters of this study will present and appraise some of the salient themes of the descriptive and theoretical literature. Our evaluation of the field will not merely list major interests and then invoke the pious ideal of scientific rigor; we shall attempt to expose specific contradictions, inadequacies, and flaws, and to point out promising new avenues of attack, in the hope of arousing discussion and, ultimately, progress by interested students. The treatment may seem harsh in some cases, but the intention of criticism is not to destroy but to stimulate further growth.

To help the student there is now available a small group of books and articles that make some critical review of the field. But there is no need to review the reviews; the student can consult the bibliography appended to this study and then turn to these works directly. Here we are concerned with making our own evaluation of the main assumptions of culture-and-personality as a branch of science.

OPERATIONAL DISCRIMINATIONS
AMONG CONCEPTS

The most celebrated definition of culture is Edward Tylor's.

Culture . . . is that complex whole which includes knowledge, belief, art, morals, law, custom, and any other capabilities and habits acquired by man as a member of society.[1]

If the word "personality" is substituted for "culture" in the above sentence and the phrase "the individual" for "man," it will serve as a passable definition of personality as well. But there are, of course, other definitions of varying levels of abstractness, each one emphasizing those dimensions of observation that are most appealing to its author. For instance, in a probabilistic mood, I suggested that culture be defined as:

1. *Primitive Culture*, Vol. I, p. 1.

those ways of behavior or techniques of solving problems which, being more frequently and more closely approximated than other ways, can be said to have a high probability of use by individual members of society.

Personality, in this context, would be simply:

those ways of behavior or techniques of solving problems which have a high probability of use by one individual.[2]

In a more idealistic mood, the writer has further suggested that culture can be thought of as the asymptote of individual behavior much as a formal system of thought like Euclidean geometry is approached but never realized by the sum of individual geometers' actual reckoning.[3] Usually the author of any such a definition has in mind some kind of observation by which individual cultures or personalities are recognized, bounded, and properly described. The ethnographer may think, when he gives a definition of culture, of a long sequence of operations beginning with learning the language, taking photographs, talking to people, and watching what goes on and trying it himself, and fifteen years later ending up with intricate comparative analysis of recorded data by the use of some specific schema, based on a particular theoretical position. An archeologist has in mind ecological parameters, digging, certain types of durable material remains, classification, labeling, and analysis by an equally specific but different schema. A psychoanalyst, when he thinks of "personality," has in mind the characteristic individual shape of psychodynamic structures whose elements are oedipal conflicts, castration anxieties, imagos, mechanisms of defense, and so forth. The clinical psychologist, describing personality structure from Rorschach test data, is visualizing a bar graph, based on frequencies of such phenomena as allusions to color, line, texture, perspective, and movement, and is inferring such characteristics as introversion, stereotypy, imaginativeness, and self-control. Thus there is no one concept

2. "Individual Differences and Cultural Uniformities," p. 750.
3. "Culture and Cognition."

of culture, or of personality, that is universally agreed upon and is universally useful.

We do not propose to list a set of definitions of the words "culture" and "personality" and then, by some suitable criteria, to select the best. Nor shall we offer new definitions. The student should realize that dozens, if not hundreds, of respectable definitions exist. Most of them, unfortunately, are ontological: that is, they assert that culture or personality *is* such and such. And ontological definitions are the bane of science. They postulate Platonic essences, states of being in a realm of absolutes, about which argument may rage endlessly without any resolution but that of authority. Discussion of such definitions is sterile, as David Hume pointed out long ago in his famous assertion:

If we take in our hand any volume . . . let us ask, Does it contain any abstract reasoning concerning quantity or number? No. Does it contain any experimental reasoning concerning matter of fact and existence? No. Commit it then to the flames: for it can contain nothing but sophistry and illusion.[4]

The more profitable procedure is to regard the words "culture" and "personality" as the names for indefinitely large numbers of different empirical operations. All of the operations under the rubric "culture" have in common certain broad and general features, as do those under the rubric "personality." An examination of textbooks and symposia concerning human personality will reveal, for instance, that a number of theories of personality dynamics and a bewildering variety of observational techniques are employed by dozens of authorities: projective tests, depth interviews, questionnaires, life histories, laboratory experiments, verbalized introspection, and so forth, and an infinitude of subject matters. And on these data various distinctive and stylized abstractive manipulations are performed, the results of which are treated as descriptive of various traits, forces, factors, vectors, structures, and so on, in many different arrangements. Similarly with materials on culture: informant interviews, participant

4. *Enquiry Concerning Human Understanding*, Sect. XII, Pt. 3.

observation, film strips and photographs, tape-recorded texts, published literature, censuses, maps, material objects, and so on, are collected and then subjected to various abstractive and analytical procedures, the products of which are regarded as constituting an ethnographic description. Obviously, whatever culture "is" and whatever personality "is," the empirical operations by which they are described vary, depending on both the observer and the situation of his observations.

It is possible, however, to discriminate between the words "personality" and "culture" and others relevant to this area of inquiry and to describe their relationship in terms of certain operational characteristics. Three dimensions are particularly relevant: the number of persons observed directly or indirectly, the number of kinds of behavior observed, and the level of abstraction achieved by various analytic and synthetic operations. All three dimensions of variation, furthermore, are to be considered under a constant condition: namely, that the observations are made of individuals within the boundaries of a specified population at a given time. The semantic relationships can best be represented in tabular form. First, we shall consider only the first two dimensions, of number of individuals and number of behavioral categories observed, allowing level of abstraction to vary. Table I[5] represents the operational differentiation of several terms (some of them to be further defined later in the text) by number of individuals and by number of behavioral categories.

The contents of Table I (and the meaning of the expression "equivalence structure") can perhaps best be illuminated by a series of nine illustrations, corresponding to the nine cells of the table:

Cell 1. We observe that an old American Indian man, who lives alone in a small house on a reservation where we are stay-

5. This table is an amplification of a smaller schema devised in manuscript by Theodore Graves to illustrate the meaning of several sociopsychological terms by reference to the concepts of behavior potential, expectancy, and reinforcement value. It is derived from his work with Dr. Julian Rotter on social learning. See Julian B. Rotter, *Social Learning and Clinical Psychology* (Englewood Cliffs, N. J.: Prentice-Hall, 1954).

Table I Culture-and-Personality Terminology Differentiated by Numbers of Individuals and of Behavior Categories Observed

---

1. When one has observed:
   one individual in a group,
   many individuals in a group,
   all individuals in a group,

2. And the behavior observed is, in the language of this investigation, of:
   one category (that is, a particular class of act, or sequence of acts, consistently performed in a class of situations),
   many categories, arranged in an equivalence structure,
   all those categories which exist in some equivalence structure,

3. Then, depending on the abstractive operations, the statement of the observations will be a description of a:

NUMBER OF BEHAVIOR CATEGORIES

	One Category	Two or More Categories	All Categories
One	habit, response, behavior potential, etc. 1	character trait, motive, complex, value, syndrome, etc. 4	mazeway, personality, psychobiological system, etc. 7
Two or More	culture trait, custom, role, alternative, specialty, etc. 2	relationship, institution, ritual, theme, etc. 5	subculture, status-personality, etc. 8
All	culture trait, custom, role, theme, universal, etc. 3	relationship, institution, ritual, theme, focus, etc. 6	pattern, configuration, culture, national character, modal personality, etc. 9

NUMBER OF INDIVIDUALS

ing, whenever he leaves the house (to walk to the general store or to visit relatives or for whatever reason), props a stick of wood against the lockless door. On being asked why he does this, he says, "It is a sign to people that I am away and that they should not enter." Without any further information about this type of behavior, we temporarily regard it as a personal *habit*.

Cell 2. On further inquiry, we find that a dozen of our acquaintances on this reservation follow the same practice when they leave the house empty: they prop a stick of wood, or a broom, against the door. They all say, on inquiry, that it is a sign of the occupant's temporary absence and of his wish that no one enter. Some aver that almost everyone on the reservation does this. We conclude that putting a stick against the door is a *custom* in this community, regularly followed by many persons when they leave a dwelling temporarily empty. Comparing notes later with another anthropologist, we learn that the same custom is practiced on a number of reservations in the area, and we begin to refer to it as a *culture trait* with an unknown distribution.

Cell 3. Although we are unable to make inquiry in every household in the community, we are told by some of our informants that almost everyone on the reservation props a stick against the door when leaving the house. We consider that it is likely that this custom is also a cultural *universal* on this reservation, but hesitate to make the claim categorically because of the difficulty and expense of even the attempt to demonstrate universality in the field.

Cell 4. Our curiosity is now piqued. We come from a city in which the custom is to lock all doors and windows when the house is empty and, if the absence is to be lengthy, to leave some sign (such as a burning light or the absence of accumulated mail) that the house is occupied. The rationale usually given for doing this is the prevention of theft and vandalism. We note that the Indian custom draws attention to the owner's absence, rather than conceals it, and that the leaning stick of wood constitutes no barrier to entry, since the door is not locked. Several speculations occur to us: First of all, we feel sure that the absent owner is confident that his neighbors will not enter his house when a stick is propped against the door; in other words, that he conceives of the two types of behavior as being equivalent and therefore expects that his house will be left alone if he plays the stick-propping role. Second, we suspect that any Indian who "stick-props" will probably display certain other behaviors as well, which have in common a quality of confidence that explicit requests will be honored. Our interest in this possibility leads us back to our earlier informant, whose habit of stick-propping had first led us to the subject. We interview him at some length, not only on stick-propping, but on matters related to confidence in the granting of wishes. We learn that he does indeed expect personal requests, both to him and from him, to be fulfilled. He makes requests of us, once we get to know him, for transportation, for errands, for legal advice, and for gifts of food, tobacco, and even money. On the other hand, he freely accedes to our wishes that he spend time as an informant without pay, accompanies us in order to introduce us to others, shares his own limited resources without stint. We feel that, at least in contrast to most whites we know, he has a characterological *trait* of expectation of wish-granting, whether he be the wisher or the granter.

Cell 5.   Indeed, as we come to know many people on the reservation, we find that this wish-granting expectancy trait is so common that we can call it a *theme* in the culture. We now observe that on several occasions, when we have gone with one or another of our informants to visit a house where someone can give us certain information, our guide will not bother to knock on a door against which a stick is propped, nor will he enter in order to look for or await the occupants. We are told several times, "You don't go into a house when a stick is propped against the door." We conclude that stick-propping and house-avoidance behaviors constitute complementary roles for many pairs of persons; the two behaviors are equivalent in the logician's sense that whenever, but only when, person A plays role a, person B will play role b. We begin to refer to this equivalence structure as an *institution*.

Cell 6. Inasmuch as we suspect, although we cannot demonstrate, that the complementary stick-propping and house-avoidance behaviors are universals, and inasmuch as this institution is only one expression of a more general theme of expectancy of wish-granting, we feel that we may now be dealing with an area of cultural *focus*. This hypothesized focus would fall on the development and maintenance of institutions that express the theme of expectancy of wish-granting. The pursuit of this hypothesis leads us to consider that wishes expressed in dreams are, indeed, historically known to have been the source of a number of cultural innovations, as for instance the cultural reforms sponsored by a religious prophet in the previous century. We observe also that many religio-medical secret societies, and even major political institutions, are said to have originated in dreams or dreamlike wishes.

Cell 7. Because we are now on good terms with the old man, we ask him whether he will tell us the story of his life, recount some of his dreams, and be a subject for several tests including the Rorschach and the TAT. Although he displays some discomfort, particularly about recounting dreams (which we expected), he feels that he must grant our wish. He excuses the indelicacy of asking for dreams on the grounds that we are whites, and white people have different customs; hence telling us his dreams is not the same thing as telling a neighbor. We thus obtain a large body of psychological materials. We regard the product of the analysis of this data as a description of the structure of his *personality*, since the statements made in this description are abstractions that we consider relevant to virtually all areas of his behavior.

Cell 8. One probable source of error in any general attribution of the modal personality description, derived by the procedures outlined for Cell 9, is the existence of sex, age, and other social differentials in the sample. Wishing to avoid the possibility of an unwary reader's attributing the modal personality type to subgroups where personality norms actually differ significantly from the modal type, we construct separate modal types for males and females, for children, active adults, and inactive ("old") adults, and for the two major ethnic groups that compose the population (approximately one-third of the tribe are sixth-generation immigrant refugees from another culture area). This refinement of the analysis reveals that there are indeed significant differences among the modal types constructed for age, sex, and ethnic subgroups within the population, and between some of these subtypes and the general type. This discovery of distinctive *status personalities,* which correspond roughly with the *subcultures* of distinctive social subgroups, does not invalidate the modal personality type characteristic of the population as a whole, of course, since its definition involved specification of its relative frequency within the population. But it makes possible much more exact understanding of the interpersonal dynamics of the society than dependence on knowledge of the general modal type would permit.

Cell 9. In addition to working with the old man, we have been obtaining similar, if less extensive, projective test data from a large number of persons on the reservation. Furthermore, with the help of several excellent informants and of our own day-by-day observation, we have been filling in the content categories of the *Outline of Cultural Materials.* We do not analyze these large bodies of data carefully in the field, but on our return to the University we work with them and produce from the projective test data a description of the *modal personality structure* of the population and, from the ethnographic data, a sketch of the *culture.*

The careful student will note, in the foregoing illustrations and in the table, that there is a certain arbitrariness in the decision to regard the product of some observation as belonging to the first, second, or third column. This arbitrariness results because, although the same category of overt behavior may be described in terms of either culture or personality, what constitutes a single category (or class) of behavior will depend on the concern of the investigator. In one study, a number of things that a mother does in relation to her offspring may be construed as a large number of more particular behaviors—such as feeding, cleaning, fondling, and so on—each of which is assignable to column 1. In this case, "the mother role" will operationally fall within column 2. This should not concern the student, however, since the important thing is not to construct an absolute classification of constructs but to specify their operational relationship within any given investigation.

Another source of ambiguity is the fact that each cell beyond 1 can contain constructs at varying levels of abstraction from the same body of primary observations. For example, in Cell 7, *mazeway* refers to the entire set of cognitive maps of positive and negative goals that an individual maintains at a given time. This set includes goals of self, others, and material objects, and of their possible dynamic interrelations. *Personality* covers the same territory, but on a higher level of abstraction, in which mazeway particulars are classified and grouped under various rubrics, such as the wish-fulfillment trait that we used in our illustration, a hysterical syndrome, or whatever. The relations among the constructs in the third column of Table I may be represented by an expansion, as in the table on page 20.

Some further discussion of the concept of mazeway may be appropriate here. Mazeway is to the individual what culture is to the group. Just as every group's history is unique, so every human individual's course of experience is unique. As a product of this experience, every human brain contains, at a given point of time, a unique mental image of a complex system of dynamically interrelated objects. This mental image—the mazeway—includes the body in which the brain is housed, various other surrounding things, and sometimes even the brain itself. It consists of an extremely large number of assemblages or cognitive residues of perception and is used by its holder as a true and more or less complete representation of the operating characteristics of a "real" world.

The mazeway may be compared to a map of a gigantic maze with an elaborate key or legend and many insets. On this map are represented three types of assemblage: (1) goals and pitfalls (values, or desirable and undesirable end-states); (2) the "self" and other objects (people and things); and (3) ways (plans, processes, or techniques) that may be circumvented or used, according to their characteristics, to facilitate the self's attainment or avoidance of values. For heuristic purposes, let us crudely categorize the content of the mazeway, recognizing that these categories (like the categories represented by different colors, shading, shapes, or thicknesses of line on a map) do not represent the only possible analytical divisions and relationships. The normal human mazeway, then, may contain representation of at least the following phenomena:

I. Values (images of situations associated with pleasant or unpleasant feeling-tone)

   A. Positive organic values

      1. Eating and drinking

      2. Sleeping, rest, relaxation, absence of discomfort or bodily tension

      3. Sexual satisfaction

      4. Optimal temperature maintenance

      5. Elimination of wastes

      6. Breathing

   B. Positive symbolic values

      1. Testimonials of love, admiration, and respect from human objects

      2. Enactment of behavior-sequences satisfying "in themselves" (for example, a game or sport, conversation, meditation) , or satisfying because they are instrumental to other values

      3. Presence of objects associated with organic and symbolic consummations (including human and non-human objects)

   C. Altruistic values (images of situations in which the primary and secondary values of others are satisfied)

   D. Negative values (associated with pain, discomfort, anxiety): the reverse of consummations outlined above

II. Objects (images, with associations, of animate and inanimate objects)

A. Self
  1. Body image
     a. surface of body
     b. bodily adornment (clothing, cosmetics, perfume, and so forth)
     c. organs and organ systems
     d. prostheses (for example, false teeth, wooden leg)
     e. defects or injuries (for example, "weak back," "shortness of breath")
  2. Self image
     a. physiological processes (for example, digestion, sexual desire)
     b. psychological process (nature of thoughts, dreams, emotions, and so forth)
     c. personality (characteristic impulse and action patterns recognized in self)
     d. evaluation (for example, good-bad, strong-weak) of parts or whole
     e. conception of the soul
B. Human environment
  1. Particular persons
     a. values of others
     b. characteristics of behavior of others (in relation to self and to others)
  2. Classes of persons
     a. particular classes defined (for example, on basis of residence, kinship, race, political affiliation, wealth, and so forth)
     b. values and characteristics of classes (in relation to self and others)
  3. Sociocultural system as a whole
C. Nonhuman environment
  1. Animals
  2. Plants
  3. Tools and equipment ("material culture")
  4. Natural phenomena (for example, fire, weather, topography, and terrain)
  5. Natural system as a whole

D. Supernatural environment
   1. Particular supernaturals (for example, ancestors' spirits, deities, ghosts, demons, and so forth)
   2. Classes of supernaturals
   3. Supernatural processes (for example, mana and taboo, witchcraft, and magic)
E. Statements of how entire sociocultural, self, natural, and supernatural system works

III. Techniques (images of ways of manipulating objects in order to experience desired end-states or values)
   A. Techniques themselves (an extremely large number of interlocking and alternative statements of "what to do when . . . ")
   B. Priority systems among values (statements of which to enjoy first, or which to do to the exclusion of something else)
   C. Priority systems among techniques (statements of which technique to use in order not to obstruct use of another, or the attainment of some other value)

These elements can be combined in an almost infinite variety of "imagined" action sequences.

The concept of mazeway thus embraces, in an organized fashion, several phenomena already generally recognized as common to human awareness: the "body image"[6]; "role," "self," "the other," "the generalized other"[7]; "behavioral environment"[8]; the "world view."[9] It is reminiscent of E. D. Tolman's "cognitive maps"[10] and of the topological concept of "life-space," and closely resembles certain concepts in cognitive theory: the "image"[11] and

6. Schilder, *The Image and Appearance of the Human Body.*

7. Mead, *Mind, Self, and Society.*

8. Hallowell, *Culture and Experience.*

9. Redfield, *The Primitive World and Its Transformations.*

10. "Cognitive Maps in Rats and Men."

11. Boulding, *The Image.*

"plan."[12] And the mazeway concept borrows from traditional psychological notions of perception, association, "integration," and patterning of experience. Evidently, the mazeway includes in one field images of phenomena that, to many an outside "absolute" observer, would fall into conceptually distinct and sometimes incommensurable categories: personality, culture, society, natural environment, values, and so on. From the standpoint of the individual mazeway-holder, however, all these phenomena normally constitute one integrated dynamic system of perceptual assemblages. Within this system, self and nonself interact according to predictable (if more or less idiosyncratic) "laws," the description of which in generalized form is the business particularly of personality psychology and of dynamic psychiatry.

REDUCTIONISM AND THE RELATION
OF PERSONALITY AND CULTURAL SYSTEMS

Anthropologists sometimes like to think of culture as a closed system and regard most efforts to consider the relation between cultural and noncultural (for example, psychological and physiological) data as "reductionism." Leslie White has been the most systematic and eloquent exponent of this tendency, and consequently a discussion of White's position on this matter offers a direct way of coming to grips with the issue. We cannot help but agree with White's essential position—that culture is "real," that cultural evolution is a major subject matter of anthropology, and that the anthropologist should be interested in culture. But some of White's arguments in justification of this position seem to be not only unnecessary, but fallacious. There are, first of all, certain questionable ontological claims: on occasion he insists upon settling the question of what culture *is* by philosophical arguments ("A thing is what it is . . . ") and dogmatic assertions that he *knows* what culture is and is not. Second, he explicitly regards the human organism and indeed all the physical universe as constant parameters without which culture could not exist,

12. Miller, Galanter, and Pribram, *Plans and the Structure of Behavior.*

*Table II Routes and Levels of Abstraction in Culture-and-Personality
Terminology*

1. If one has derived an approximation to a complete description of
   one mazeway, or
   one culture,

2. Abstractive operations, involving classification of content into fewer,
   broader categories, will yield descriptions of, respectively,
   personality, or
   national character.

3. If one has derived an approximation to a complete description of
   one mazeway, or
   one personality,

4. Operations, involving addition of all individual cases to the pool of
   data, without altering the level of abstraction, will yield descriptions
   of, respectively,
   culture, or
   modal personality structure.

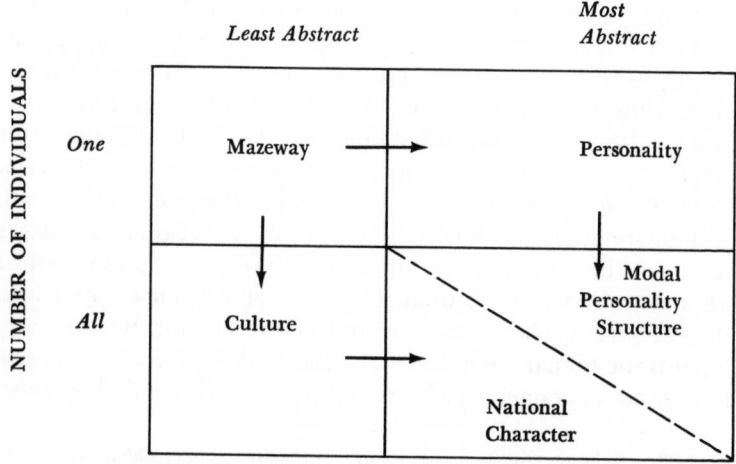

but which, once given, have no bearing on the variables involved in cultural process. "A consideration of the human organism, individually or collectively, is irrelevant to an explanation of the processes of culture change."[13] This position could only be successfully maintained if it were the case that "the human organism, individually or collectively," which White has already admitted is a parameter (albeit, in his view, a single-valued one) of cultural process, were indeed a changeless, uniform, absolute, univalued parameter. But the human organism, individually and collectively, is not uniform. It has been grossly variable, in physical evolution, synchronically in any population in response to genetic, ecological, and cultural circumstances, and in the individual in response to growth, accident, and disease. Indeed, the anthropologist must take the position that the processes of culture change (including the process by which human culture emerged) cannot be explained adequately without a consideration of the human organism, individually and collectively, and of that organism's physical environment, as well as of culture, per se. Any other position will inevitably yield a science of culture that is no science at all, but rather a sterile catalogue of cultural forms.

What sort of consideration of "the human organism" does culture-and-personality undertake in the interest of extending our knowledge of cultural process? First of all, the physiology of the organism is considered, insofar as it is relevant. The areas of relevance, however, are broad: endocrinology; neurophysiology, particularly of the limbic system; diet and nutrition; sickness and health; physical evolution; the general adaptation syndrome (of Selye); maturation, sexual differentiation, and aging; psychopharmacology (particularly in relation to narcotics and hallucinogenic agents like peyote). All of these, and more, are intimately related to both psychological and cultural processes. In regard to specifically psychological subjects a number of traditional areas are relevant: learning, perception, cognitive process, group dynamics, the structure of affect distribution (a conventional sense of "personality"), and existential phenomen-

13. "The Concept of Culture," p. 240.

ology (the attempt to describe what another person perceives in categories isomorphic with those in which he perceives it). And, most importantly, the human organism is creative: it selects, rejects, seeks information, thinks, makes decisions, and ultimately modifies the systems of which it is a part. In addition to "interacting" externally with other components of social and other systems, the human organism does systematic internal work, the magnitude of which, even in a grossly physical sense, is measured by metabolic assays.

In culture-and-personality analysis, as was implied in the discussion of operational definitions, a society is usually considered to be a system on a higher level of organization than are the individual organisms, or even the social groups, that are the components of that society. There are available to the student of culture-and-personality two major, and to a degree antithetical, conceptions of the nature of the relation between cultural and personality systems; and at this point, perhaps, the dialectic should be presented, for it will sooner or later be translated into the student's research operations. These conceptions may be construed, respectively, as emphasizing the *replication of uniformity* and the *organization of diversity*. We shall discuss them at greater length later; for the moment, it will suffice to contrast the world view behind each.

THE REPLICATION OF UNIFORMITY

In many investigations, the anthropologist tacitly, and sometimes even explicitly, is primarily interested in the extent to which members of a social group, by virtue of their common group identification, behave in the same way under the same circumstances. For the sake of convenience in discourse, they may even be considered to have learned the "same things" in the "same cultural environment." Under such circumstances, the society may be regarded as culturally homogeneous and the individuals will be expected to share a uniform nuclear character. If a near-perfect correspondence between culture and individual nuclear character is assumed, the structural relation between the two becomes nonproblematical, and the interest of processual research lies rather in the mechanisms of socialization by which each generation becomes, culturally and characterologically, a replica of its predecessors. This viewpoint is particularly congenial to the world view associated with dynamic psychology, ultimately based on Freud's psychoanalytic theories but modified by conceiving the personality to reflect faithfully the culture in which it was formed and not merely universal constants, such as the Oedipus conflict and the stages of psychosexual maturation. The sense of tragedy implicit in this world view is, as everyone knows, very different from that which preceded it. From the days of the Greeks to the Industrial Revolution, Western man had, most commonly, conceived of the essence of tragedy as lying in the inevitability of sin, that is, of sacred crime, the intentional or unintentional violation of "the Law." Different as the Greek plays are from the Christian gospels, they agree on one theme: sin is unavoidable. Beginning with Freud, and increasingly with his successors, the inevitable tragedy of man's situation was seen not as sin, but as the conflict of wishes, in themselves neither evil nor good, and often growing from contradictions inherent in the person's culture. Thus, to the student who emphasizes the replication of uniformity, the point of tragic concern is the fate of those whose cultures, internally rent with contradictions, unavoidably instill painful conflict.

THE ORGANIZATION OF DIVERSITY

In other investigations, it is sometimes more interesting to consider the actual diversity of habits, of motives, of personalities, of customs that do, in fact, coexist within the boundaries of any culturally organized society. When the fact of diversity is emphasized, the obvious question must immediately be asked: how do such various individuals organize themselves culturally into orderly, expanding, changing societies? When the process of socialization is examined closely, it becomes apparent that, within the limits of practical human control and observation, it is not a perfectly reliable mechanism for replication. And culture, far from being, with the one exception of recent Western civilization, a slowly changing, sluggish, conservative beast, appears to be a turbulent species, constantly oscillating between the ecstasies of revitalization and the agonies of decline. Culture shifts in policy from generation to generation with kaleidoscopic variety and is characterized internally not by uniformity, but by diversity of both individuals and groups, many of whom are in continuous and overt conflict in one subsystem and in active cooperation in another. Culture, as seen from this viewpoint, becomes not so much a superorganic entity, but policy, tacitly and gradually concocted by groups of people for the furtherance of their interests, and contract, established by practice, between and among individuals to organize their strivings into mutually facilitating equivalence structures. Nor can the phenomeno-logical world of an individual, or of a people, be assumed to be understood by the anthropologist, once he can predict the move-ments of their bodies; rather, he must recognize the possibility of a radical diversity of mazeways that have their orderly relation-ship guaranteed not by the sharing of uniformity, but by their capacities for mutual prediction.

From this organization-of-diversity viewpoint grows a different sense of tragedy. The unwanted inevitability is not sin, nor con-flict, but loneliness: the only partly bridgeable chasms of mutual ignorance between whole peoples and the failures of understand-ing between individuals. A modicum of this loneliness would appear to be as irreducible in interpersonal relations (including the relation of the anthropologist to his subjects) as is the com-plementarity of perceptions in physical observation.

THE PSYCHIC UNITY OF HUMAN GROUPS

One of the most hoary assumptions of the uniformitarian view-point is the belief that a society will fall apart and its members scatter if they are not threaded like beads on a string of common motives. Numerous sources may be quoted that attest to the "common thread" belief. Thus Aberle, Cohen, Davis, Levy, and Sutton[14] in an essay on the functional prerequisites of a human

14. "The Functional Prerequisites of a Society."

society, include as prerequisites a "shared, articulated set of goals." Erich Fromm asserts that a nuclear character structure must be shared by "most members of the same culture" in order for the culture to continue; socialization must make people "want to act as they have to act."[15] Emile Durkheim's thesis that society depends for integration upon the "common sentiments" of its members is a similar view.[16] John Honigmann expresses the position in the plaintive assertion, "In any community, there must be some congruence between what different people do, believe, and feel, otherwise social order would be impossible."[17] Margaret Mead has carried the argument to the point where cultural heterogeneity is conceived as almost ipso facto pathogenic:

in a heterogeneous culture, individual life experiences differ so markedly from one another that almost every individual may find the existing cultural forms of expression inadequate to express his peculiar bent, and so be driven into more and more special forms of psychosomatic expression.[18]

Social philosophers, less humane than the scientists quoted above, but equally disturbed by the problems of their societies, at times have found the "common motive" theme a congenial one and have used the threat of social disintegration and individual degeneration to justify draconian measures for the standardization of sentiments.

It is, however, impossible to demonstrate empirically that any social system is operated by individuals all driven by the same motives; indeed, the data of personality-and-culture studies, as well as clinical observation, show conclusively that a sharing of motives is not necessary to a sharing of institutions. But is cognitive sharing a functional prerequisite of society? Here we enter the domain of the ethnographer who may not wish to

---

15. In Sargant and Smith (eds.), *Personality*, p. 5.

16. *The Elementary Forms of the Religious Life.*

17. *Culture and Personality*, p. 220.

18. "The Concept of Culture and the Psychosomatic Approach," p. 72.

tread the spongy ground of motive-analysis, but who finds it both necessary and painless to make inferences from overt behavior about cognitive matters, such as the criteria for discrimination of kinsmen by terminological category, the substantive beliefs about the order of the cosmos, and the rules of procedure by which a shaman arrives at his differential diagnosis over a sick child. The minimum task of the ethnographer, of course, is simply to describe overt human behavior. "Description," in this minimum sense, is the formulation of a set of statements that will predict, for the ethnographer, what a class of subjects will do and say under various circumstances. Accordingly, any complete ethnographic statement will include a specification of both a configuration of circumstances and of a behavior sequence that a class of subjects produces (presumptively as a result of learning) whenever that configuration presents itself. Usually, the "circumstances" that elicit a certain behavior sequence on the part of one class of subjects will include the acts and utterances of another class. Therefore, most ethnographic descriptions primarily concern repetitive patterns of reciprocal interaction in which the behaviors of each class are the circumstance for the behaviors of the other class.

It has been sometimes assumed that such systems of reciprocal interaction, in which different classes of subjects play specialized roles, as well as general norms describing constant act-and-circumstance relations for a single class of subjects, require not merely a set of cognitive maps, but a uniformity of cognitive maps among the participants for their continued successful operation. For example, in their previously quoted essay on the functional prerequisites of a human society, Aberle, Cohen, Davis, Levy, and Sutton postulate the necessity of "shared cognitive orientations," as well as a "shared, articulated set of goals."[19] Yet what few formal attempts have been made, by techniques such as componential analysis, to define the cognitive maps necessary to culturally correct behaviors have demonstrated unambiguously that it is often possible for the ethnographer to construct several different maps, each of which will predict

19. "The Functional Prerequisites of a Society."

adequately the overt behavior of subjects. Let us therefore now ask the question directly: is it necessary that all participants in a stable sociocultural system have the same "map" of the system in order that they may select the correct overt behaviors under the various relevant circumstances?

1. Minimal Sociocultural Systems

A system may be defined as a set of variable entities (persons, objects, customs, atoms, or whatever) so related that, first, some variation in any one is followed by a predictable (that is, non-random) variation in at least one other; second, that there is at least one sequence of variations which involves all of the entities.

Let us define the properties of the least complex system that an ethnographer might describe. Such a system must satisfy the following minimum requirements: first, that two parties, A and B, the initiator and respondent, respectively, interact; second, that each completion of one sequence of interactions be followed, sooner or later, by a repetition of the same sequence. Representing the acts of A by the symbols a_i, those of B by the symbols b_j, and temporal relationship by the symbol $\rightarrow$, to be read "is followed by," we assert that the simplest such system has the following structure:

$$a_1 \longleftrightarrow b_1$$

Since it is legitimate to regard the sense of the symbol $\rightarrow$, "is followed by," as a reasonable interpretation of the logical relationship of material implication (whenever x, then y), we may refer to the structure $a_1 \longleftrightarrow b_1$ as a *primary equivalence structure* (ES_1). In such a structure, whenever A does a_1, then (sooner or later) B does b_1; and whenever B does b_1, then (sooner or later) A does a_1.

Interaction structures of ES_1 type seem too simple to serve as useful models of the components of sociocultural systems. The *secondary equivalence structure* (ES_2), however, looks more interesting:

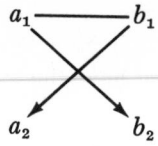

Here we may interpret acts a_1 and b_1 as instrumental acts and acts a_2 and b_2 as consummatory acts. The distinguishing feature of ES_2 is that the consummatory act of each party is released by (but is not necessarily exclusively conditional upon) the instrumental act of the other. The equivalence between a_1 and b_1 describes the repetitive nature of the interaction. A little ritual commonly found among the present inhabitants of the eastern coast of the United States (its wider distribution, in time and space, is unknown to me) provides a whimsical but culturally valid example of a secondary equivalence structure. When a child loses one of his baby teeth, he places the tooth under his pillow at night when he goes to bed; the parent, after the child has fallen asleep, comes and replaces the tooth with a coin $(a_1 \rightarrow b_1)$. The child, on awakening, takes the coin and buys candy with it $(b_1 \rightarrow a_2)$. (Possibly, he thereby loosens another tooth, if it is caramel candy!) The parent, meanwhile, after replacing the tooth with a coin, delightedly reports the transaction to his spouse $(a_1 \rightarrow b_1 \rightarrow b_2)$. And with the next tooth he sheds, the child, who has observed that tooth-placing is followed by candy and who likes candy, repeats a_1 and thus continues the process $(b_1 \rightarrow a_1)$. This simple custom is (for reasons that I shall mention later) not unlike the silent trade, so widely reported among primitive peoples. It may be diagrammed as follows:

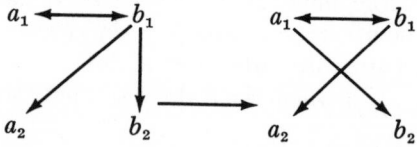

More complex structures, involving two parties, can obviously be constructed out of the same relationships. Thus a tertiary equivalence structure (ES_3) has the form:

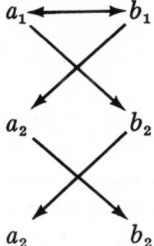

Structures of quaternary and still higher degree evidently can be made by a simple process of extension. Structures involving more than two persons also can be designed, although they are more difficult to represent on a plane surface. In general, we can consider that the two-party secondary equivalence structure, which we have suggested as the smallest practical model of a stable sociocultural system, is only one of a class of equivalence structures $^{m}ES_{n}$, where $m > 1$ denotes the number of parties to the system, and $n \geq 1$ denotes the number of levels of equivalences $a_i \longleftrightarrow b_j$ incorporated. It would be interesting to investigate in detail the logical properties of these systems and to speculate that, in principle, *any* sociosystem, involving m parties in repetitive interaction, can be described by some equivalence structure of the class $^{m}ES_{n}$. However, these exercises would carry us beyond the purposes of this discussion.

We now conclude that the simplest possible social-interaction system that an ethnographer might describe has the form of a two-person secondary equivalence structure. This structure is, however, a model of what the ethnographer perceives; it is the ethnographer's cognitive map. We wish now to discover with what combination of maps, α_i and β_j, held by the two parties A and B, the ethnographer's model is compatible.

2. Minimal Cognitive Maps of Participants in Sociocultural Systems

At this point, we must make explicit two conventions that have been employed in the foregoing analysis. These are: first, that the ethnographer's map is valid ("true"); second, that the systems are "perfect," in the sense that there are no exceptions to the regularity of the relationships indicated by the symbols →. We know, of course, that in "real life" ethnographers make errors and that human behavior is not perfectly predictable. Although it would not invalidate the reasoning to introduce these qualifications (since a probabilistic logic would do just as well as the strict two-valued logic we are using), it would make the demonstrations more tedious. These conventions are now also applied to the cognitive maps maintained by the participants: we assume that the relationships are two-valued ("yes" or "no" rather than a probabilistic "maybe").

We have suggested already that a_1 and b_1 be regarded as "instrumental" acts and a_2 and b_2 as "consummatory." It is important to recognize that this classification is only a relative one; that is, a_1 is instrumental with respect to a_2, and b_1 with respect to b_2. In teleological terms, A does a_1 "in order to be able" to do a_2, and B does b_1 "in order to be able" to do b_2. But we do not actually need to invoke any panel of needs, drives, tensions, instincts, or whatever, the satisfaction of which makes an act ultimately consummatory, since we assume that the maps validly describe real events. It is therefore true by definition that neither A nor B will continue to participate in the system unless, first, each perceives that, *within the limits of the system,* his ability to perform his own consummatory act depends upon his partner performing his instrumental act; second, that when he performs his own instrumental act, its function is to elicit his partner's instrumental act; third, that he repeatedly performs his own instrumental act.

The simplest (but not the only) possible cognitive maps for A and B, respectively, which satisfy the foregoing requirements, are the following:

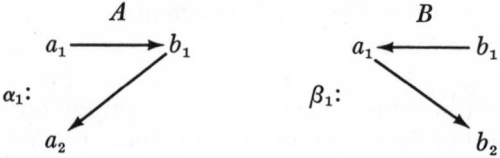

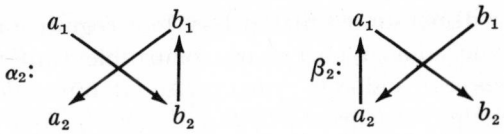

These maps are to be interpreted as follows:

α_1: A knows that whenever he does a_1, B will respond with b_1, and A will then perform a_2.

α_2: A knows that whenever he does a_1, B will respond with b_2 and then b_1, and A will then perform a_2.

β_1: B knows that whenever he does b_1, A will respond with a_1, and B will then perform b_2.

β_2: B knows that whenever he does b_1, A will respond with a_2 and then a_1, and B will then perform b_2.

Each possible combination of these cognitive maps will yield a structure that is identical with, or logically implies, $^2ES_2$. Thus:

$\alpha_1 \wedge \beta_1 =$

$\alpha_1 \wedge \beta_2 =$

$\alpha_2 \wedge \beta_1 =$

$\alpha_2 \wedge \beta_2 =$

We have now demonstrated that at least four cognitive maps, in addition to the ethnographer's, are compatible with the continued existence of a simple system of social interaction. The four maps of the participant parties can exist in four possible combinations, each of which sums to $^2ES_2$ or to a form that implies $^2ES_2$. Evidently, it is not *necessary* that both participants share the same map; and we have answered our original question: is cognitive sharing a functional prerequisite of society?

3. How Many Combinations of Cognitive Maps Will Yield the Secondary Equivalence Structure?

Even a casual comparison of the ethnographer's model with the four participants' models will suggest that a number of unique cognitive maps are possible which are different from, but contain, either or both of the A structures and/or either or both of the B structures. The basic model of $^2ES_2$ itself, for instance, contains both α_1 and β_1; $^2ES_2$ added to itself will yield $^2ES_2$; $^2ES_2$ added to α_1 will yield $^2ES_2$; $^2ES_2$ added to β_1 will yield $^2ES_2$, and so on. Let us therefore inquire, out of curiosity, just how many unique combinations of α-maps and β-maps there are where the sum equals, contains, or implies $^2ES_2$, with the proviso that each component α-map include either or both α_1 and α_2, and each component β-map include either or both β_1 and β_2. The number is well over a million. The number of unique α-maps is over a thousand and the number of unique β-maps is also over a thousand. Thus it is apparent that even when one considers extremely simple systems, a very large number of different cognitive maps of such systems are, for all practical purposes, interchangeable as system components.

What are the implications of these considerations? Evidently cognitive sharing is not *necessary* for stable social interaction. The two parties to systems of form $^2ES_2$ do not need to know what the "motives" of their partners in the interchange are. Indeed, they need not even correctly know *who* their partners are. In the tooth exchange ritual alluded to earlier, the child at first believes that a good fairy, whom he never sees, takes the tooth, for motives unexplained, and leaves the coin. This relationship is not unlike the silent trade. Later, the child may know that the parents are responsible, but he does not "let on" from a benevolent wish not to spoil his parents' fantasies about *his* fantasies. One or the other or both of the parties may be able to perform his consummatory act *only* after the partner performs his instrumental act; or other circumstances may also permit it.

But, the advocate of togetherness may argue, whether or not it is necessary that *all* members of society share all cognitive maps, they must share at least *one*. Such an argument, however, is not convincing. I know of no criteria that would specify the one map all members of a given society should share. One cannot argue empirically that all members of all societies are *known* to share at least one map, for the data to support such an argument do not exist. And merely demonstrating that some defined group of human individuals, or even all the members of some one society, share a particular map, is irrelevant to the discussion. (Such a society would have to be peculiarly simple and at the same time clairvoyant.) Two or more parties may indeed share a common cognitive map, but such a circumstance is, in a sense, wasteful, since at least two, and therefore all, of these maps must be larger than the minimally necessary ones. And only when each actor is cognizant of the other's "motive" (consummatory act), can the actors' cognitive maps be identical and still contribute to system maintenance.

It may appear to be a bleak prospect to consider that human beings characteristically engage in a kind of silent trade with all their fellow men, rarely or never actually achieving cognitive communality. Indeed, one may suspect that the social sciences have nourished the idea of cognitive sharing for so long, just because the world may seem rather a lonely place if the wistful dream of mutual identification is abandoned. Still another anxiety may now arise: for an implication of our researches is that individuals can produce a sociocultural system that is beyond their own comprehension. If, for instance, α_k is as complex a map as A can maintain, and β_1 is as complex as B can maintain, their sum (*unless* they are identical) will be a structure *containing* $^2ES_2$, but in its totality *more* complex than one or both of them can grasp. If one of these parties is an anthropologist, who is attempting to construct a general *ES* that he will call "culture," then, alas, he may be a participant-observer in a sociocultural system that is more complex than he can describe ethnographically! Even if he cannot describe the system fully, he must be able to construct a cognitive map that is more complex than that of any of his subject's.

But perhaps the most significant point to be made is a relatively practical one, growing out of concerns with the application of anthropological knowledge to psychiatric research. A principal problem for the research anthropologist, in a mental hospital setting, is to explain how a person comes to be extruded from his sociocultural system. Is it because he is a "deviant," one whose cognitive maps are not shared by other members of the community? Or is it because he has been unable to maintain stable cognitive maps sufficiently complex for them to sum to an equivalence structure with those of his fellows? From the viewpoint of the organization of diversity, it would appear that the most generally adequate explanation is the latter: particularly in a large and complex society, equivalence structures normally will be the articulation of uniquely private cognitive worlds. The measure of individual value will not be conformity, but complementarity.

4. Is Cognitive Nonsharing a Functional Prerequisite of Society?

Finally, we ask whether the fact that cognitive sharing is not a *necessary* condition of society does not mask an even more general point. Not only *can* societies contain subsystems, the cognitive maps of which are not uniform among participants, but they *do*, in fact, invariably contain such systems. Ritual, for instance, is often differently conceptualized by viewers and performers; public entertainment similarly is variously perceived by professional and audience; the doctor (or shaman) and patient relationship demands a mutual misunderstanding. Even in class and political relationships, complementary roles (as, for instance, between the holders of "Great" and "Little" Traditions) are notoriously difficult to exchange. Administrative personnel and leaders generally must understand the system on a "higher" level of synthesis than their subordinates, a level that demands a different, because more abstract, cognitive map. Indeed, we now suggest that human societies may characteristically *require* the nonsharing of certain cognitive maps among participants in a variety of institutional arrangements. Many a social subsystem simply will not "work" if all participants share common knowledge of the system. It would seem therefore that cognitive *non*uniformity may be a functional desideratum of society (although, by the criteria we have used above, it is certainly not a formal prerequisite any more than is uniformity). For cognitive nonuniformity subserves two important functions: (1) it permits a more complex system to arise than most, or any, of its participants can comprehend; (2) it liberates the participants in a system from the heavy burden of learning and knowing each other's motivations and cognitions.

If sociocultural organization is not necessarily dependent upon a community of motives or cognitions, then by what psychological mechanism is it achieved and maintained? This mechanism is evidently the perception of partial equivalence structures. By this is implied the recognition—as the result of learning—that the behavior of other people under various circumstances is predictable, irrespective of knowledge of their motivation, and thus is capable of being predictably related to one's own actions. Evidently, groups, as well as individuals, can integrate their behaviors into reliable systems by means of equivalence structures, without extensive motivational or cognitive sharing. The equivalence structure model should be congenial to that tradition in social anthropology which interests itself in the relations between organized groups. Thus reciprocal interactions between the representatives of geographically separate groups as alien as American Indian tribes and colonial or state governments have proceeded for centuries, with only minimal sharing of motives or understanding, on a basis of carefully patterned equivalences. Similar observation might be made of the relations between castes, social classes, professional groups, kin groups, factions, parties, and so forth. In no case is it necessary that a basic personality or a basic cognitive framework be shared, but it is necessary that behaviors be mutually predictable and equivalent.

We may say that as any set of persons establish a system of equivalent behavioral expectancies, an organized relationship comes into existence. Such a system of equivalent mutual expectancies may be termed an *implicit contract,* in the general sense of the word "contract." In this sense, and not in the sense of any formal document, society is, as Rousseau intuited, built upon a set of continually changing social contracts that are possible only because human beings have cognitive equipment adequate to their maintenance and renewal. Culture can be conceived as a set of standardized models of such contractual relationships, in which the equivalent roles are specified and available for implementation to any two parties whose motives make their adoption promising. The relationship is based not on a sharing, but on a complementarity of cognitions and motives. Marital relationship, entry into an age grade, the giving of a feast—in all such contracts the motives may be diverse, but the cognitive expectations are standardized. Thus the relationship between the driver of a bus and the riders is a contractual one, involving specific and detailed mutual expectancies. The motives of drivers and riders may be as diverse as one wishes; the contract establishes the system. From this standpoint, then, it is culture that is shared (in the special sense of institutional contract) rather than personality, and culture may be conceived as an invention that makes possible the maximal organization of motivational and cognitive diversity. This it is able to accomplish because of the human (not uniquely human, but preeminently so) cognitive capacity for the perception of systems of behavioral equivalence. (See Chapter III for further discussion of cognitive sharing and diversity.)

FALLACIES, FADS, AND SPECIALIZATIONS

The progress of research in culture-and-personality is, at times, hampered by the common use of fallacious metaphors and by faddish enthusiasms for particular jargons and techniques. But it is important to distinguish between fad and fallacy, on the one hand, and legitimate specialization, on the other.

Conspicuous examples of the fallacious metaphor are the frequently mishandled words "internalization," "impact," and "mold." It is sometimes said that personality *is* (ontologically) culture "internalized" in the individual; that culture change has an "impact" on the individual; that culture "molds" the individual. Such expressions, and theoretical formulations based on them, are meaningless in any literal sense. As Alfred Radcliffe-Brown once remarked, "To say of culture patterns that they act upon an individual . . . is as absurd as to hold a quadratic equation capable of committing a murder." As we observed in connection with systems analysis, culture and personality are constructs of different "logical type," in Bertrand Russell's sense; that is, the concept of a culture is a set of propositions about some of the same propositions which are included within the concept of one or more of the personalities within the society. Thus to use transitive metaphors like "internalize," "impact," "mold," and so on, to describe the relation between culture and personality, is precisely comparable to claiming that a circle has an "impact on," "molds," the points that constitute it, or that the points are "internalizations" (or "expressions," or "phrasings," or "transforms") of the equation describing the circle.

The obverse of the "internalization" fallacy is the "statistical" fallacy, which offers an enumeration of the properties of individual persons as if it were a description of a social or cultural system, without any demonstration that a nonrandom relationship obtains among the dimensions considered. Such statistical "structures" are mere archival material unless a systematic relationship among the dimensions can be demonstrated.

Fads in culture-and-personality, as in other fields of endeavor, are sometimes difficult to distinguish from new specializations. To some, the projective techniques have been a fad, now happily passing; to others, they appear as legitimate, highly specialized tools that will be continuously refined and employed by a few individuals concerned with particular kinds of problems for a very long time. The fad for projective techniques saw them being used for a time uncritically, as novelties, by dozens of field workers, often in inappropriate situations. Now that the fad stage has worn off and sober reflection has begun, the projective techniques and other test and measurement devices are being used by fewer but better-trained persons for the special tasks to which they are suited, or to which they may be adapted; and we may expect continuous improvement of the tools themselves and of their interpretation as this specialization continues.

A similar observation may be made with respect to a number of conceptual schemes and research procedures "borrowed" from other disciplines. Psychoanalysis, for instance, is a highly specialized branch of psychiatry, particularly successful in dealing with the character disorders and symptomatic neuroses of upper- and middle-class people who can afford and will accept protracted verbal treatment. Much of psychoanalytic theory has been, in one form or another, used by culture-and-personality workers. For a time, it was something of a fad to sprinkle psychoanalytic jargon over the pages of ethnographic reports, like the water of baptism, in order to make them read like personality descriptions. This faddish misuse of psychoanalytic theory, by both psychiatrists and anthropologists, is waning; what remains is a specialized body of concepts and research techniques that will continue to be used wherever profitable by properly trained men. Comparable remarks may be made about the utility of communication theory, reinforcement learning theory, the life history, and other special techniques and bodies of knowledge. Their incorporation into anthropological thought is regularly accompanied by inflated claims that they are universal theoretical or methodological solvents, and students flock to try them out. Enthusiasm wanes when they are recognized as being useful only in solving particular kinds of problems, and they assume the humbler but more enduring role of specializations.

chapter two
THE EVOLUTION
OF CULTURE AND
THE EVOLUTION
OF BRAIN

The concept of personality generally connotes not only an organization of motives, but also a repertoire of cognitive processes. Contemporary dynamic psychology, in contrast to the early Freudian approach, is very much concerned with these "ego functions," for they provide the "organization factor"[1] that makes the difference between the intricate emotional architecture of mental health and the shambles of mental illness. Furthermore, these cognitive, or ego, functions govern the individual's relation to the world around him via perception, learning, language and other forms of symbolic communication, and by "insightful," "creative," or "imaginative" restructuring. Cognitive processes both organize the motives of the individual and relate them to his environment.

The study of cognition has been, at least until recently, one of the least thoroughly developed aspects of academic psychology, but it is certainly one of the oldest. It is also an ancient preoccupation of anthropologists. With or without the blessing of psychologists, anthropologists—even those outside the conventional culture-and-personality tradition—always have used assumptions above cognitive process as the foundation for culture theory. The rational calculations involved in adaptive behavior, psycholinguistic relativism, the study of "symboling," teleological functionalism, and the rational creativities of innovation—these and similar issues long have been of central concern in anthropological literature. The general point of cultural relativism—that, as Kurt Koffka put it, "the fact that things are as they are does not explain why they look as they look"—has been a commonly accepted methodological principle among most anthropologists for generations.

But we cannot here examine the whole subject of culture and

1. Rashkis, "A General Theory of Treatment in Psychiatry."

41

cognition. In this chapter, we have a more restricted aim: to consider the implications of the principle that a certain complexity of cognitive apparatus is necessary to the development and maintenance both of the complexity of culture and of the complexity of personality characteristic of modern man. As we look back over the last few million years, we observe that recognizably human cultures and personalities have developed in an evolutionary process that seemingly has been dependent upon the evolution of an increasingly large and complex brain. Or, more precisely, these developments have been concomitant with the evolution of an increasingly large cerebral cortex—that part of the brain in which those mental functions that we call cognitive are performed for the most part.

MAN'S EXPANDING BRAIN

Let us first take the long view. In the perspective of the past few million years, two major events in the history of the hominids are outstanding: (1) a rapid, progressive, and cumulatively vast increase in the size of brain in certain hominid lines; (2) a similarly rapid, progressive, and vast increase in the complexity of culture in the same hominid lines. These two events, furthermore, have been concurrent rather than successive. It is the concurrence of the changes, in time, that poses the significant scientific problem: the elucidation of the interdependence of the evolution of culture and the evolution of brain.

The probable magnitude of the impact of cultural evolution on brain evolution may be judged from the simple fact that at least one-half of the modern human brain's total volume and all of the difference in cranial capacity between modern man and the earliest known fossil members of his genus have been accumulated in the million and a half years following the adoption of upright posture and invention of chipped stone tools. This is a conservative estimate, based on an assumption of mean modern *sapiens'* cranial capacity at 1,350 cc., mean *Homo habilis* at 700 cc., and the proposition that *Homo habilis* was the first maker of stone tools.

But this sort of heuristic arithmetic will not carry us very far, and serious conceptual blockages from the start will impede further progress both in defining the problem and in obtaining relevant data. We must therefore examine some of these conceptual difficulties, first from an historical, and later from an analytical, standpoint. Such an examination will lead to the chief purpose of this chapter: the outlining of a loose but general theory of brain and culture relationships.

HISTORY OF DEFINITION OF THE PROBLEM

Although the evolutionary relation between culture and brain may seem to be far removed from the conventional concerns of culture-and-personality, a moment's reflection will show that the subject is not merely relevant, but is central. This is because, as Hallowell,[2] La Barre,[3] Henry,[4] Spiro,[5] and other writers in the culture-and-personality tradition have pointed out, the development of man's capacity to form his present kind of complex personality structure is an evolutionary process worthy of study. This process has yielded a brain that is anatomically distinctive in size and structure, most conspicuously in the mass of the cerebral cortex. Increase in size is not, in itself, necessarily a sign of improvement in function, but it is an empirical correlate of such an improvement in the hominid evolutionary series. Hence, in the following discussion we shall treat gross increases in size—readily observable and measurable—as valid indices of those enlargements of hominid cognitive capacities that have accompanied the evolution of human varieties of culture and personality.

Awareness that the relationship between brain and cultural evolution is problematical has been slow in developing. In the nineteenth century, the matter was handled by citing convenient

2. "Personality Structure and the Evolution of Man."

3. *The Human Animal.*

4. "Culture, Personality, and Evolution."

5. "Human Nature in Its Psychological Dimensions."

assumptions. Many nineteenth-century scientists were still influenced by the ethnocentric belief that "civilized" cultures were excreted by "civilized" physical types, and "primitive" cultures by "primitive" physical types. The fundamentalists disposed of the issue by invoking the *deus ex machina*. Charles Darwin, of course, was concerned with applying the same principles of natural selection to human evolution as to the evolution of other organisms. Darwin, however, tended toward uncritical emphasis on sanguinary individual competition for food (natural selection) and mates (sexual selection) as the social processes in which selection occurred; the cooperative institutions were not taken as his model. Furthermore, the supply of spontaneous genetic variations, even in Darwin's eyes, appeared to be inadequate to account for the innovations in behavior that we would call culture today (and that Darwin tended to label as "half-art and half-instinct"). Consequently, he was forced to postulate the inheritance of selected acquired characteristics to account for the differentiation of men from animals and of primitive from civilized men. This led him to an analytical model that has the advantage of recognizing the mutual interaction of brain evolution and cultural evolution but the disadvantage of invoking the now unacceptable Lamarckian hypothesis. Darwin's theory may be exemplified by the following quotation:

A great stride in the development of intellect will have followed, as soon as the half-art and half-instinct language came into use; for the continued use of language will have reacted on the brain and produced an inherited effect; and this again will have reacted on the improvement of language. As Mr. Chauncey Wright has well remarked, the largeness of the brain in man relatively to his body, compared with the lower animals, may be attributed in chief part to the early use of some simple form of language,—that wonderful engine which affixes signs to all sorts of objects and qualities, and excites trains of thought which would never arise from the mere impression of the senses, or if they did arise could not be followed out. The higher intellectual powers of man, such as those of ratiocination, abstraction, self-consciousness, &c., probably follow from the continued improvement and exercise of the other mental faculties.

The development of the moral qualities is a more interesting problem. The foundation lies in the social instincts, including under this term the family ties. . . . It is not improbable that after long practice virtuous tendencies may be inherited.[6]

We may smile at the simplicity of some of Darwin's assumptions, such as the inheritance of acquired virtue, but the Darwinian hypothesis did not suffer from two weaknesses that have afflicted some later and more sophisticated formulations. Specifically, he posited no discontinuity between evolutionary processes in man, in animals, and in the transitional forms; and he recognized that what we would call culture today developed concurrently with brain in some process of mutual dependency.

A. R. Wallace, who independently had discovered natural selection as an explanatory principle in physical evolution, sensed another aspect of the brain-and-culture problem. As Loren Eiseley points out, Wallace had absorbed, in the course of his travels, some of the culturally relativistic attitude of ethnology. He used the concept of culture and he recognized that men of such "low" cultures as might be found in primitive societies possessed ample brains. (Darwin naively assumed a race-and-culture equivalence.) Wallace asserted:

Natural selection could only have endowed the savage with a brain a little superior to that of an ape, whereas he actually possesses one but very little inferior to that of the average member of our learned societies. . . . among the lowest savages with the least copious vocabularies, the capacity of uttering a variety of distinct articulate sounds, and of applying to them an almost infinite amount of modulation and inflection, is not in any way inferior to that of the higher races. An instrument has been developed in advance of the needs of its possessor.[7]

But Wallace himself was unable to do much with his insights; he hinted at mystical, quasi-supernatural interventions in human

6. *Descent of Man*, p. 624.

7. In Eiseley, *Darwin's Century: Evolution and the Men Who Discovered It*, p. 311.

evolution, and increasingly dispensed with selection (whether of genetic or acquired characters) as a principle to explain the sudden and spectacular evolution of other specialized parts after the upright posture had been achieved. He doubted, indeed, what Darwin and his contemporary (and later) disciples never questioned, that the great increments of hominid intellectual capacity, accumulated since Miocene times, had any survival value at all. But (in common with later evolutionists) he felt that other evolutionary processes had stopped, once the hominid brain had achieved human status.[8]

Twentieth-century biology has worked hard to resolve the ambiguities and to prune away the excrescences of evolutionary theory, as left by Darwin, Wallace, Thomas Huxley and other nineteenth-century pioneers. Modern population genetics has indicated that, because of the large number of gene *loci* in man (in the neighborhood of 40,000), and because of the variety of alternatives at many *loci* resulting from genetic mutation, under certain population conditions a sufficient body of diversified genetic raw material exists for natural selection to do its work. It is not necessary to call upon the inheritance of habit as an auxiliary source of variations. Genetic theory has also provided interesting, if difficult to test, theories of evolution that permit, given the necessary data, prediction of the rates and boundaries of change in genetic complexes. Anthropology, comparative biology, and psychology have demonstrated that cooperative social systems should select for intelligence as strictly as competitive societies. Paleontology and comparative anatomy have documented various phylogenetic histories in considerable detail.

But these developments have, paradoxically, been of little use in the elucidation of the relationship between cultural evolution and brain evolution. The reason lies in the divergence of specializations: biologists, physical anthropologists, and cultural anthropologists have increasingly gone their own way since Darwin's time. Cultural anthropology, in particular, during the first half of the twentieth century, did not maintain intense concern with the theory of cultural evolution; instead, it emphasized close ethnographic description on a relativistic matrix. Both physical

8. *Ibid.,* Chap. XI.

and cultural anthropologists eschewed the early "social Darwinism" theories that rather crudely rationalized ethnic, class, and other biases. Furthermore, a philosophic doctrine, central in Darwin's thinking, has been partially abandoned by the biologists. Uniformitarianism, as a guiding principle in the study of man-animal relationships, has been replaced by a concern with man's uniqueness, and that uniqueness has been conceived to reside in man's possession of culture.[9] A traditional, but gratuitous, distinction between "natural" and "artificial" selection further emphasizes man's uniqueness. These currents of thought have conspired to make culture appear to be mainly an epiphenomenon: a product of physical evolution and not a determinant thereof. The problem has been neatly cut in half: biological theory is addressed largely to the explanation of how man came to have a brain big enough to entertain symbols and thus create culture; and what happened to culture and the brain thereafter is, by and large, handed over to the anthropologists (except, of course, by some eugenists who deplore the supposed diminution of the operation of natural selection on cultured man).

Julian Huxley has been perhaps the most eloquent and most popular exponent of the epiphenomenal theory of culture, which has, as its corollary, the concept of the uniqueness of man. In an essay urging anthropologists to emulate evolutionary biology in the study of cultural evolution ("the adoption of a broadly similar outlook would permit real progress in anthropology"), Huxley is explicit:

it appears that before the mid-Pliocene period some five million years ago, all the purely physiological and material possibilities of life had been exhausted—size, power, speed, sensory and muscular efficiency, chemical coordination, temperature-regulation, and the rest. After nearly two thousand million years, biological evolution on this planet had reached the limit of its advance.

But evolution was by no means at an end. Major advance was still possible, for other major potentialities of life had not been realized, one of its most important capacities scarcely exploited. . . .

9. Etkin, "Social Behavior and the Evolution of Man's Mental Faculties"; Huxley, *Man Stands Alone;* Simpson, *The Meaning of Evolution.*

[i.e.,] the cumulative transmission of experience. The resultant shareable, transmissible, and progressively transformable tradition gave rise to the new type of entity or organization technically called cultural, and evolution in the psycho-social phase has been essentially cultural, not biological or genetic.[10]

Some biologists view the supposed cessation of physical evolution with alarm. George G. Simpson dolefully observes:

Man has so largely modified the impact of the sort of natural selection that produced him that desirable biological progression on this basis is not to be expected. There is no reason to believe that individuals with more desirable genetic characteristics now have more children than do those whose genetic factors are undesirable, and there is some reason to suspect the opposite. The present influence of natural selection on man is at least as likely to be retrogressive as progressive. Maintenance of something near the present biological level is probably about the best to be hoped for on this basis.[11]

Similar ominous predictions are commonly made by other biological theorists when the subject of postcultural human evolution is broached. Urgent pleas for eugenic legislation and eugenic education are uttered in tones implying the imminent end of civilization if this negative evolution is not checked by such heroic measures as the sterilization of the mentally ill, criminals, national enemies, and other "unfit" members of society.

But such oracular pronouncements as these, contained in philosophical epilogues and popular expositions of evolution, serve more to obscure the problem than to clarify it. Actually, they are reassertions of belief in the continued operation of the selective law, for to assert that modern culture has eliminated all but "retrogressive" bodily and mental evolution is merely to pass a personal value judgment on the products of selection.

Of late, however, some scientists have taken up the problem from the other direction: culture as prime mover and brain as

10. "Evolution, Cultural and Biological," pp. 6–7.
11. *The Meaning of Evolution*, p. 344.

epiphenomenon. Empirical studies have revealed probably continuing evolutionary processes in such genetic traits as blood groups and other racial characters in recent millennia. Theodosius Dobzhansky, although he repeats the clichés about cultural heredity and the uniqueness of man, emphasizes in his textbook:

The adaptive advantage of the ability to acquire even the most rudimentary forms of culture must have been so great in the early stages of human evolution that natural selection rapidly propagated the genotypes which permitted the acquisition of culture throughout the human species. The gene-controlled capacity to learn, absorb, and use new techniques and tools was, then, developed, intensified, and diffused by means of biological evolution, making our species more and more human.[12]

Hayes and Hayes, reflecting on the cultural capacities of their adopted baby chimpanzee, went so far as to suggest that man's brain probably increased greatly in size *after* man's chimpanzee-like forebears graduated to a cultural level of existence.[13] Physical anthropologists and cultural anthropologists alike have, in fact, begun to consider seriously the role of culture itself as the determinant of man's capacity for culture. A number of anthropologists have contributed to this viewpoint but Neil Tappen first asserted the argument explicitly in a brief paper in the *American Anthropologist*:

Ancestors of the human group must have made the shift over to symbolic communication to initiate specifically human evolution. Such an adaptive change corresponds to Simpson's evolutionary mode, the *quantum evolution*. Once such a shift toward this new adaptive zone was initiated, a high selective advantage for individuals better adapted to learned behavior and symbolic communication must have ensued. . . . The progressive increase in brain size is interpreted here as indicating the process involved in the evolution of a species adapting better to a cultural way of life. In terms of selection theory, individuals with better brains would be better adapted to a cultural environment, with resulting superior

12. *Evolution, Genetics, and Man,* pp. 339–340.
13. Hayes and Hayes, "The Cultural Capacity of Chimpanzees."

viability and greater reproduction of culture-adapted characteristics.[14]

Carleton Coon, in one of the Cold Spring Harbor Symposium
papers,[15] added a significant additional suggestion: that "the
recorded changes in the size of the human brain are in some way
associated with increases in cultural complexity." A radically
epiphenomenal view of culture thus seems, on the face of it,
unreasonable, as well as empirically undemonstrable.

THE EVOLUTION OF CULTURE

Culture and Protoculture

A. I. Hallowell, in a pair of significant papers,[16] has observed
that a discontinuous concept of culture—as something that came
into being with a kind of mid-Pleistocene thunderclap—is fundamentally antievolutionist. He points out that presapiens hominids must be assumed to have lived in social groups. The data
of primatology indicate that these social groups were characterized by territoriality and by some form of the biparental family
(that is, a perennial association of two or more adults of both
sexes who, as a group, care for offspring). Enduring, transgenerational territorialism and biparental family structure in primates
imply not merely learning, but social learning. Furthermore,
subhuman primates display various learned skills and have a
certain tradition of technical knowledge. They recognize and
avoid poisonous berries; they use (but rarely make) traditional
implements; they construct and inhabit domiciles ("nests"); they
intercommunicate by signs, such as gestures and sounds; they live
in bands that frequently are larger than the biparental family,
and in which a variety of social roles are played by individuals.

14. "A Mechanistic Theory of Human Evolution," p. 606.

15. "Human Races in Relation to Environment and Culture with Special Reference to the Influence of Culture upon Genetic Changes in the Human Population," p. 248.

16. "The Structural and Functional Dimensions of a Human Existence" and
"Behavioral Evolution and the Emergence of the Self."

As Hallowell remarks, such pretool, prelanguage, prefire systems of learned social behavior cannot be maintained by organisms that are incapable of concept-formation (intrinsic symbols); and concept-formation can be demonstrated at least in chimpanzees by discrimination-and-learning experiments.[17]

Now extrinsic symbols (such as spoken words) are the signs of concepts. Many anthropologists regard the extrinsic symbol as the criterion of culture. Many anthropologists also deny that any animal, except man, is an extrinsic-symbol user; thus they justify the denial of culture to nonhumans. But this view is questionable. An animal that forms concepts, and recognizes and produces signs, can hardly avoid associating signs with concepts, albeit on a simple level and perhaps depending more on the language of body movement than the language of sounds.[18] Etkin, a biologist, in a review of primate social behavior, does concede a limited ability for the use of extrinsic symbols, that is, a few "words," to the great apes,[19] and more recent studies have shown that chimpanzees can develop a respectable vocabulary in sign language![20] And some comparative psychologists freely use the word "culture" for subhominid behavior systems.

In the presence of these elaborate, learning-dependent social systems among the apes and monkeys, irrespective of the presence or absence of extrinsic symbols, Hallowell, like David Bidney,[21] finds it difficult to support the notion of a radical discontinuity. He therefore suggests the term "protoculture" to denote the systems of socially learned behavior among the higher primates below man, particularly including his protohominid ancestors. I would suggest (although Hallowell would not go so far) that the term "protoculture" be extended, in order to make it logically independent of biological taxonomy, to denote any system of socially learned behavior, irrespective of species, genus, order, of even phylum. While this extension would permit protoculture

17. Kelleher, "Concept Formation in Chimpanzees."

18. Cf. Birdwhistell, "Body Motion Research and Interviewing" concerning a "lexicon" of kinesic symbols.

19. "Social Behavior and the Evolution of Man's Mental Faculties."

20. Kellogg, "Communication and Language in the Home-Raised Chimpanzee."

21. *Theoretical Anthropology.*

to range over the socially learned behaviors of various birds, insects, and other creatures far removed from man (a distasteful prospect, perhaps, to those of us who wish to emphasize the uniqueness of our own species), it has the advantage of implying a behavioral continuity between man and other animals. This last implication should also be made explicit: both culture and protoculture are phenomena of the same class: namely, the class of transgenerational, socially learned, socially organized behavior. This more inclusive class may also, in the context of this discussion, be labeled "culture."

What, then, are the distinctions between culture and protoculture? The fundamental distinctions would seem to be three: the vastly greater use of extrinsic symbols by man, making spoken language possible; the control of sources of energy outside the human body; and the proliferation of technology (traditions of complex manipulative skills in the transfer and application of energy). Language, energy control, and technology would seem to be the necessary conditions for both the self-conscious, self-evaluating, constantly striving, moral character of human society that Hallowell stresses as a *sine qua non* of humanity, and the process of cumulative technical and scientific invention that marks the archeological as well as historical record. The extensive use of symbols, furthermore, would seem to be conducive to that difference between protoculture and culture which is of central importance in this inquiry: protoculture changes relatively slowly; culture changes relatively rapidly.

Levels of Organization of Culture

Although comparisons of particular cultures are usually qualitative, concerned with pattern and the presence or absence of specific traits, anthropologists continually invoke notions of order and magnitude. Cultures are ranked on single or multiple dimensions, such as level of industrial development, relative competitiveness or cooperativeness, degree of fulfillment of internal potentialities, degree of approximation to or removal from some index culture type (as in acculturation, diffusion, and culture area analyses), absolute level of evolutionary advancement, per capita energy output, absolute quantity of energy exploited, and so on. Simple ranked dichotomies are also often invoked: simple versus complex, primitive versus civilized, low versus high, and so on. These rankings are often conceptually metric but empirically nonmetric; that is, the user of the ranking conceives of the dimension as a continuous variable with measurable intervals between all pairs of values (like the series of real numbers), but the data may permit only a crude rank ordering of values without measurement of intervals. We are interested here in the possibility of treating these metric or nonmetric cultural variables as functions of time in evolutionary models.

The mathematical concept of a partial ordering offers itself as a useful nonparametric device for describing evolutionary series. A partial ordering may be defined as a set of attributes so ordered that each successive attribute implies all the preceding attributes. We may, for brevity, call such a partial ordering a scale. Thus in the scale $a \leftarrow b \leftarrow c \leftarrow d$, if d is true, then a, b, and c are true as well; if c is true, but d is not true, then a and b are true; d cannot be true without c being true; c and d can be equivalent, and so on. Certain cultural attributes of the primates, as ascertained from comparative psychology and anthropology, closely approximate such a scale, and that scale is in fact both a useful description of the empirical course of cultural evolution in the hominid family line and a statement of the scaling of cultures among the living primates (see Table III).

Table III Scale of Cultural Attributes in Primates

1. Territoriality	
2. Domiciles	
3. Band organization	*protoculture*
4. Biparental perennial family	
5. Implements	
6. Language	
7. Tools	
8. Controlled use of fire	
9. Cultivation and/or domestication	*culture*
10. Urbanism	
11. Industrial civilization	

The scale of cultural attributes in primates presented in Table III is a partial ordering of empirical data, with the qualification that "Language" may properly belong after either "Tools" or "Controlled use of fire." It is, however, nonmetric; that is, it does not tell us in any quantitative sense *how much* more of anything is contained in 11 than in 10; nor does it even tell us whether there is just as much, or more, or less increment in 11 over 10 as 10 over 9.

But anthropologists do often place cultures on an implicitly metric dimension (for which, alas, no practical observational devices yet exist): the dimension of level of complexity or level of organization. Coon, for instance, explicitly states:

> The essence of the quantitative approach in cultural anthropology lies in the thesis that the main stream or streams of human culture must have proceeded from simpler to more complex. The evidence of archaeology and of history supports this thesis, which in turn accords with all that we know of life in general. It must be equally apparent that the living cultures of the world vary in degrees of complexity, and that whole cultures can be listed and studied with greatest profit on the basis of such a progressive scheme.[22]

Mere complexity, however, is not the best criterion, for in a given system complexity may be accompanied by varying degrees of orderliness. An intuitively acceptable measure of the quantity of organization of a system should increase both with the orderliness of the system and with its complexity. Complexity essentially is a function of the number of possible events within the system. Orderliness, on the other hand, is a function of the relative probabilities of these events. Quantity of organization is the product of the orderliness and the complexity of the system.[23]

In fine, then, we claim that an evolutionary scale of primate cultures can be constructed on the basis of available data that will approximately fit the model presented in Table III. This scale probably correlates with a progressive increase in the quan-

22. *A Reader in General Anthropology*, p. vii.

23. See Wallace, "The Psychic Unity of Human Groups" for a mathematical definition of these concepts.

tity of organization of the corresponding culturally organized social systems, quantity of organization being understood to be the product of both complexity and order (smoothness of function). Coon, in the work quoted above, describes a series of levels of complexity on a group of (putatively) closely interrelated dimensions and sums them to define one major dimension of "cultural complexity." This dimension spans points 8, 9, and 10 on the scale in Table III. The values on Coon's dimensions can be readily translated into the notion of number of possible events: number of occupational specialties in the society; number of institutions to which an individual may belong; variety of articles traded, and so on. Coon apparently assumes equivalent smoothness of functioning at all levels as the parameter of complexity. Other anthropologists, however, have deeply concerned themselves with precisely this notion of smoothness of functioning, using such terms as "cultural integration," "morale," and "vitality." The two conceptual dimensions of complexity and orderliness therefore are themselves conventional in anthropology, and their relationships may be considered without doing violence to anthropological tradition.

Rates of Culture Change

During the last 50,000 years or so of human culture history, it is commonly conceded, the rate of culture change generally has been accelerating. Archeologists contrast the slowness with which the stone tool traditions changed during the lower Paleolithic and the rapidity of recent technological changes. Some anthropologists and sociologists, attending to these massive sweeps of time, have suggested that the complexity of various aspects of culture (measured by such indices as number of components in technology), and probably the complexity of whole cultures, have been increasing exponentially. The empirical observation underlying the assumptions of the exponential model is that the frequency of innovation in a given field increases with the number of extant components in that field.

When, however, we examine culture change more closely, we

find, as might be expected, that this smoothly accelerating curve of cultural-organizational increase is the sum of brief or specialized processes of change, many of which do not fit an exponential model, and which tend to differ markedly from one another in rate and direction. Some glotto-chronologists, for instance, have asserted that the rate of linguistic drift is relatively constant for the "basic vocabulary" of all languages, and that a count of differences between the basic vocabularies of related languages may be used as an index of absolute time elapsed since their social separation. (The logic is similar to logic in radium-lead and carbon-14 methods of dating geological and paleontological specimens.) Data bearing on differential rates of change are widely gathered and discussed: suggestions are made that some aspects of culture, such as religion and social organization in our own society, change more slowly than others (the "cultural lag" theory); that culture changes most rapidly in the areas of cultural focus; that cultures and civilizations grow, and decline, over centuries, with different rates at different times. Cultural anthropologists, including archeologists, have been very much interested in the phenomena of diffusion of culture traits over wide areas, the rates at which various culture traits have diffused, and the processes of selection, resistance, and acceptance that facilitate and impede acculturation (the process by which diffusion through an intercultural boundary occurs). Recently, considerable attention has been paid to the phenomenon of extremely rapid and widespread acceptance of innovation that occurs in connection with revitalization movements.

These various empirical studies of rates of culture change may, for our purposes, be summarized briefly: changes in the culture of a given localized segment of the human population will tend to be uneven in rate, to the point of being sporadic, and to proceed with different rates (including, occasionally, constant or even negative rates) in different aspects of the culture and in different social subgroups; furthermore, different segments of the human population at any given time have different cultures, all of which are changing in somewhat different directions and at different rates. These conditions are highly relevant to any discussion of processes of selection in man.

Culture Change and Genetic Change

In summarizing the present position of cultural anthropology on the general relation between genetic and cultural change, in the context of concern with brain-culture relations, four fundamental generalizations may be made: (1) in any given period of time, the human population will be found to exist in numerous distinct societies, many of which are demonstrably undergoing cultural change; (2) during a given generation, culture change usually occurs without concomitant biological change[24]; (3) the direction of future culture change to some extent can be predicted from a knowledge of the present state of a cultural system, and past changes can be plausibly explained in part by describing their antecedent cultural conditions; (4) usually, in culture change different parts of a population (either subgroups within a society or different societies within an area of interaction) at any given time will be accepting and using an innovation effectively, while others will not, and frequently this differential may be related to differential survival and reproduction rates in the two groups.

Culture Change and Cognitive Capacity

Although specific culture changes not only can but usually do occur without measurable concomitant genetic change, it would be a mistake to suppose that culture can therefore be treated as a closed system that—transforming but conserving some mysterious inner source of cultural energy—evolves according to its own plan with neither input nor output. The cultural system is manifestly an open system and phylogenetic change in physical constitution, climatic change, faunal change, and changes in physical environment have demonstrably played a part in its evolution, both special and general. The immediate source of culture

24. This view has received classic expression by A. L. Kroeber in his paper "The Superorganic" and by Leslie White in his essays on "culturology" in *The Science of Culture.*

change is the brain itself, in which changes of state, within the lifetime of the organism, lead to the changes in overt behavior that are the visible substance of culture change. Hence without evolutionary advance in the brain as an organ, culture cannot exceed a certain degree of complexity because the necessary innovations cannot be made. To summarize the argument in crude metaphor: the Pithecanthropines *did not* exploit atomic energy, because their *culture* had not yet evolved to the point where atomic energy was an inevitable next step in cultural evolution; but *their* culture *could never* reach this point because a brain of 900 cc. is not enough to produce an atomic physics.

THE EVOLUTION OF BRAIN

In an earlier passage we observed that a major increase in brain size has taken place among the hominids since the invention of stone tools, from about 700 to about 1,350 cc. (considering mean values for the most advanced varieties). Since the data are of necessity fairly crude estimates, subject to errors of sampling, errors arising from unreliable and different methods of measurement and computation (the use of estimates from living species to represent skeletally similar extinct ones, and so on), the figures are not precise; the order of magnitude, however, would not seem to be in doubt. What is important is that there has occurred in primates "a special evolution of the brain in the direction of the development of additional cerebral tissue, the weight of which is independent of body weight,"[25] and that this "special evolution," as Eiseley repeatedly has pointed out, has been not a singular "saltation," but an evolutionary "explosion." While other orders also show increase in brain size (for example, the horses during the Tertiary, as described by Tilly Edinger[26]), the recent primates are unique, both in rate of acceleration and (if index of cephalization be the measure) in level achieved.

We shall now consider, as the phenomenon to be explained and

25. Jerison, "Brain to Body Ratios and the Evolution of Intelligence," p. 449.
26. *Evolution of the Horse Brain.*

understood, this unique "explosive," exponential increase in the size of brain and shall introduce culture change as a possible determinant of this "explosion." In thus focusing on size, of course, we do not imply that an increase in mere mass of tissue has been responsible for the changes in man's abilities; as Ralph Holloway[27] argues effectively, other kinds of subtle modifications of the primate brain, including changes in the limbic system to raise the rage threshold, may very possibly have occurred. As is well known, furthermore, normal human brains today vary through a range of about 1,000 cc. Nonetheless, the increase in mean size is a paleontological fact to be explained and tissue reorganization and neurochemical changes are speculations; and, presumably, the change in brain size was accomplished by the natural selection of animals with better brains.

The Determinants of Increase in Brain Size

The increase in brain size observable in the paleontological record, and inferable from comparative primatology, is a change in phenotype. Three groups of factors may be, and probably are, involved as determinants: (1) the dependence of brain weight on body weight in phylogenetic process; (2) the dependence of brain weight on environmental conditions affecting ontogeny; (3) the evolution of genes affecting brain size independently of body size.

1. Dependence of Brain Weight on Body Weight. Within most of the mammalian orders, brain weight is a definite and characteristic mathematical function of body weight and can be satisfactorily predicted (in an actuarial sense) from knowledge of body weight. But the phylogenetic increase in brain weight, within the primate order, is larger than can be accounted for by the phylogenetic increase in body weight alone. The largeness of modern man's brain, in other words, is not simply the consequence of his having a larger body than his ancestors, although

27. "Cranial Capacity, Neural Reorganization, and Hominid Evolution: A Search for More Suitable Parameters."

some part of the phylogenetic increase in brain size may be attributed to an increase in body size.[28]

2. Dependence of Brain Weight on Environmental Conditions.
Although there is little to suggest that physical environmental conditions (other than such as produce gross pathologies) directly and independently affect brain size, it is not inconceivable that historical changes in the milieu of the primate brain could be also responsible for part of the phylogenetic increase in the size of phenotypes. Several well-known anthropological studies have demonstrated that changes in the cultural and geographical milieu of populations can affect phenotypic characters, such as head form, body height, and body weight, presumably via such factors as nutrition, stress, and disease. There is also evidence from studies with laboratory animals that "rich" environments, which provide the organism with relatively complex and frequent social and perceptual stimulation, directly cause increases in brain size and weight in comparison with "poor" environments (a finding relevant to efforts to improve the circumstances of the culturally deprived). Nevertheless, such processes on the face of it would seem to be insufficient to account for more than a small part of the vast increase in size of the primate brain during the past fifty-five million years. Actually some of these factors could as easily be considered responsible for reducing, rather than maximizing, the phenotypic differences expected from genetic evolution—as, for instance, in the reduction in hominid brain size from its maximum among the Neanderthals, whose average brain capacity exceeded modern man's by about 100 cc.

3. Genetic Evolution Involving Genes Affecting Brain Size Independently of Body Size. In view of the fact that phenotypic evolution in brain size has occurred, and that other processes are inadequate to account for it, it must be presumed that genetic evolution is largely responsible. The genetical theory of evolution, as developed by Sewall Wright, J. B. S. Haldane, R. A.

28. Jerison, *op. cit.*

Fisher, and others,[29] is primarily a rational mathematical theory, rather than an empirical one: that is, the equations that describe the distribution of genes are derived from reasonable assumptions, rather than from empirical data, and the entities represented in the equations are not readily observable. Several independent variables, according to this theory, are involved in genetic evolution, particularly mutation, random drift, and selection. It would seem that random drift is unlikely to be the sole explanation: random drift alone, without selection, would tend either to extinction, in small populations, or would be too slow, in larger ones; and mutation rates alone are probably too low to produce the effects observed in the last two million years. Both mutation and selection must therefore be invoked.

This raises the question of the selective advantage of genes conducive to large-brained phenotypes. While it is conceivable that brain could increase in size—not because size of brain is of advantage in phenotypic selection, but because it is genetically linked to some other, noncerebral, advantageous phenotypic character—it is simpler to make the obvious, if equally difficult to prove, assumption: that brain size, to some significant extent, is correlated with brain function, and that larger brains tend to have an advantage in phenotypic selection. It is not necessary to postulate a close correlation; it is only necessary that the correlation be sufficient to yield the gene for large brain a reproductive advantage under phenotypic selection substantially greater than twice its countermutation rate.

At this point it must be recognized that, since it is phenotypes which are "selected" for survival and reproduction, it is probably genetic complexes, rather than single genes, among which selection pressures discriminate most effectively. Thus, in all likelihood, a major increase in phenotypic cognitive capacity must have been the result of the selection of a complex of genes responsible for not merely brain size, but also for size of female pelvis, rate of growth, length of parental life, continuous sexual excitability of the female, appropriate enzyme systems control-

29. See Gerard, Kluckhohn, and Rapoport, "Biological and Cultural Evolution: Some Analogies and Explorations" for a summary of this theory.

ling brain metabolism, and so forth; in other words, for that whole set of behavior potentialities that is required for the maintenance of the conditions under which a primate with a large brain can be born, survive infancy and childhood, and reproduce its kind. Undoubtedly, a large number of genes are involved in this process, *all* of which are necessary to the success of the large-brained primate phenotype.

The large number of genes presumably involved carries a further interesting implication: it is highly improbable that any single gamete should be the site of all the necessary multiple mutations; furthermore, since most mutations are recessive, it is still less likely that such a mutational constellation would at once be expressed in phenotypic form. A more likely process would be that of the genetic preadaptation of a whole population, in which the recessive mutant alleles, each with a negligible individual selective value, occurred at random in a population and were diffused by the process of genetic drift. Once the gene pool contained a measurable "solution" of the constituent genes, even random mating, in the course of time, repeatedly would bring together all the ingredients of the criterion complex in single homozygous individuals. Such individuals, phenotypically, would possess selective advantage and would tend to increase the proportion of the criterion genes in the pool, even if several generations of their immediate descendants might lose the phenotypic evidences of the genes. Eventually, however, the proportion of criterion genes would become so large, and the "evolution of dominance" would have proceeded so far, that the corresponding phenotype would be displayed frequently and would be selectively favored in certain local groups, thereby possessing a *group* advantage and eventually outbreeding and replacing other groups.

Culture as a Determinant of the Variables in Genetic Evolution of Brain

To describe a culture is to describe certain properties of a population which are closely related to three of the evolution variables and may be related (at least today) to a fourth: gene migration, population size, selection pressure, and (possibly) mutation rate. Let us, for the moment, discount the last as more applicable to the future than to the historic past that we are considering.

1. Culture and Gene Migration. Culture immediately affects gene migration not only via a host of regulations on residence and marriage, but also by the most multifarious and indirect means. Anything that determines the social boundaries of sexual relations will affect gene migration: the technology of transportation, the system of trade, the nature of warfare, religious and magical beliefs, ethnic prejudices, institutions such as slavery and the adoption of captives, ideals of sexual beauty, and so on. The cumulative significance of all these factors lies in their contribution to the degree of relative genetic isolation of a culture-bearing population. It is evident that purely geographical factors affect gene migration, too, by determining the mutual accessibility of populations; but choice of geographical location, and its significance in relation to accessibility, are also heavily influenced by culture. Modern studies tentatively conclude that the typical human mating pattern is for a given area's population to be broken up into a large number of "partial isolates," within which fairly free interbreeding is guaranteed (and rationalized) by prohibitions against marriage between the near degrees of kinship, as locally defined. This human tendency to partial isolation of small breeding populations, to the extent that it is general and ancient in time, lays down one of Wright's hypothesized conditions for the most rapid kind of evolution.

2. Culture and Population Size. The same sort of cultural factors that determine group isolation are also active in determining the size of a culture-bearing population. Customs in regard to age of marriage, abortion, contraception, infanticide, and taboos on sexual activity immediately affect the dynamics of reproduction. Age- and sex-specific mortality and morbidity rates are functions of warfare patterns, sanitation, medical care, treatment of the aged, and so on. Fertility is affected by nutritional level, occupation, psychological stress, and so on, and technology and social structure determine the size of group that can maintain continuous existence as a freely intrabreeding partial isolate. Empirically, the partial isolates, discussed above, for modern European populations range between 400 and 3,000 in numbers; among simpler peoples, they are reported to range from 100 to 1,500. American Indian "political" tribes (the equivalent of partial isolates), in the northeastern agricultural area, ranged in size from 200 to 6,000, with few tribes larger than 3,000. Ward Goodenough has shown, with cross-cultural materials, that the size of face-to-face groups ranges between about 13 and about 1,000.[30] City planners have suggested that, even in a metropolis, the maximum size of the "neighborhood" cannot be more than a figure variously estimated at 2,000 to 6,000 persons. Since the "effective breeding populations" to which the evolution models refer are bounded not by genetic characters, but by the social relations of the phenotypic carriers of the genes, it would seem that the figures cited above all suggest that the size of human breeding populations, while variable culturally, largely varies between the limits (roughly) of about 100 and 3,000 persons. Effective breeding population generally is taken as one-third of the total population. Thus effective breeding population in humans lies between 33 and 1,000, probably tending toward the lower figure in early times at the protocultural border, and toward the higher figures only after the neolithic revolution.

If we take these figures as a basis for calculation, we arrive at the conclusion that the total gene pool of any hominid species, numbering 100,000 individuals or more, will be distributed among 100 partial breeding isolates, at the very least. The precise size of the isolates, and the index of their isolation, is largely dependent on culture. In all probability, in early times the number of isolates per 100,000 individuals would have been closer to 3,000, since the isolates themselves probably would have been smaller. These conclusions suggest that the typical hominid breeding structure is precisely that envisaged in Sewall Wright's hypothesis for rapid evolution: a relatively large population "cellulated" into a number of freely intrabreeding partial isolates.

30. Quoted in Murdock, *Social Structure*, p. 81.

3. Culture as a Selection Agent. We now consider the effects of culture on the differential reproduction of groups defined with respect to phenotypic mental functions, such as intelligence, educability, concept formation, self-awareness and self-evaluation, reliability of performance under stress, attention span, sensitivity in discrimination, creativity, and so forth. We suspect, but cannot prove, except via comparative psychology, that such functions to some degree are dependent on brain size. In order to simplify our own prose, we shall use the expression "cognitive capacity" to denote any subset of the set of functions mentioned above, on the grounds that they all contribute to maximizing the quantity of organization in the cognitive tasks that are imposed by culture, and that more than simply "intelligence," in the I.Q. sense, is involved.

The study of culture-and-cognition, as this area of interest may be called, has been slow to emerge, but research is now actively going ahead among anthropologists, linguists, sociologists, and psychologists, in the analysis of the cognitive tasks implicit in minimally adequate cultural behavior. The development of the technique known as componential analysis for the study of meaning, in linguistics and anthropology, and the application to it of the principles of logical semantics, is already yielding fruitful results. The description of cognitive task and motivation in innovation, and other aspects of culture change, presents an even more formidable challenge. Initially, it would seem that tension-reduction theories of learning, extended to innovation via the formula, "Necessity is the mother of invention," are inadequate alone to explain all of the phenomena, and that the cultural anthropologist, like some, at least, of the comparative psychologists, will be required first to postulate, and eventually to demonstrate, a primary "play" or "exploratory" or (as I like to call it) "organization drive."[31] As Ralph Linton put it some time ago:

the development of culture has become an end in itself. Man may be a rational being, but he certainly is not a utilitarian one. The constant revision and expansion of his social heredity is a result of some inner drive, not of outer necessity. It seems that man en-

31. "The Psychic Unity of Human Groups."

joys playing with both his mind and his muscles. The skilled craftsman is not content with endless repetitions. He takes delight in setting and solving for himself new problems of creation. The thinker derives pleasure from speculating about all sorts of things which are of no practical importance, while the individuals who lack the ability to create with either hand or mind are alert to learn new things. It seems probable that the human capacity for being bored, rather than man's social or cultural needs, lies at the root of man's cultural advance.[32]

The bearing of these considerations on the relationship between cultural evolution and brain evolution should now begin to be apparent. At a given time, individuals and groups differ, depending on various parameters (such as genetic endowment, health, age, stress level, motivation, and other factors), with respect to the complexity of the cognitive tasks that they can learn and perform in an orderly way. If this capacity chronically falls below that required by the task, their cultural participation will be restricted ipso facto, and they will tend to be subject to negative phenotypic selection; that is, they will not survive, or, if they survive, will reproduce at a lower rate. This capacity, it should be noted, is related to, but is not identical with, "intelligence" as it is measured by psychological tests, since it must include such qualities as reliability of performance under stresses of various kinds; stability of the physiological determinants; preconscious attention span, measured in periods of time up to and including years; readiness to increase performance on call, and probably other qualities that these tests do not generally measure. These qualities will determine, among other things, the *kind* of personality organization of which the individual is capable. Furthermore, it is evident that individuals frequently are faced, in the course of their lifetime, with the necessity of learning new and sometimes more complex cognitive tasks. These new tasks are often presented by new cultural material that has been invented and is diffusing, or is being imposed in the course of change by an interest group or by another society, or is possessed by a competing interest group or society. Such situations like-

32. *The Study of Man*, p. 90.

wise bring phenotypic selection for cognitive capacity to bear on a population.

In order to obtain some notion of how selection for cognitive capacity must operate, let us consider the cognitive tasks implied by the controlled use of fire, apparently first achieved by the Sinanthropines with a mean cranial capacity of about 1,100 cc.[33] The control of fire by a species has four components: (1) keeping the fire alive over extended periods of time (days, weeks, months, even years); (2) maintaining its size and position within definite boundaries; (3) being able either to transport or to kindle it; (4) using it for some useful purpose or purposes (light, warmth, frightening carnivores, driving or blinding game, tempering wooden implements, keeping away insects, cutting wood and hair, drying wet clothes, cooking, and so on). These four desiderata are both complex and interrelated and they require the cooperation of the group.

Maintenance of a fire means, first of all, bringing to it fuel: wood, or some other combustible material, recognizable from its appearance and tangible qualities. The fire must be close enough to the fuel supply to make the trip convenient. Since not all woods burn equally well and cleanly, the right kind of wood must be used. Furthermore, it must be reasonably dry; and, since in most places where wood can be found, protracted rain occurs from time to time, this means that it must be stored in a dry place. Storage is also desirable to reduce the frequency of trips.

Keeping the fire the right size and in the right place means that it must be large enough to be useful and secure from imminent failure, but not so large as to burn people, food, implements, or clothing, or to smoke out the user, or to use up the fuel too rapidly. It must be insulated from contact with combustible things, such as its own fuel supply, both in order to prevent loss and to keep it from spreading out of control. It must be located where it will not interfere with various activities and yet be where it will be usable; where it will not be in too much draft, nor where it will smother; where it will not be drowned by rain or flood.

33. See Oakley, "Fire as Paleolithic Tool and Weapon" for a review of paleolithic fire use.

Fire must be transportable; otherwise, unless kindling arts are known (and these are of fairly recent origin, coming into use, apparently, long after early Sinanthropus), fire-users will be geographically immobilized. Transporting fire requires at least care not to burn oneself, either directly with the brand or coals, or indirectly by firing the prairie or forest. If long distances are to be traversed, special insulating containers are needed.

And finally, fire must be useful. In Sinanthropine times, apparently, it was not used for cooking, but for warmth and dryness, and probably for light and protection. Effective use of open fire for warmth requires that people, gear, and a fire of proper size be carefully placed into a pattern that exacts maximum body warmth from minimum fuel.

In order to accomplish all these tasks, without interfering with other necessary activities, fairly complex cognitive operations are necessary. Types of fuel and location must be discriminated; there must be planning and foresight for replenishment and for such emergencies as rain and high wind; continuous, even if subliminal, attention must be paid to the condition of the fire; infants must be kept from falling into it; and so on. All this, in a group, requires some differentiation of responsibility and also shared responsibility; it requires some instruction of the young; above all, it demands continuous "back-of-the-mind" attention by every member of the group. Language would probably not be necessary, but would be very helpful, for immediate communication and the transmittal of traditional concepts.

Now, from the standpoint of selection, two points may be made: first, a group with fire is, in any environment, in a better position to survive various threats from cold, exposure, and predatory animals than is a group without fire and will also be able to live in colder regions than its fireless confreres; second, within the group, any individual who is unable to perform the cognitive tasks necessary to fire control is endangering both himself and his group, and he is apt to be negatively selected by his group if he fails to perform adequately. He will find it more difficult to attract a mate and to maintain a sexual relationship; his shivering or baking mate and offspring will have a lesser chance of survival; he himself may be burned or frozen or punished by contempt, assault, or ostracism for his failings. Other things being equal, an individual unable to perform the cognitive tasks required by the social use of fire, in a group in which the controlled use of fire is becoming or has become a culture trait, is less likely to survive and reproduce; but his group (with or without him) has a greater chance of survival than another competitive group without fire.

It is possible to obtain some clues as to the intensity of phenotypic selection for mental faculty in man in modern culturally organized societies. We do not intend to invoke here the commonly asserted, and patently ethnocentric and class-conscious, assumption that number of years of formal schooling, annual income, occupational status, and other such indices of social class are reliable measures of inheritable cognitive capacity. Such characteristics are phenotypic; their relevance to either heredity or cognitive capacity is very doubtful, and they are more properly described as subcultural differences than as phenotypic evidences of genetic endowment. (Indeed, this sort of class-and-caste eugenics is the intellectual successor to phrenology. Bumps for friendliness, religiosity, pugnaciousness, and so forth, have merely been replaced by genes for farming, banking, college education, mechanical drafting, income over $10,000 per year, and so on, *ad nauseam*.) More appropriate for our purposes are gross contrasts between normal and pathological or clinically deficient mental functions (at least some of which do have demonstrable genetic determinants).

We can obtain an initial orientation to this problem by observing that all social groups are forced to make one of four dispositions of those of their members who cannot safely and adequately perform the cognitive tasks required for participation. This disposition may be physical detention (institutionalization, chaining to a post, and so on), banishment, death, or the assignment of a limited (sometimes very useful) role that absolves the holder from some of the general tasks, such as food production, marriage and the rearing of children, military service, and so on. But in general those of minimal cognitive capacity have both a lower survival rate and a lower net reproduction rate precisely because they cannot perform the tasks necessary to stay alive and reproduce in a culturally organized society. Mentally defective individuals have a much lower life and reproductive expectancy than normals. For instance, in Massachusetts, as reported in 1932, the probability of an idiot female reaching reproductive age was about .2 (by contrast, for a normal female it was about .8); the probability of an idiot female living through the reproductive period was about .1 (for a normal female, about .7). It hardly seems far-fetched to suggest, in the light of these considerations, that even under the supposedly lax and dysgenic conditions of modern urban civilization, cultural selection still operates on phenotypic cognitive capacity with a severity that would be sufficient to produce substantial vertical evolution in a comparatively short time. This holds true even in cases involving recessive genes, provided sufficient genetic variations are available.

Genetic evolution in brain size may be reaching a plateau, however. The intensity of selection in comparison with mutation rates, and the cellulated nature of the breeding structure, seem to have reduced the hominid store of variability in many genetic characteristics. Adolph Schultz has cited the remarkable anatomical homogeneity of modern man, including all races, in comparison with wild primates (and, one may suspect, with the notoriously variable extinct hominoids); and David Wechsler (the author of the well-known intelligence test) similarly has remarked on the extremely small variance of several human physical and psychological dimensions.[34] Indeed, of all the indices of human capacity chosen by Wechsler, brain weight and cranial capacity are the most narrowly distributed—more narrowly, for instance, than intelligence, body weight, or memory span. Little evidence is available to suggest any substantial interracial differences in cognitive capacity. If it is true that human evolution has been using up the "capital" of genetic variability more rapidly than it has been replaced by mutational "investment," then it would seem that two more conclusions are indicated: (1) in regard to brain, modern man represents a highly selected and segregated combination of genetic characters present in small

34. Schultz, "The Specializations of Man and His Place Among the Catarrhine Primates," p. 49, and Wechsler, "The Range of Human Capacities."

numbers as new mutants (and only rarely phenotypically realized) in very primitive and highly heterogeneous, but genetically preadapted, populations (perhaps on the level of *Sinanthropus*, for instance); (2) after this store of variability in some significant characters has been substantially exhausted, physical evolution with respect to them will perforce slow down in pace to a rate controlled by mutation (if it has not already slowed down, as evidenced by the relative constancy of brain size since Neanderthal times). This will, in turn, if not slow down, at least help to determine the direction of cultural evolution, probably toward the development of cultural systems so devised that machines can take up an increasing share of cognitive burdens as the total culture increasingly outstrips individual human cognitive capacities. This process, indeed, is already becoming important. Furthermore, continuing vertical selection for any characteristics (such as reactions to stress, fatigue, emotion, disease, and so on) that temporarily reduce cognitive capacity, can be expected as demands for reliable performance become more intense. This demand for reliability of performance, as opposed to level of peak performance, may be reflected in the phenomenon of schizophrenia.

CONCLUSION: A THEORY OF CULTURAL SELECTION

In the preceding pages the relationship of the evolution of culture to the evolution of brain has been examined from various positions. On the basis of modern knowledge, it seems that several propositions are now reasonably well established:

> The distribution of the genetic determinants of cognitive capacity in a population, of which one rough index is brain size, sets upper bounds for the quantity and direction of culture change which is possible without genetic change.
>
> 2. Culture can and does change independently of prior genetic change, within the aforesaid genetically determined limits and, since the protocultural period among hominids, culture has increased in quantity of organization at an accelerating rate.

3. Culture acts as a powerful agent of phenotypic (and probably of genotypic) selection for cognitive capacity.

4. Because of the intensity of cultural selection, despite the contribution of mutation, a large proportion of genetic evolution in the *sapiens* ancestry may have been the result of genetic fixation, at the expense of intraspecies variability.

5. Continuous culture change has probably maintained an especially high selection pressure and may be producing a plateau, with respect to determinants of cognitive capacity.

6. Culture change (not, as some theories have had it, just "culture") is probably largely responsible for the observed increase in brain size in the hominid line.

chapter three
CULTURE AND COGNITION

The long-standing dispute among anthropologists over the relative merits of "emic" and "etic" in ethnographic description is essentially an argument over a behavioristic versus a cognitive definition of culture. A similar, and independently evolved, clash of traditions has existed in experimental psychology for some time, the learning theorists (such as Pavlov, Hull, Skinner, and Osgood) explaining behavior by reference to one or another model of directly observable stimulus-response-reinforcement sequences, and the cognitive theorists (the Gestalt school, the psychodynamic tradition, and such recent experimental investigators as Jerome Bruner and Leon Festinger) explaining it in terms of schemata stored in the brain as a result of learning and inferable from performance and verbal report. Since much of ethnography is, from the standpoint of this book, a description of cognitive systems, it is desirable to review certain aspects of the issue in psychology for the light it may shed on anthropological approaches to cognition.[1]

SOME ASPECTS OF THE PROBLEM OF COGNITION IN EXPERIMENTAL PSYCHOLOGY

The so-called S–R and information-processing approaches to cognition are both confronted with the problem of accounting for certain phenomena of learned behavior that have been demonstrated in laboratory experiments. Conspicuous among these phenomena are "stimulus equivalence" and "response equivalence."

1. For psychological approaches see Bruner, Goodnow, and Austin, *A Study of Thinking*, and Harper, *et al.*, *The Cognitive Processes: Readings*; for a selection of anthropological writings see Tyler, *Cognitive Anthropology*, and Garvin, *Cognition: A Multiple Approach*.

"Stimulus equivalence" is the tendency of a subject to respond in the same way to different conditioned stimuli (not merely objectively different by finely honed technical measurement but different within the capacity of the subject to discriminate). For instance, the actual stimulation of receptors (sense organs) by a given object or event may vary widely depending on such factors as intensity, distance, lighting, and position in space; merely "similar," and not identical, stimuli are adequate to elicit a given response; the condition of the organism with respect to hunger, fatigue, stress, and so forth, may vary widely without obstructing performance. In other words, the organism "generalizes": it classifies a range of objectively different stimuli as equivalent. In human beings, this is impressively demonstrable in semantic conditioning. In these experiments, a human subject learns to salivate, or respond in some other reflex modality such as vasoconstriction or blood coagulation time, in response to a particular word or phrase. Acoustically identical but semantically different words, visually presented, do not evoke the response. Acoustically different but semantically identical (or at least closely related in meaning) words do evoke the response. Thus to a subject conditioned to drool at the words "style, "urn," "freeze," and "surf," the words "stile," "earn," "frieze," and "serf" are not stimulating; but his mouth waters at "fashion," "vase," "cold," and "waves."

Correspondingly, "response equivalence" may also be regarded as a kind of classification. For example, Bruner and his associates over a period of time trained rats to run a certain maze whose pattern was $LRLRLR$ ... Those rats who had learned this pattern of responses thoroughly took far less time to learn a maze whose pattern was reversed $RLRLRL$ ... The experimenters concluded that the rats had learned, not just the original $LRLR$ pattern, but a more general principle (whether it was acquired during the learning of the initial sequence or after the first few trials on the new sequence is not clear). On the human level, a similar point has been urged by Noam Chomsky[2] who argues convincingly that because a person can produce an infinite num-

2. *Language and Mind.*

ber of grammatical sentences in his language, he has not learned particular strings of words, or parts of speech, or even a stochastic matrix for generating such strings, but rather a basic grammatical structure from which, by applying transformation rules, he can generate any number of sentences. Similarly, Miller, Galanter, and Pribram[3] and others point out that often a "response" is not a particular and finite sequence of muscular contractions but an open-ended effort to achieve a given effect on the environment by one means or another.

Such considerations as these lead both learning theorists and cognitive theorists to look at the old paradigm anew. Evidently it is the mediating schemata that reinforcement reinforces, rather than a unique relationship between a single sequence of receptor images and a single sequence of muscular contractions or glandular secretions. Hence one must ask what previously had not been a serious question: what are the mediating schemata—structures or processes—in the brain that must be assumed to account for such phenomena as stimulus equivalence and response equivalence?

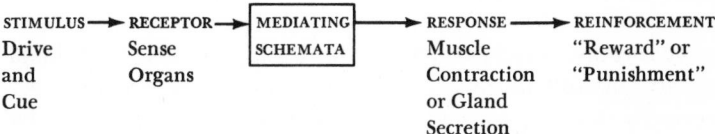

STIMULUS → RECEPTOR → MEDIATING SCHEMATA → RESPONSE → REINFORCEMENT
Drive and Cue — Sense Organs — — Muscle Contraction or Gland Secretion — "Reward" or "Punishment"

The learning theory answer in general is that the brain contains complex S–R circuits, including internal reinforcers, which are somehow established in learning and are operative in such "cognitive" processes as perceptual classification and planning. To speculate about such circuits is awkward, however, for learning theory has prided itself on its objectivity and reliance on the measurement of hearable, seeable, countable physical objects and physical events; yet now it must speculate on the nature of physical objects and events that are not hearable, seeable, or countable in order to preserve the claim to universality of explanation. The cognitive theory answer in general is to concentrate

3. *Plans and the Structure of Behavior.*

attention on "what is learned" and to describe information-processing structures (also denoted as schemata, plans, strategies, classifications, images, maps, codes, and so forth) on the basis of inference from performance (and, in the case of human beings, to some extent from introspection and verbal report, in the language in which such structures are customarily communicated by one person to another). It even becomes permissible to question whether reinforcement in any but the most metaphysical sense is necessary for all learning or for the preservation of schemata from extinction (*vide* curiosity learning, latent learning, and imprinting).

But the last question requires a corollary. If, as both human intuition and laboratory experiment suggest, reinforcement is *not* necessary for all learning, knowing, and thinking, then even where reinforcement *is* at work, there may be another process that contributes to the formation and maintenance of schemata. Thus the corollary question is: what processes are there in addition to S–R learning that might contribute to the formation, maintenance, and application of schemata? Two sorts of answers suggest themselves, which are not mutually exclusive, and both of them of traditional interest to anthropologists: first, there may be certain cognitive capacities for forming kinds of schemata that are neurologically "wired into" all human beings, are genetically determined, and are presumably a product of evolution; second, there is a phenomenon that might be called "autistic thought" (without implying necessary psychopathology) that is responsible for reorganizing what has been learned, constantly recombining and differentiating elements in novel arrangements, going beyond information given, solving contradictions, and sometimes innovating new schemata. The first kind of answer is explicitly asserted by Chomsky for the capacity to form a grammar and by Claude Lévi-Strauss for certain principles of classification and analogical and dialectical reasoning. The second kind of process (for which the capacity, to be sure, is assumed to be innate and biologically based) is suggested by such familiar phenomena as dreaming, meditating, and thinking, personality development by the use of defense mechanisms and psychotherapy, and "creative" work of various kinds. ("Autistic thought" in the pathological sense then would be merely a condition of preoccupation with autistic thought in a person whose automatic synthesizer is not producing adequately.)

Indeed, it is difficult to dispense with the notion of an automatic synthesizer, which mechanically manufactures possible new schemata, as a contributor to the formation of schemata even in an S–R model of cognitive process. For the automatic synthesis must play the role, in any mental process in which new environmental information is *not* coming in, that the experimenter plays in the typical learning procedure where cues and reinforcements are environmental. The *experimenter* (whose role is usually not adequately represented in psychological analyses of the learning process) himself invents the alternate schemata that are imposed by design and schedule on the subject—rat or man—for reinforcement to select. Inside the experimenter's head, however, there is no homunculus to perform the task he performs for the rat. Without an automatic synthesizer to produce alternates as grist for the reinforcement mill, it is difficult to see why reinforcements are needed at all. The problem is not unlike a problem in the theory of natural selection: just as Darwin had to assume a supply of "variations" among which selection could select, so the learning theorist must assume variable behavior in the subject—subject must be able to do at least two things in any situation—in order for reinforcement to select (if there is no variation, reinforcement would be gratuitous; thus a simple reflex is not learned and need not be reinforced). But where does the supply of variations come from? For the evolutionist, the answer has been mutation (and, for some, acquired characteristics); for cognitive theory, the answer has to be an automatic alternate-schemata synthesizer. And this answer is relevant to anthropology, for the cultural anthropologist must also ask: how are the innovations produced that lead to culture change?

THE GENERAL CHARACTERISTICS OF SCHEMATA

With relatively little intercommunication on the subject, and for the most part (but with some interesting exceptions that we shall discuss later) working on different bodies of data, anthropologists, linguists, and psychologists have come to rather similar conclusions about the general characteristics of the schemata that they discover. The dimensions on which these general characteristics are located are four in number: level of abstraction, degree of complexity, the nature of interschema linkages, and extent of verbalizability.

Any kind of "concept-formation," whether or not the concepts are represented in language or merely demonstrated in stimulus and response equivalences, by definition implies abstraction. The abstraction involves a restriction of attention to selected dimensions both of the environment and of the organism's own response potentialities, and the exclusion of others as irrelevant; it necessarily also involves the ignoring of variations within the minimum resolution range permitted by the physiology of the animal. In these senses, the schemata are both insatiable and inexhaustible: an unlimited number of different actual stimulus situations can be recognized as the same, and an unlimited number of actually different responses can be generated by the same schema. Furthermore, it seems to be the intuitive practice of both anthropologists and psychologists to "empty" the schemata they describe as much as possible of particular content and if possible to describe it as a "total" abstraction with minimal restrictions as to context. Thus Bruner describes the rat schema as "single alternation" in the most general terms, although he does raise the question of whether it applies only to walled mazes or whether the rat would apply it to, for instance, color alternation on a painted board. Linguists do their best to describe languages in terms free of particular utterances or of "meaning"; a list of phonemes does not specify a lexicon and a grammar does not contain any single sentence. Lévi-Strauss[4] intuitively proceeds to treat "a myth" as the set of all its variants and to describe "it" as a transformation rule describing the relationships among elementary themes; indeed, he argues that all myths are generated by one single schema represented by the mystic formula:

$$F_x(a):F_y(b) \simeq F_x(b):F_{a-1}(y)$$

Whether the formula adequately represents the schema of myth

4. "The Structural Study of Myth."

may be argued, but it represents very well the effort to "empty" schemata and to represent them in a content- and domain-free algebraic or geometrical formula. The same principle applies to the work of anthropologists on kinship systems: the terminological structures, and the rules of marriage, residence, and descent are as soon as possible reduced to abstract forms whose structures can be represented in a symbolic notation usually derived from logic, algebra, or geometry.

The use of such totally abstract notations, however, begs a question of importance: in what domain of experience is the schema valid? Let us return to Bruner's rats. What *did* they learn? Was it the abstract series *ababab*..., potentially discoverable as a progressive shortening of transfer learning time not only in the color alternation experiment but also in such conceivable other experiments as learning to press two bars alternately, then learning to lift first one paw and then the other, then learning to stand first in one corner and then the other, and so forth? Or is the domain restricted to turning left, then right, wherever the stimulus also has the form *LRLR*...? Or is it restricted simply to pairs of *LR* mazes differing only in the direction of the initial turn?

Similar questions are of interest to the anthropologist, who tries to identify the same formal structure in diverse domains. Given an analysis of a kinship terminology and the description of its taxonomic structure in an algebraic notation, are the formal characteristics of the taxonomy (such as, for instance, a perfectly orthogonal matrix) found also in other taxonomic domains in the same culture such as plant classifications, color terminology, and so on? Are the same dimensions repeatedly used for concept formation in diverse domains? The continuing currency of interest in such descriptive concepts as values, national character, ethos and eidos, world view, the Sapir-Whorf type of speculation, and so forth, all depend upon an intuitive feeling that certain schemata are so "basic," so "deep," and so abstract that they give structure to many domains of experience and thus can be said to characterize the culture as a whole.

All this suggests that schemata have a kind of nesting structure, the deepest being the most abstract and least restricted as to domain, and the most superficial being the most concrete and most similar to environmental stimuli and responses in its imagery. For instance, in respect to taxonomy, the deepest level is given in the abstract structure of the type of semantic space on which taxonomies are constructed; next, perhaps, one finds the dimensions as such identified for various domains; next, the variability characteristics of the dimensions are specified; next, the intersections and other logical relationships are detailed; and at the surface the appropriate, verbalizable lexicon is assigned to the taxonomic structure.

With respect to level of complexity, it appears that for human beings, at any level of abstraction, similar conclusions are reached from both laboratory and ethnographic evidence. Speaking about discrimination responses, George Miller[5] has suggested the "magical number seven" as the comfortable limit for discriminations on a scale and for the number of binary dimensions that can be conveniently handled in concept formation. Working with cultural data, Wallace suggested a 2^6 rule: that folk taxonomies are typically built out of contrast sets requiring no more than six binary dimensions.[6] With respect to continuous variables, most human beings (I think) have difficulty in handling more than three dimensions simultaneously in mental arithmetic (although of course the use of writing and other objective symbols, models, and computational aids makes it possible to go far beyond this). There is no particular reason why, when working with discrete variables, the size of contrast sets should be in the neighborhood of 2^6 or 2^7 cells, other than the limitations of the neurological equipment involved. One is reminded in this connection that the information processing equipment in the individual cell (the "genetic code") also operates at the 2^6 level; and one may speculate that if this equipment is involved in cognitive processes, the human capacity for concept formation and that of simpler species is actually the same, being restricted to building blocks (contrast sets) of constant size (2^6), the human

5. "The Magical Number Seven, Plus or Minus Two: Some Limits on Our Capacity for Processing Information."

6. "On Being Just Complicated Enough."

advantage lying simply in the capacity to link contrast sets in enormously larger structures.

We are now led directly to the question of relationships among schemata. As we have already suggested, one kind of relationship is certainly formed by extending a given schema over other domains. This principle is invoked repeatedly by Lévi-Strauss who sees it operative in analogical and metaphorical reasoning not only in "the savage mind" but also among his sophisticated and scientific contemporaries. He points out, for instance, that many "totemic" cultures use the taxonomic structure applied to the local flora and fauna as the conceptual schema for human groups: the names of animal species will be used to denote human sibs, and the relationships among the clans will be construed as being of the same kind, involving the same dimensions, as the relationships among the species: thus

$$\text{clan 1:clan 2} \simeq \text{species A:species B}$$

But while this phenomenon does occur—and is, indeed, of great importance in theory development among scientists as well as among Australian aborigines—it hardly exhausts the human capacity for formulating relationships among schemata. There is, first of all, in taxonomic schemata themselves, an impelling tendency to arrange such structures in the form of hierarchical graphs or trees, whose nodes consist of contrast sets and whose successively higher nodes consist of more and more abstract values representing the domains differentiated below them. Such structures are certainly visible in the belief systems embodied in culture. Relationships of contradiction and dissonance also exist, sometimes in happy insulation and sometimes in conflict, and much human energy would seem to be devoted to the process of relating such contradictory schemata, either by resolving the oppositions or by dissociating the schemata so that the contradictory schemata are not simultaneously invoked. Clinical psychologists (whether behavioristic or psychodynamic) concern themselves actively with such structures in the individual; anthropologists outside the Lévi-Strauss tradition have tended to assume that such contradictions do not occur in culture except between sociologically distinct subgroups, such as youths and adults in the socialization process, or progressive and conservative factions in acculturation situations, and that here they are either normally handled by ritually institutionalized defense mechanisms or by cultural reformulations.

Finally, I think it is generally agreed that the relatively "deep structures," the very general and very abstract schemata, are not really verbalizable by individual subjects without a great deal of coaching by an investigator who is inferring hypothetical schemata and feeding back his inferences. The psychologist does not expect his experimental subject, whether rat or man, to be able to describe the schema that he has learned in clear, exact, English prose. The linguist does not expect his informant to be able to expound in abstract terms the phonemic, morphophonemic, and syntactical system that actually guides his language behavior. The psychotherapist does not expect a new patient to be able to understand the symbolic equations and the interpersonal strategies by which he strives to avoid anxiety and attain libidinal satisfaction. The ethnographer does not expect to find an informant who can clearly and succinctly describe the semantic structure of his kinship terminology or precisely articulate the values of the community. All these schemata are "unconscious" in the sense that they cannot be stated in abstract form by the subject even though his perceptions and responses are precisely determined by them; they must be inferred from behavior, both verbal and nonverbal.

CULTURAL SCHEMATA

Some of the psychologists who have investigated the relationships of schemata to learning have been concerned with those deep structures which are embedded in culture. Charles Osgood and his associates have studied connotational meaning and other properties of language; mathematical psychologists have explored the formal properties of marriage and descent rules. But much of the labor of description of cultural schemata, both deep and superficial, has been carried out by anthropologists, who have recorded what men in various cultures have learned, and the archives of ethnography and ethnology are the repository of most of the data on human cognition. Inasmuch as a large proportion of any one person's cognitive structures are described in ethnography, it would appear that it is the cultural anthropologist who knows what man knows.

The schemata delineated in formal terms by anthropologists and their colleagues in other disciplines may for convenience of discussion be divided into three categories: semantics, relations, and processes. We shall review some of the work that has been done, and some of the issues involved, in each of them.

Semantic Structures

A semantic structure generally consists of a covert taxonomy whose categories correspond to a set of overt index behaviors, such as a phonemic system, a terminology, or other differential responses. Incoming information is assumed to be classified according to the taxonomy (that is, "understood" or "recognized") and the appropriate response then automatically indicated; in reverse, perception of the overt index behavior is interpreted by matching it with the proper taxonomic information. Most of the work of anthropologists in ethnoscience has dealt with the taxonomies associated with terminologies in restricted domains, such as the categories of kinship, colors, diseases, and plants. The methodological problem is to infer the covert taxonomic schema from the objective characteristics of the phenomena to which the terminology seems to refer and from the subject's manipulation of the overt symbols themselves. The theoretical goal is to characterize the formal structure of a given taxonomy at a level of abstraction adequate for comparison with other taxonomies.

Much of the work in this area has made use of a method called "componential analysis." This term was first used to refer to the analysis of the matrix of articulation behaviors associated with the phonemes of a given language. Thus sound could be classified by whether it was voiced or voiceless, by the position of the tongue, by the position of the lips, and so forth. Each of the mutually exclusive alternatives on one of the dimensions was a "component" and each phoneme represented a unique combination of components, one from each of the dimensions or contrast groups. Although individual phonemes generally do not have a meaning in the lexical sense, they are semantic at least to the extent that words differing in only one phoneme generally mean different things; thus the phoneme is the minimal semantic differentiator in language. This general method was applied by Ward Goodenough and Floyd Lounsbury, two linguistically oriented anthropologists, to the analysis of the meaning of kinship terms. In general these and subsequent componential analyses follow the original phonemic model, conceiving of the covert taxonomy as a logic of classes, and of a given taxonomic category as a class product. It is now conventional to represent the categories either by algebraic formulae or as cells arranged in rectangular grids, with hierarchical relations of inclusion and differentiation indicated algebraically or by drawing a simple graph. For instance, the English word "father" means the following components: male on the dimension of sex, one generation above ego on the dimension of generation, consanguineal on the dimension of consanguinity-affinity, and lineal on the dimension of lineality (which differentiates the component consanguineal). By symbolyzing the dimensions $A, B, C,$ and $D,$ then, the formula might be written $a^1\ b^1\ c^1\ d^1$ or represented as a unique cell on a grid representing the same class-product space.

CONSANGUINEAL

		Lineal	Colineal	Ablineal
Male	+gen	Father		
	0 gen			
	−gen			
Female	+gen			
	0 gen			
	−gen			

Such spaces of course may be further analyzed and compared in regard to their size, their hierarchical structure, and their orthogonality.

Some tentative generalizations appear possible with regard to these folk taxonomic schemata. First, they seem to be composed of contrast-sets (that is, perfectly orthogonal paradigms) containing no more than 2^6 cells; second, in most cases, and especially if the taxonomy requires more than 2^6 categories, the contrast sets are arranged nonorthogonally in a graph or branching structure; and third, taxonomies frequently provide cells for which no term exists in the language and provide cover terms that ignore some of the distinctions implicit in the taxonomy.

A principal research problem with regard to the models that can be generated by componential analysis and related methods is their psychological validity. Such a model generally claims implicitly, if not explicitly, to represent the actual semantic calculus by which the native thinks and not just an equivalent calculus that will permit the ethnographer to predict the native's overt behavior accurately. The distinction can perhaps be made clear by a simple example from another schematic area. In order to multiply two numbers, say 24 by 17, I proceed to set them forth, mentally or on paper, in the following way: write the numbers on two lines, justifying the right hand margin and arranging digits on a rectangular grid; then, using a memorized "multiplication table," multiplying the top line by the right digit of the lower; then, multiplying the top line by the next digit to the left, and writing the product offset one space to the left; then adding the two product lines, counting blank spaces as zero. Thus:

$$
\begin{array}{r}
24 \\
17 \\
\hline
168 \\
24 \\
\hline
408
\end{array}
$$

But one can also—and this in effect is the way my desk calculator does it—achieve the same answer by adding up a column of seventeen 24s. Thus:

$$
\begin{array}{r}
24 \\
24 \\
24 \\
24 \\
24 \\
24 \\
24 \\
24 \\
24 \\
24 \\
24 \\
24 \\
24 \\
24 \\
24 \\
24 \\
24 \\
\hline
408
\end{array}
$$

Although the multiplication operation can be transformed into the additive one by a set of rules, when *I* multiply *I do not perform the additive operations.* A psychologically valid account of how I produce the product 408, then, is given by the first example; the second, although it will enable the analyst to predict my answer, does not replicate but merely simulates the cognitive schema I use.

Actually there are various other calculi that can be used for multiplication; and in general the same can be said for semantic calculi: several schemata will enable the analyst to predict correct terminological or other index behavior. If all of these possible schemata can be considered to be hypotheses about the identity of the actual schema or schemata in use, then obviously some experimental or observational procedure is required to validate or invalidate each of them. Unfortunately insufficient attention has been paid to this problem either by anthropologists or by mathematical psychologists who work in these areas.

Beyond questions regarding the correctness of any particular semantic hypothesis constructed in the familiar class-product form lies the larger question of the general adequacy of simple class-product logics for semantic analysis. Granted their validity in many instances, their universal applicability may be questioned. There may be some semantic domains recalcitrant to analysis in terms of neat either-or distinctions and there may be domains that require relational logics.

Lexical domains recalcitrant to componential analysis are apt to be those characterized by the following features: there is no set of objective denotata (people, plants, kin-types, and so on) to which the terms manifestly refer and which may be objectively analyzed in order to infer the covert taxonomy; the boundaries of the lexical domain are uncertain; and the relevant dimensions are continuous rather than discrete variables. Such a difficult domain, for instance, is emotion. The list of emotion terms in English is much larger and more difficult to bound than the list of kinship terms; there is no finite set of objects, events, or other physical stimuli to which the terms refer; and some of the relevant dimensions seem to be continuous variables, such as the continuum from unpleasant through neutral to pleasant, and degree of intensity. In such a situation, the neat algebraic formulae and square boxes of componential analysis, while they may give some approximation to the taxonomy, immediately and intuitively feel wrong. Their psychological validity, in other words, seems to be low.

The logic of relations in addition to, and perhaps sometimes rather than, the logic of classes would seem to be appropriate to some domains. In English, for instance, while most natives probably can be taught to reckon kinship in a class-product calculus, most intuitively use a relational logic for inferring the relationship from the term or from other information. Thus if one asks a naive English informant to define a word like "aunt," one is apt to hear initially something like "that's my mother's sister or my father's sister," then a pause, and then, "and also the wife of my father's brother or my mother's brother." Rarely will one elicit "female, one generation above me, if consanguin-

eal then colineal, if affinal," and so forth. If someone is introduced to me as my cousin ("This is your cousin Mary"), then I
am apt to get the explanation, "you know, Uncle Joe's daughter,"
or I am apt to say, "Let's see, are you Uncle *Joe's* daughter?" In
these situations, the calculus is not of class-product form but of
relational logic form, with the reckoning concerning relationships of paternity, siblinghood, and marriage, along with an
auxiliary use of class-product logic divorced from the ego base
("daughter" means *any* female child to anyone, not just speaker's
daughter). Thus in relational logic form, "aunt" means anyone
related to anyone by one of the following four strings:

1. sister of mother
2. sister of father
3. wife of brother of mother
4. wife of brother of father

Pursuing this line of analysis, and disregarding sex (a class-
product distinction applied routinely to each category except
cousin), one finds that there are essentially five types of strings
employing three primitive terms—child, parent, sibling—that
differentiate all English consanguineal terms:

1. *child of sibling of parent* (all cousins)
2. *sibling of parent* (all uncles and aunts)
3. *child of sibling* (all nieces and nephews)
4. *parent of parent* (all grandparents)
5. *child of child* (all grandchildren)

Degrees of distance as marked by such prefixes as great, grand,
first-, second-, once-removed, twice-removed are indicated by
iteration of primitives either at the beginning or the end of the
strings. Such a taxonomic structure cannot be represented as a
class-product space because the *order* in which the primitives are
combined determines the meaning.

The fundamental difference between the two systems of taxonomy lies in the manipulation of sets. In class-product analyses,
each term refers to any element in a unique subset that is the

intersection of sets; a dimension is a set of nonintersecting subsets. Thus "father" as a class product may be conceived in set terms as the intersection of the sets male, higher generation, and lineal:

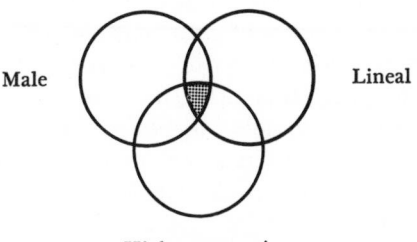

In relative product terms, however, a term is defined as an element in a set to which ego belongs or in another set that is connected to ego's set by sharing a common element; this process of intersection of connecting elements can be extended, in principle, to chains of great length but in practice the chains are apt to be short. Thus "cousin" as a relative product may be represented in set diagrams as follows:

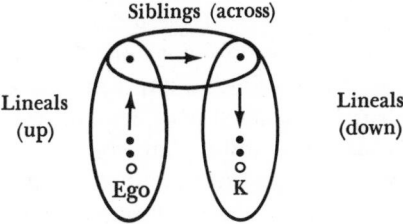

The reckoning procedures are therefore different: in the class product, one asks in effect a series of questions, one for each dimension, in order to identify the sets whose intersection includes kinsman K; in the relative product one traces the relationship through a series of one-element intersections until one reaches the designated kinsman.

The defining sentences for kin terms appear, indeed, to be a particular grammatical domain, with a finite and small number of transformations of the kernel *K is a kinsman of E* sufficing to account for the generation of the possible sentences in kinship syntax. This leads to the more general question of syntactic structures, which are in effect the rules for generating meaningful sentences. Since this is not an essay in linguistics, the reader should refer to the works of Chomsky[7] and others for analyses of the formal characteristics of grammars generally. But continuing the kinship example, it may be observed that there seems to be a rather similar grammatical structure in most if not all systems of kinship terminology: the sentences are constructed in relative product form and refer to no more than three interconnecting sets in the definition of consanguineals: two sets for lineal relationships and one for a collateral relationship. In most systems other than the Murngin type, furthermore, the order of reference is *lineal-collateral-lineal;* in systems of the Murngin type, the order is *lineal-lineal-collateral.* Differentiation is introduced, of course, by various conceptions of lineal and collateral sets, and by various combinations of iteration rules. This similarity of basic conceptual structure, despite the gross and important social consequences of the differences in the definitions produced, suggests, like the 2^6 rule for contrast sets, the working of a psychic unity factor.

A third kind of semantic structure, in addition to taxonomic and syntactical ones, must still be mentioned—symbolism. In this context, the term "symbol" does not refer in some general sense to any sign that stands for any concept, but rather to a special kind of value-associated complex concept. This kind of symbol is, essentially, a stimulus that evokes in the perceiver a complex structure of images, ideas, and emotions, some of which in turn may be symbols in the same sense.[8] This notion of the symbol is used extensively in psychoanalytic theory, which heavily depends upon the intuition that the meaning of some symbols is more complex than can be easily articulated and may even be largely unconscious. In psychoanalytic theory, various body parts and processes, and the images of important early

7. *Syntactic Structures.*

8. See Turner, "Myth and Symbol."

figures in a child's life—like mother, father, and siblings—come to stand for a wide range of things, events, types of people, and relationships, all of which share various significant and often complex, even contradictory, characteristics. The symbol "father," for instance, may stand for persons who are powerful, have authority, are jealous, threaten castration as a penalty for sexual impulses, and so forth, and may extend to not only the "real" father but to other relatives, teachers, employers, supervisors, supernatural beings, and so on. Contact with one of the exemplars will elicit a response to the symbol in addition to a response to the unique characteristics of the person himself and to his ordinary social identity.

The domains of literature, religion, and political belief provide examples of still more complex symbolism. The cross, the swastika, the Virgin Mary, the hammer and sickle, the flag, the mandalla, and so forth, evoke what may be extensive sets of ideas and values whose articulation require equally extensive exposition. A given symbol, of course, need not have the same meaning for all; the meaning, indeed, resides in the perceiver rather than in the symbol itself. Thus the meaning of a symbol may change over time and, of course, differ from person to person and from group to group. Symbols of this kind are apt to be central organizing points in a personality or in an ideology, bringing together diverse domains of experience and producing a kind of consistency and character in behavior on a very abstract level.

The Christian symbol of the cross, for instance, evokes the story of the life of Jesus as it is told in the New Testament, particularly his death by crucifixion, which secured man's redemption. There are important associated values, such as uncomplaining personal sacrifice, confidence in salvation, and love of neighbor. These concepts may serve to rationalize behavior in many domains: aggressive war ("crusades"), submission to political authority, assertion of moral superiority, endurance of privation, pain, and ridicule, tolerance of disagreement, evangelism. The full explication of "its" meaning, of course, has occupied theologians, ministers, and laymen for centuries.

Relations

Developing from a very different tradition, the work of Lévi-Strauss has opened up the analysis of another aspect of cognitive structures in culture: the relations of concepts or "symbols" outside the taxonomic frames that define them. Although there is repeated deference shown to the concepts of descriptive linguistics, the analytical models exploit less linguistics than philosophy. The domains of interest are "symbols," in the third sense discussed above, analogical reasoning, and a Hegelian dialectic of binary oppositions and their resolutions. Proceeding from an assumption of psychic unity that unites both primitive and civilized, Lévi-Strauss proposes broad principles of cognitive structure at the basis of such nearly pan-human institutions as totemism and mythology.

The Lévi-Straussian method of analysis is most simply expounded in the analysis of totemism. The procedure involves four steps:

1. Identify an empirical phenomenon (in this case, an example of totemism).
2. Define the phenomenon as one of several possible relations among two or more "terms."
3. Construct a table of possible permutations among these terms.
4. Take this table as the general object of analysis, the empirical phenomena observed being viewed only as realizations of the various permutations of the complete system.

Thus any one arrangement in observable ethnographic reality is only a local and perhaps transient expression of a many-faceted ideal form that exists as a kind of Platonic essence, a generative paradigm which like a grammar has a reality on a higher level of abstraction than the sentences that it produces.

With respect to totemism, the analysis proceeds as follows. Totemism is taken to refer to relations between two series of concepts: *nature* and *culture*. Nature is dichotomized into *category* ("species") and *particular* (individual animal); culture, into *group* (for example, sib) and *person*. A four-celled matrix is thus generated, and for each of the four cells there are ethnographic illustrations of the implied totemic combinations.

NATURE

		Category	Particular
CULTURE	*Group*	Australian (moiety, section, etc.)	Africa (veneration of sacred animals)
	Person	North American Indians (guardian spirit)	Banks Islands (child as incarnation of plant or animal ingested by mother)

Lévi-Strauss points out that his analysis includes under the rubric of totemism phenomena that have often been excluded by others who have approached the subject. He goes on to argue convincingly that the relation between man and totem is an ideological one: it expresses the idea that human-to-human relations, such as the relations among sibs, are analogous to the relations among the totems. The point being conveyed in the analogy is not that men are animals, plants, insects, or whatever, but that their relationships to each other share a property of the relationships among the totems. It may be merely a principle of duality; it may be the idea of a status hierarchy; it may be a certainty of separate descent; in any case, the relations among humans are being expressed by drawing attention to familiar relationships in the natural world according to the simple formula

$$a:b \simeq A:B$$

But the simplicity of the basic formula is deceptive; it conceals large assumptions about the character of human thought. For one thing, the relation of principal interest is that of contrariety or opposition; and this in turn leads to the notion of a term that "resolves" or synthesizes the contradiction and, by associationist thinking, at the same time generates its own opposite. An elementary formula thus contains within itself not only the four- (or more) celled matrix in which the "phenomenon" is located, but it is also subject to transformations of both an algebraic and a dialectical kind. In the case of myth, Lévi-Strauss argues that "a" myth as recorded is merely one of a family of transformations, each of which states a constant analogical and dialectical structure even though the empirical terms move from place to place and may be replaced by opposites. The function of myth is said to be the mediating, or blurring, of contradictions inherent in the cosmology, values, or other domain of the symbol structure of the culture. The Oedipus myth, for instance, is analyzed as a statement that excessive kinship solidarity (incest) is to deficient kinship solidarity (patricide) as the denial of the autochthonous origin of man (Oedipus killing the sphinx) is to the affirmation of the autochthonous origin of man (Oedipus being himself after all a chthonian figure).

On close inspection these logical models look very fuzzy. The presentation of the Oedipus analysis, for instance,[9] is itself contradictory (that is, there are internal contradictions in the analysis independent of the oppositions discovered in the myth). Thus in paragraph 4:9, it is said that "column four is to column three as column one is to column two." Column one includes the incest motif and has to do with overrating blood relations; column two has to do with underrating blood relations and includes the patricide motif; column three includes killing dragons—the "attempt to escape autochthony" theme; and column four introduces the etymologies of the names Oedipus, Laius, and Labdocos, all alluding to crippledness, and thus (by deduction from a generalization of Lévi-Strauss's concerning "men born from the earth") to autochthonous birth. But in the next paragraph, it is asserted that "the overrating of blood relations [1] is to the underrating of blood relations [2] as the attempt to escape autochthony [3] is to the impossibility to succeed in it [4]." In sum, paragraph 4:9 says

$$1:2 \simeq 4:3$$

and paragraph 4:10 says

$$1:2 \simeq 3:4$$

9. See Lévi-Strauss, "The Structural Study of Myth."

One can also ask whether, to a Greek, Oedipus was really over-rating blood relations when he engaged in sexual intercourse with his mother or whether, in fact, his sin was not regarded as an underrating of blood relations of the same order of gravity as killing the father. Furthermore, does it really make any difference anyway, since *all* pairs in a Lévi-Straussian analysis have the same relationship, that of contrast (analogously to phonemic contrast) and since by "associationist" thinking one can discover a contrast to any term and a "mediator" between any two contrasts?

The value of the Lévi-Straussian approach would seem to lie more in its heuristic eloquence than in its logical rigor. The ethnologist's attention is directed to the possibility of finding sets of simple binary oppositions related by a variety of logical devices that generate such structures as analogies, dialectical processes, and permutation groups. The timelessness of such cognitive structures, which are neither savage nor civilized in their nature, quite properly makes them suitable for examination in cross-cultural studies.

More rigorous approaches to relations are embodied in the application of certain formal mathematical models to ethnographic data. An example is Goodenough's use of the Guttman scale[10] to arrange data on the reciprocal rights and duties implicit in a series of role pairs (such as male and female, father and son, and so on). Guttman scaling techniques measure the degree to which a set of data approximate a perfect partial ordering. A partial ordering is a series of terms such that the occurrence of each successive term implies the occurrence of its predecessors. Thus in the array

$$a \quad b \quad c \quad d$$
$$b \quad c \quad d$$
$$c \quad d$$
$$d$$

10. "Some Applications of Guttman Scale Analysis to Ethnography and Culture Theory" and "Rethinking Status and Role: Toward a General Model of the Cultural Organization of Social Relationships."

if a occurs, b, c, and d all occur too; if b occurs, then c and d; and if c, then d. Goodenough shows that Trukese courtesy behaviors form an almost perfect scale of essentially this kind, with the duty to pay the "highest" courtesy implying the duty to pay a partial ordering of "lesser" courtesies. In a Guttman scale, however, early elements may drop out if the scale is large, so that it may have a form like this

$$
\begin{array}{cccccc}
a & b & c & d & & & \\
& b & c & d & e & & \\
& & c & d & e & f & \\
& & & d & e & f & g \\
& & & & e & f & g \\
& & & & & f & g \\
& & & & & & g \\
\end{array}
$$

The tendency for orderings in empirically observed cultural materials to display this shifting property of Guttman scales may have to do with the cognitive complexity limits of a "magical number seven" and "2^6" kind.

The elementary taxonomies that we discussed earlier are based, in principle, on intersections of unordered sets of indeterminate size. The Lévi-Straussian oppositions are still elementary in the sense that they are binary and the order of the relationship is irrelevant. In the scale, however, serial order is an essential feature and the set is not necessarily restricted to two members. But, as in the case of the dichotomies, the empirical dimension to which the order refers is free. An ordering may refer to time, to space, to value, to dominance, to status, and so forth. A partially ordered set does not strictly imply a number system but a completely ordered set a, b, c, d, e, . . . , n does.

Although all cultural systems seem to have developed some sort of numbering structures, some are apparently very simple indeed. There seem to be cultures, or institutions within cultures, that, in effect, operate with a two-element or three-element number system (1, 2, and 1, 2, 3), which without a place system such as sophisticated arithmetics employ severely limits calculation. A (1, 2) number system is embodied in the kinship reckoning procedure of the Murngin. The Murngin count generations by modulus 2: that is, if ego's generation is 1, then mother's is 2, MoMo's is 1, and MoMoMo's is 2; sister's daughter's is 2, SiDaDa's is 1, SiDaDaDa's is 2, and SiDaDaDaDa's is 1. But the Murngin also employ a kind of three-place system that groups sets and numbers these sets in the same way. Thus a particular generation can be specified (as it must be for certain kin terms) by three numbers. The system works like this:

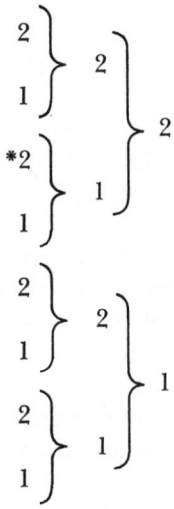

For instance, the generation with the asterisk can be specified as $2 - 1 - 2$. Apparently no more than three places are used and thus the maximum number for effective calculation is 8. Modulus 3 numbering is implicit in the pollution-purity cycle of Brahmins. There are three degrees of ritual cleanliness; if one labels the highest as 1, then one can descend from 1 to 2 and from 2 to 3. From 3 one can only proceed to 1 (completing the modular cycle) or return to 2 (by reversing direction).

Perfect orderings of this kind, especially with numbers for zero and infinity, make possible the development of arithmetic and other calculi and have led to complex cultural developments in mathematics and logic that cannot be discussed here. To judge from the scattered evidence available, it would appear that com-

plete orderings are the latest relational structures to evolve
culturally. An evolutionary scale may be reflected, however, in
the fact that taxonomies and relations of roughly the same level
of complexity are universal; that paired binary oppositions
(analogies) are probably universal; that partial orderings (scales)
are at least widely distributed; but that number systems larger
than mod 2 or mod 3 may be recent and restricted in
distribution.[11]

Processes

The relational and semantic structures discussed above are
static in the sense that they do not refer to processes in time
(although their reckoning of course follows a processual path).
In this section we shall take up processual structures. Processes
have in common the property that time, and often physical space
too, is a dimension of the structure, and that the structure is
divided into a sequence of steps or stages corresponding to the
successive values on the time/space dimension. Each stage then
can be considered as a single value on a dimension that corresponds precisely in number of values to the time/space dimension;
but each of these values on the stage dimension can be decom-
posed into a complex structure whose matrix may be (but is
not necessarily) unique to that stage. Consider, for instance, the
stages of man's life contained in the old riddle, "what is it that
goes first on four legs, then on two, and finally on three?" Here
a three-stage life cycle is depicted with each stage defined by the
number of supports employed in locomotion, this number drawn
from the set of integers 2, 3, and 4. In ordinary American conversation, by contrast, the stages of life recognized are apt to be
six in number: infancy, childhood, adolescence, young adulthood, middle age, and old age. These stages, furthermore, are not
defined so simply: the concept of "infancy" invokes images and
considerations that are in contrast with some other stages (for

11. In this connection see also Berlin and Kay, "The Evolution of Color
Categories."

instance, radical dependency versus independence), but there are a large number of such dimensions, and it is the context of the conversation that determines which of them are relevant at any moment. In those processes which may be called "plans" (or "instructions" or "rules"), the independence of matrices at each stage is more explicit. Consider for example the plan for hanging a picture on a wall. It involves at least the following instructions:

1. Carry picture, hammer, and hook to wall.
2. Locate correct position for placing hook.
3. Hammer hook into wall.
4. Hang picture on hook.

Each of these stages is in itself complex and susceptible of further definition as a sequence. Furthermore, it would strain common sense to insist that each stage be defined in terms of meaningful contrast with the other stages. Each stage is rather a unique assemblage containing some dimensions not even relevant to other stages, although some dimensions remain throughout: what to do with picture; what to do with hammer; what to do with hook. This suggests that processual structures generally contain three kinds of dimensions: time/space; a core matrix that is shared by all stages; and peripheral matrices relevant to only some of the stages. Some simple structures contain only the first two.

We have discussed the question of the size of semantic structures. One can also ask a similar question about processes: what is the optimum number of stages for cultural standardization of processual structure? The range would seem to run from two (which is of course the minimum) to about seven. This estimate, as in the other case, refers to "folk" processes, rather than to scientific or technical ones, and furthermore assumes that these limits do not necessarily reflect the way the natural world "really" is processually structured (any more than a kinship taxonomy obeying the 2^6 rule describes the "real" categories of kinship). For instance, in American English, the life cycle is commonly divided into six or seven stages; while this probably does reflect a natural division into stages at one level of abstraction, for some purposes two or three might be more meaningful, and for others perhaps ten, or twenty, or fifty might *technically* be more revealing. Cross-cultural data on such questions have not to my knowledge been generally assembled, but it is my impression that a seven-stage rule would come close to the mark; and, indeed, the size of folk taxonomies may itself be limited by the number of stages convenient in the formulation of reckoning rules. In the social sciences, one suspects, the seven-stage rule is intuitively obeyed even in supposedly "objective" analysis.

Some folk processual structures can be readily analyzed in the abstract. This is the case, for instance, with identity transformation systems, which are culturally universal. By identity transformation system I mean a set of states, each state different in some respects from the others, which a given entity may according to folk theory occupy at one time or another. The entities relevant to anthropological consideration are preeminently individual human beings and individual institutions, but animals, plants, and so forth, may also be considered to be subject to transformation. Thus, for instance, a person in some culture may be considered, without losing all the aspects of his identity, to pass through several states of development: infancy, childhood, adulthood, old age, and spiritual survival after death. He occupies these states successively, and is different in each, without however completely losing his continuity as a unique entity. In transformation systems in general, the number of possible states may vary, as well as the rules governing the succession of states and the value attached to being in one state or another.

A classic illustration of such a system is the Hindu system of belief concerning ritual pollution among Brahmins. My attention was drawn to this material by Dr. Edward B. Harper, then of Bryn Mawr College, and preliminary analysis was conducted with the assistance of Mrs. Lucile Malim, a student of mine. In brief, the Brahmin postulates three states: *madi,* the state of ritual purity; *muttuchittu,* the state of ordinary everyday purity; and *mailage,* the state of ritual impurity. An elaborate system of behavior governs the Brahmin with respect to these states: certain rituals can be performed only when he is in a state of *madi;* elaborate precautions must be observed to prevent his moving unintentionally from *madi* to one of the other two states; and special rituals exist for effecting the transformation from *mailage* or *muttuchittu* to *madi*. In a ritual sense, a value hierarchy exists among the states, with *madi* the most valued state and *mailage* the least valued.

Let us generalize the description of this system and delineate certain formal properties of such three-place systems, which are not uncommon, at least in literate cultures (witness the formally similar three class social system—upper, middle, and lower—of the United States).

Let us call the type of system being considered a three-place free transformation system. It will be defined as a set of three states, in one and only one of which a given entity must be at any time; an entity can move from one state to either of the other two, or remain in the same state, during any period.

The states will be termed A, B, and C. There are seven possible transformations of state:

A——B
B——C
C——·A
A——C
C——B
B——A
stay in same place

These transformations can be conceptualized as two circles, a clockwise and a counterclockwise, G_1 and G_2:

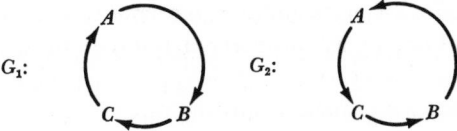

Each of these circles can be interpreted as a group, in the algebraic sense, comparable to the group of integers mod 3. Let us represent one step clockwise by the symbol $+1$, two steps clockwise by $+2$, one step counterclockwise by -1, two steps counterclockwise by -2, and staying in the same place by 0. The operation "followed by" will be represented by the symbol o.

Then for G_1 we have:

o	0	1	2
0	0	1	2
1	1	2	0
2	2	0	1

Similarly for G_2 we have:

o	0	-1	-2
0	0	-1	-2
-1	-1	-2	0
-2	-2	0	-1

The structures G_1 and G_2 separately satisfy the four axioms of the Galois group.

1. *Axiom of closure.* For each ordered pair, a and b in G, a o b is a unique element of c of G.
2. *Associative axiom.* For each triple, a, b, and c in G, $(a$ o $b)$ o $c = a$ o $(b$ o $c)$.
3. *Identity axiom.* There exists a unique element of e of G, having the property that for every a in G, a o $e = e$ o $a = a$.
4. *Inverse axiom.* Corresponding to each a in G there is a unique element a^1 having the property that a o $a^1 = a^1$ o $a = e$.

The structures also satisfy a fifth axiom:
5. *Commutative axiom.* For every a and b in G, a o $b = b$ o a.

Although the structures G_1 and G_2 form commutative groups, their sum is not a group, as may be seen from the resulting matrix:

o	2	1	0	−1	−2
2	1,−2	0	2,−1	1,−2	0
1	0	2,−1	1,−2	0	−1,2
0	2,−1	1,−2	0	−1,2	−2,1
−1	1,−2	0	−1,2	−2,1	0
−2	0	−1,2	−2,1	0	−1,2

The complete three-place free transformation system satisfies the associative and identity laws but none of the others; it has the interesting property that going two steps in any direction is the equivalent of going one step in the other direction, and that going one step in any direction is the equivalent of going two steps in the other direction.

Despite my disclaimer of interest in the application of this analysis to other problems, I would like to advance a speculation. It may occur to the ethnologist that group structures (that is, certain cyclical unidirectional transformation systems) might be culturally prior, and prerequisite, to the free transformation system, which can be treated as a sum of groups. Such speculation would suggest, first, that a group concept (for example, a concept of world cycles and of death-and-rebirth of individuals) historically precedes the development of the free transformation concept and, second, that the simplest cultures may not contain, or may not have contained, the concept of the free transformation system (that is, of reversible cyclical processes). It is worth noting also that such modular systems, when applied to such cultural domains as disease and treatment, imply very different plans. For instance, a one-way modular system of psychotherapy would view a return to health (position A) as *requiring* passage through increasingly severe stages of illness; a two-way modular system (like the one analyzed above) as *permitting but not requiring* return to health via deeper stages of illness; but a noncyclical concept, like that in the West, as *requiring* a return "upward" through the same stages of illness traversed on the way "down."

A second ubiquitous kind of processual structure is implicit in systems of exchange. The classic examples of these in the anthropological literature are prescriptive marriage systems, in which, in effect, groups exchange women. Various Australian kinship systems, and that of the Natchez, have been subjected to mathematical analysis by psychologists, sociologists, and mathematicians and the resulting cyclical structures delineated.[12]

Kariera society, for example, is divided into four "marriage classes" called Banaka, Burung, Palyeri, and Karimera. A specific rule specifies that the Banaka and Burung classes exchange women for wives and that Palyeri and Karimera also exchange women for wives. The descent rule is a bit more complex: the child of a Banaka man is Palyeri, of a Burung man a Karimera, of a Palyeri man a Banaka, and of a Karimera man a Burung. The underlying mathematical structure can be described by the use of a concept of marriage type and the application of a group of permutation matrices to represent the descent rules. There are four marriage types: (1) Banaka man and Burung woman, (2) Burung man and Banaka woman, (3) Palyeri man and Karimera woman, and (4) Karimera man and Palyeri woman. If we consider this series as a column vector (X) then we can define two permutation matrices F and G such that FX will yield the proper sequence of marriage types that the sons must contract, and GX the proper sequence for the daughters. Thus:

$$FX = \begin{bmatrix} 0 & 0 & 1 & 0 \\ 0 & 0 & 0 & 1 \\ 1 & 0 & 0 & 0 \\ 0 & 1 & 0 & 0 \end{bmatrix} \begin{bmatrix} 1 \\ 2 \\ 3 \\ 4 \end{bmatrix} = \begin{bmatrix} 3 \\ 4 \\ 1 \\ 2 \end{bmatrix}$$

$$GX = \begin{bmatrix} 0 & 0 & 0 & 1 \\ 0 & 0 & 1 & 0 \\ 0 & 1 & 0 & 0 \\ 1 & 0 & 0 & 0 \end{bmatrix} \begin{bmatrix} 1 \\ 2 \\ 3 \\ 4 \end{bmatrix} = \begin{bmatrix} 4 \\ 3 \\ 2 \\ 1 \end{bmatrix}$$

12. See the papers of Weil, "Sur l'Étude de Certain Types de Lois de Mariage (Système Murngin), Bush, "An Algebraic Treatment of Rules of Marriage and Descent," and the exercise of Kemeny, Snell, and Thompson in *Introduction to Finite Mathematics*, pp. 343–353.

The operators F and G have two properties that describe other essential features of the system: they commute ($FG = GF$), and their squares $(F)^2$ and $(G)^2$ yield the identity operator. These Galois group properties account for the alternate generation cycling of class membership and for preferential cross-cousin marriage. Other analyses of the Kariera system have been suggested, one of them[13] suggesting that full explication requires the recognition of eight latent and unnamed "clans," two for each class. It is interesting to note that here, as in the case of the pollution cycle problem, and of Lévi-Strauss's treatment of mythology, the algebra of groups proves to be a useful tool in reducing a series of rules to simple mathematical elements. In effect, the group model of cyclical processes avoids the problem of beginnings and endings and defines each successive stage in a process, from some arbitrary starting point, as a new arrangement of constant elements produced by the operation of the permutation matrix associated with each step.

A third, and equally ubiquitous, kind of processual model is the noncyclical goal-directed program. In these models, there is a beginning, a middle, and an end (although iteration or cycling may occur internally). Such models are necessary in technological matters involved in transportation, manufacture, hunting, and the like, and have been regarded by some psychologists as the most basic model of cognitive process, perhaps because their finite quality permits intellectual *rapprochement* with reinforcement theory. Miller, Galanter, and Prabram, for instance, in discussing "plans" propose an elementary test-operate-test-exit (TOTE) sequence for plans, the organism acting, testing the results, then acting again, until the desired goal is reached, and then stopping. Wallace has suggested[14] that process models for technical tasks have the following components: Action Plan (the stage structure, specifying the origin state, goal state, and intervening transitional states at which instrumental choices must be made); Action Rules (general rules for making choices among possible alternative actions); Control Operations (specification

13. White, *An Anatomy of Kinship.*

14. "Driving to Work."

of the minimal behavioral responses available to the actor); Monitored Information (specification of types of data relevant to choice of response); Organization (pattern of interpretation employed in relating data to action). Within any one individual's mazeway, such plans are evidently extremely complex, even at the level of conscious awareness, but culturally standardized plans are perhaps less formidable, and in any case can be analyzed into relatively simple components that are assembled in detail by individual experience. It is a common enough observation that "the culture" (represented by teacher, or book, or other standard communicator) can only provide the major framework of plans, presented more or less haphazardly, in many domains of behavior; the enculturee must "learn by doing," "gain experience," "work it out for himself," in order to put a full plan together cognitively in sufficient detail to enable him to act effectively. Reading the ethnography of a hunting culture does not make one a hunter. For instance, young men may be schooled in the arts of war in training camps for months: taught the elements of sanitation, discipline, communication, weaponry, tactics, survival techniques, and so forth; but the bits and pieces of the plan for operating a radio in a vehicle in combat, or of participating in an infantry attack, or whatever, actually get fitted together in the course of "combat experience." Green troops, however well trained and motivated, are apt to be relatively inefficient because they have neither assembled plans in organized structures internally nor articulated them adequately with the plans of other members of the team.

The problem in assembling plans into a mazeway is the need to discover and eliminate gaps and contradictions. In order for a plan to be effective, the instrumental connections need to be tight (but not so tight that innovative changes cannot be made): that is, the actor must not discover that he does not know how to get from stage A to stage C because he doesn't know what happens in stage B. Maps must specify what to do at all decision points (such as road intersections); technological instructions such as are involved in the making of pottery[15] must specify what

15. Cf. Sabloff and Smith, "Ceramic Wares in the Maya Area: A Clarification of an Aspect of the Type-Variety System and Presentation of a Formal Model for Comparative Use."

to do, how to initiate, control, and stop each physical or chemical process involved; relevant contingencies must be anticipated as much as possible. In regard to contradictions, it is necessary that different plans, perhaps directed toward "unrelated" domains of experience, not require behaviors that interfere with or invalidate each other. Thus the soldier's weapon must not use such heavy ammunition that he cannot carry both an adequate supply of cartridges and other essentials such as water. In plans affecting interpersonal relations, a classic difficulty is variously called by such terms as "role conflict," "conflict of interest," "moral conflict," and the like. In such dilemmas, the person discovers that he may have to sacrifice some important value, whose incompatibility with another plan was not anticipated, unless he can somehow reformulate or adjust both, and much cognitive work (and much emotional stress) may be precipitated by such a discovery.

In a radical sense, then, it would appear that much of every culture must be literally rediscovered in every generation because of the impossibility of describing, and therefore communicating, the relevant plans in sufficient detail for their effective execution. The best a culture can do is communicate the general framework of "its" plans and ensure that the new generation is placed in situations in which they will have to reinvent the details, probably with minor modifications. No lecture, training manual, film, or demonstration can fully "get across" all the skills involved even in driving a car; a few rules for manipulating a small and finite set of objects, in order to control the vehicle in certain ways in certain situations, is about all that can be done by instruction; the art must be continuously relearned by practice.

THE ORGANIZATION OF COGNITIVE DIVERSITY

In an earlier chapter, the argument was developed that no culture in its entirety is cognitively shared, or internalized, by all members of its society, and that to the contrary not only is a great deal of cultural content not shared empirically, but it is necessary that diversity exist. All societies are, in a radical sense, plural societies. The problem for ethnographic analysis, then, beyond the initial level of describing "the" culture as a pattern, is to discover how diverse elements are organized into patterns. We have in this chapter discussed some of the kinds of elementary cognitive structures of which cultures are composed. Now let us inquire further into the problem of organization. According to what principles are the disparate cognitions of the individual members of any society shaped and coordinated into the relatively consistent and elegant models that ethnographic analysis reveals? How do societies ensure that the diverse cognitions of adults and children, males and females, warriors and shamans, slaves and masters articulate to form the equivalence structures that are the substance of social life?

We may start out with a zero principle: one way of handling diversity is to eliminate it, to ensure uniformity, as much as possible, by early training and by the application of rewards and punishments to those supposedly already trained. Certainly there are domains of culture in which fairly high levels of conformity are achieved: language, customs of courtesy, methods of numerical reckoning, names for places, the use of common tools, and so forth. But the general social science experience has been that cultural constants, when examined closely, turn out to be variables. Sociolinguistics, for instance, is discovering the magnitude of speech variation in supposedly monolingual communities and the important role these variations play in communication. It would be difficult to find *any* single cognitive structure that is uniformly shared by all members of any community (except by excluding from membership by various arbitrary rules those persons who do not share it) for the members of any community do in fact include social categories such as speechless infants, senile old people, persons deaf and dumb, village atheists and nonconformists, immigrants, prisoners from other tribes, and so on; to exclude them is merely to beg the question. But nonetheless we must include as a principle of organization of diversity the zero principle of exacting as much conformity as possible, both because it is attempted for whole communities and because it is sometimes applied rather strenuously to subgroups, such as particular occupational categories, age groups, and so forth.

In contrast to the extreme principle of zero diversity, there are occasions where, in the interest of survival, the culture encourages unorganized diversity or randomness. Where decision is difficult or likely to arouse dispute, or where too great consistency would be dangerous, randomization processes may be instituted, as in various divination practices[16] and in planning sessions where maximum variety of viewpoint and formation is wanted. Such randomization, however, is generally a temporary phase of an orderly plan.

The other principles are based on the acceptance and organization of diversity. There are at least four of these that we shall discuss here: (1) ad hoc communication, (2) inclusion, (3) end linkage, and (4) administration. They are certainly visible in any culture but cultures probably differ widely in their reliance on various combinations of them, primitive societies for instance placing far less dependence on administrative processes.

Ad hoc communication. No group of human beings working together to accomplish some, or several, ends finds it easy to continue the process without depending upon frequent verbal and nonverbal communication. Both the inevitable diversity of which we have been talking, and the errors of enculturation, make any human group very different from a set of perfectly programmed, inertially guided robots designed to interact flawlessly over long periods of time. Most human activity requires a constant flow of communication that, among other things, enables the participants continuously to readjust and expand their own cognitions, including their knowledge of the communication system itself. The content of this flow is not culture, but the language—verbal or nonverbal—in which it is conducted is. It is as if everyone is imperfectly trained in an incomplete cultural system and for any complex task must communicate with his fellows lest the system rapidly plunge into a chaos of mutual ignorance and misunderstanding. The studies of Erving Goffman, Raymond Birdwhistell, and sociolinguists generally are contrib-

16. See Moore, "Divination—A New Perspective," and Potter, *Biological Disorder and the Uncertainty of Man's Future.*

uting extremely important knowledge about how communication processes of this sort actually work and about the consequences of their failure for social and mental order. From brief encounters of strangers in the street, to extended relationships among the members of families or highly trained teams, the need for ad hoc communication is continuous.

Take, for example, a psychiatric team investigating the relationship between emotion and urinary excretion of corticosteroids in a ward of psychiatric patients. One of their tasks was to record the emotional state of each patient during an interview. They found great difficulty in agreeing, first, on a standard and manageably small vocabulary to use in recording emotion; and further, they found that they tended to disagree with each other about the patient's emotional state. They found it necessary, therefore, to constantly "talk over" their rating scale and its use, in order to achieve reliability, and to "discuss" the patient interviews. A colleague and I were asked to study the semantic problem that they were attempting to solve (with some success) by this process of communication. We discovered some extremely interesting facts about the problem of semantic diversity with which they were confronted and which they were handling by ad hoc communication.

First, we found that of the 2,000 or so terms for emotion that *we* recognized in the listings of *Webster's Collegiate Dictionary* and the *Dictionary of Slang,* our subjects were ready to use about 1,000. We elicited terms from subjects by reading them up to 250 brief anecdotes, in five to eight sessions, and asking them how they would feel in or about the situation described. Some words were used much more frequently than others by any one informant; these "core vocabularies" were on the order of 2^6 to 2^7 in number. The core vocabularies of different informants were considerably different, however. Among the five most carefully studied subjects, the distribution was as follows:

Proportion of terms	unique to one subject	15%
	shared by two subjects	22%
	shared by three subjects	28%
	shared by four subjects	24%
	shared by all five subjects	11%

Among those terms shared in core usage, furthermore, there was considerable variation in the nuances of meaning. The term "anger/angry," for instance, was found in all core vocabularies, on the negative side of the primary qualitative dimension; but the group of other terms from which the informant differentiated it by intensity contrast alone was different from one informant to another. The intensity contrast groups were, for six subjects:

> mad, furious/fury
> mad, furious
> bored, disappointed, resentment, disdain, hostility, fear, anxiety, repulsion
> hate, shocked, disgusted, dislike, annoyed
> annoyed
> shocked, horror/horrified

In order to estimate the level of semantic consensus a psychiatric research team might achieve, we collated a standard check list of sixty-one terms from core vocabularies and asked a pair of research personnel to check off on a mimeographed form for each of fourteen patients seen by both in the same interview, the emotions each thought the patient was experiencing. The average number of items checked was ten and the average agreement matrix for the two judges was as follows:

JUDGE A

		+	−
	+	5	5
JUDGE B	−	5	46

Although the homogenized matrix is statistically significant of better agreement than chance, there were four out of fourteen subjects about whom agreement was not significantly better than chance. Part of the source of disagreement is word preference or meaning: for instance, A described one patient as "gay"; B on the same occasion did not check "gay" but did check "loving," "light-hearted," and "unconcerned" (not checked by A). Part of the disagreement grew from other cognitive differences, however, of mood, personality, or theoretical orientation. For instance, one of the patients was rated thus by the two judges:

A	B
contrary	afraid
cross	agitated
grim	insecure
mean	lonely
serious	miserable
solemn	overwhelmed
tense	sad
	threatened

The point of the illustration is not that psychiatric evaluation and diagnosis, and psychiatric communication with patients, is *uniquely* hampered by cognitive diversity of various kinds, but, rather, that a well-trained and successful team of psychiatric researchers should even after a great deal of ad hoc communication *still* be unable to reduce their cognitive diversity in this domain, and the resulting language use, below the level of unreliability we observed. One recourse for them, of course, was the usual one used in coding operations in behavioral science research—to approach conformity by reducing the range of allowed observer response to an absolute minimum (such as using a seven-term scale) but this obviously merely replaces one problem by another, for by grossly oversimplifying the allowable common language, they were creating a smaller jargon than that employed by the subjects (or by the observers themselves in other settings).

Inclusion. The principle of inclusion applies particularly to the relation between a specialist and his client and between the cooperating members of highly differentiated work teams. In the case of the specialist and client, the client knows that the specialist has a plan and is able to describe it, perhaps with reasonable accuracy, as a broad framework. The doctor and patient provide (in fortunate cases, at least) a good example. In general the patient who suffers from some complaint knows that the doctor first makes a diagnosis from information the patient supplies, then prescribes some treatment, and then, at least if the treatment is not effective, reevaluates and prescribes something different quantitatively or qualitatively. Thus the patient is prepared to cooperate while the physician secures information by asking questions and "making tests" and to delay demands for prescription and treatment until the doctor has had a chance to find out what is wrong with him. Then he is prepared to follow orders and submit to the treatment itself, and finally to come back and complain if it doesn't relieve him within some agreed-upon limits of time and degree of discomfiture. But the doctor has a much richer plan. The patient's simple two- or three-stage model is further subdivided into finer stages; the matrices of information, decision, and control contain elements of which the patient is not at all aware. But the patient also knows that the doctor's plan has a high degree of complexity, compared to his own. The details of the doctor's plan, then, are in a sense included in the broad categories of the patient's knowledge of the doctor's plan. If the two models are not thus related, it becomes difficult for the patient to coordinate his behavior with that of his doctor; he may be unable to understand why the doctor is asking all these questions and giving all these tests, instead of treating the complaint immediately; he may be unwilling to return if relief is not quick and complete.

But the relationship must go the other way too. The patient has his own plan for the sick role, which may involve very detailed procedures for suspending, or carrying on, other important activities and securing financial and other support from relatives or friends. Unless the doctor is able to take into account the broad categories of the patient's plan for illness, within which the details of this plan are included, he on his part may find it difficult to work successfully because he may expect forms of "cooperation" that in effect would unnecessarily invalidate the patient's other life plans.

End linkage. Inclusive structures tend to occur in relations involving dominance and subordination. End linkage, by contrast, is associated with team organization, where the participants do not have authority relationships with one another but are specialists of equal status performing tasks within separate domains of expertise. There may indeed be inclusive knowledge of others' plans but these are not necessary and may even be prohibited. The articulation is achieved by a precise complementarity of subplans that sum to a complete plan. Small teams of highly trained co-workers—for instance, a surgical team, the members of an interdisciplinary research group, the crew of an aircraft, a domestic household, the operatives in a factory assembly line, or the agents in an intelligence network—must be able to carry out their several components of the total task in such a way that the products sum to a coherent and effectively tight program. The signals for commencement of each component may be quite arbitrary and convey little or no information about the overall design (as in the minimal equivalence structures discussed in an earlier chapter).

Consider, for instance, economic cooperation in a husband-wife team in a hunting culture. The production of food and a set of garments for the members of the household involves an alternating sequence of highly specialized plans by husband and wife. The husband's plan for tracking and killing a fur-bearing animal is articulated with the wife's plan for locating, carrying back, and skinning the carcass; this in turn is articulated with the husband's plan for butchering and distributing the meat; this then is fitted to the wife's plan for cooking and serving meals; and dressing the skin, designing, and sewing the garment remain as the final contribution of the wife. Neither knows how to carry out the other's task and no one needs to organize the program administratively; but the ability of each to do his own part depends on the fit of the other's plan to his own, in time, in space, and in the form of result. They sum to a smoothly articulated process.

A different sort of end linkage is implied in the Lévi-Straussian set of mythic transformations discussed in a previous section. The several purveyors of different versions of a myth hold different cognitions; the articulation of these different stories is described by the transformation matrix itself. Here we deal not with a team of specialists but with a group modifying a story according to a logical·plan to which all unconsciously subscribe. More conscious, but similar in principle, is the elaboration of a scientific or artistic paradigm over time by workers in a continuing tradition. We shall discuss the process of paradigm development later in the chapter on culture change.

Administration. The larger the number of cooperating individuals, and the more complex the individual component plans, however, the more need there is for a regulation of communication, inclusion, and end linkage relations by administration. Administration provides for the design and continuous adjustment of diverse component plans in a group of cooperating individuals. It requires a hierarchy of authority relations, with an individual or executive group "at the top" whose plan in principle includes at least the abstract framework of all the subplans of the group and who have a recognized right, and duty, to ensure that the several relationships of inclusion and end linkage are mutually consistent, adequately tight, and sum to a productive total plan, and that ad hoc communication is always effective enough to ensure the correction of errors. Even the most primitive cultures employ administrative processes—even though there may be no full-time administrative role as such—by providing for ad hoc leaders in kin group activities, in group hunting, in combat, in the management of complex tasks like sailing large vessels, and the like.

The elaboration of administrative systems increases with technological complexity and population density. Full-time administrative roles probably began with the early urban cultures of the Near East, where the need to manage large irrigation systems and to maintain military organizations of some size, and to rationalize their use to the dependent population, led to centralized royal administrations and associated technologically skilled priesthoods. With the development of industrial civilization and the rise of vast urban populations, the need for the organization of diversity by administrative process has led to those large structures known as bureaucracies. In modern society, virtually all aspects of life are dependent upon an intersection of bureaucracies. The provision of water, food, clothing, shelter, transportation, courts, records, communication, education, medical care, sanitation, fire control, police and military protection— to name some of the major categories—requires a level of coordination in plans of extremely high complexity that only those organizations called bureaucracies can supply. To maintain a population of more than a few thousand people in a "city" without some sort of central system of communication and control is probably impossible; to maintain, as modern cities do, up to ten million persons in one area, none of whom can individually supply himself with the necessities of life, is completely inconceivable without bureaucracy.

One can, indeed, take the view that the principal social, and cultural, problem of the modern world is to design more effective bureaucracies. The age of European exploration and the industrial revolution spawned a set of immediate social problems that led to the rise of ideologies of the right and left which competed for the power to resolve such issues as racism, economic exploitation of industrial workers, and the displacement of peasantries from the land. To cope with these problems, both left and right turned to essentially the same old models of bureaucratic process in industrial management and government. But these horizontal ideologies of left and right have become almost irrelevant. The similar horrors of Hitlerism and Stalinism arise with equal facility under capitalist and communist systems; and one of the impressive features of the contemporary world is the widespread dissatisfaction expressed by the young people in all advanced countries, on both sides of the ideological frontier, with the functioning of the vast bureaucracies of education, of government, and of industry. The intellectual conflict increasingly focuses on the problems of vertical ideology—the ideology of administration—with positions ranging from a sort of administrative nihilism to a concern with the perfection of management. In other words, the interface between bureaucracy and its clientele, rather than the interface between classes or races, is increasingly perceived as a major problem that does not disappear under *any* horizontal ideological system, but in fact increases constantly with technology, urbanism, and population.

To what sort of problems do we refer? There are perhaps two that must be mentioned. Most conspicuous is the susceptibility of a large bureaucracy to seizure by those who consciously exploit it as an instrument of private economic gain and political terror, as has been done repeatedly and most dramatically by totalitarians in this century. It is the bureaucratization of theft, terror, torture, and murder that has made—to use Hannah Arendt's felicitous phrase—evil so banal. On a lesser scale, of course, similar misuse of bureaucracy is visible wherever payrolls are padded with absent persons and goods are systematically diverted into black markets.

A second problem, less dramatic, but no less destructive in the long run, is the low level of responsiveness of many bureaucracies to the claims of its clientele. Bureaucracy is apt to fail to serve those dependent upon it for services, not through any intention of harm, but from a host of difficulties that can perhaps be lumped together under the rubric of insensitivity. It is a typical situation that an administrator—or a machine acting on his plan—must, after a few minutes of reflection on very limited information, make a decision that profoundly affects the life or perhaps even determines the survival of a person whom the administrator does not know and about whom he can care only in the most abstract and categorical way. Such decisions about academic standing, about draft eligibility, about hospital admission and release, about taxation, and so forth, can with difficulty be appealed and even if there has been a manifest error, the error cannot easily be corrected. The impersonality of the evil thus wreaked by mistake by honest and well-intentioned people cannot be corrected by moral exhortation nor, in many situations, by the sort of "sensitivity training" that a liberal education or group encounter therapy supposedly conveys. The propensity for frequent error may be built into the system by gaps, or outright fallacies, in scientific knowledge, or by shortage of trained personnel, or by even a faulty system of record-keeping. Whole groups of potential clients may be excluded from service by the unintentionally faulty phrasing of a law or an administrative directive. It would be comforting to believe that all such miscarriages of administrative process can be charged to the personal inadequacies—moral or psychiatric—of the personnel involved, or to the collective guilt of groups; but unfortunately neither the moral virtue nor the psychiatric health of its staff guarantees that a bureaucracy will do a good job.

Since the task of any culture, and particularly the cultures of large industrial societies, is to organize diversity rather than to destroy it, and since large industrial societies are increasingly dependent upon bureaucratic systems of management, a major task of cultural reform for continued human progress must be to design bureaucracies that are resistant to exploitation and are adequately sensitive to their clienteles. This enterprise calls for an awareness of the real technical problems involved in the analysis of the cognitive structures of groups.

chapter four
THE CULTURAL DISTRIBUTION OF PERSONALITY CHARACTERISTICS

In this chapter, we deal with the aspect of culture-and-personality studies that has produced the bulk of the literature in the field. For many people, indeed, this aspect *is* culture-and-personality. But because of certain conceptual ambiguities, which gave rise to fruitless controversy and tautology, culture-and-personality studies some years ago reached an impasse in this area. We have attempted to clear away a part of the debris by drawing attention to the distinction between replication and organization theories; and new insights are being provided by the reinterpretations of human nature suggested by ethology.

REPLICATION THEORY AND
ORGANIZATION THEORY

In the introductory chapter, we distinguished between two approaches to culture-and-personality, one emphasizing the replication of uniformities, and the other the organization of diversity. Both approaches attempt to explain the systems of interaction among individuals by saying something about what goes on inside them. For descriptive purposes serving only to delineate the preponderant characteristics of a group, particularly in comparing them with some other group (for example, in comparing one tribe with another, or one generation with another), the replication-of-uniformity approach is convenient and serviceable. But for the purpose of developing empirical support of theoretical analysis of the relation of sociocultural and personality systems, the organization-of-diversity approach is essential; in such contexts, the replication-of-uniformity approach is actually misleading.

One extreme formulation of the replication approach—the microcosmic metaphor—is so nearly tautological as to make

123

empirical investigation unnecessary. It takes many forms, but
they convey in common the proposition that inside the head of
"the ———" (adjectival form of name of group inserted here) is
a little replica of his group's culture, systematically transformed,
point for point, to fit neural tissue, which he has "internalized."
This replica is "the ———" personality. With some such formula
in mind, it has been asserted that "all culture and personality
studies . . . are focused on the way human beings embody the
culture they have been reared in, or to which they have immi-
grated."[1] To a few persons in every group, of course, the formula
does not apply; these few may be called "deviants." Such deviants
excluded, the metaphor implies, first of all, a conformity of all
personalities within a given culture-bearing (or subculture-
bearing) group to a single personality type; second, it implies a
perfect association between culture type and personality type.
From the latter assumption, accordingly, inference can supposedly
proceed in two ways: culture can be deduced from personality,
and personality can be deduced from culture, using the standard
syllogism. The process by which the internalization is accomplished is the process of child development as it is phrased in the
given culture.

The confusions produced by attempting to interpret empirical
data from the standpoint of the microcosmic metaphor are well
exemplified in a famous analysis of Alorese personality materials.[2]
The psychoanalytic consultant, working with field data brought
back by the anthropologist, assumes that all Alorese share a basic
personality structure because all have been exposed to the same
cultural influences. But he also finds empirically that each of the
four males from whom autobiographical and dream material
were secured is a "highly individual character." "Each has some
features of the basic personality structure, but each in turn is
molded by the specific factors in his individual fate." The analyst,
in fact, has great trouble in relating the character structures of
his four males to any basic personality norm. Thus, on initial
presentation, he observes, "It is difficult to decide how typical

1. Mead, "National Character," p. 642.
2. DuBois, *The People of Alor.*

Mangma is. I would venture to say that if he were typical, the society could not continue to exist." Yet, later he asserts, "Mangma is the most typical, and his character corresponds to the basic personality structure." Rilpada, a second male, is "atypical" because he is passive and has a strong superego, owing to good maternal care and a powerful father. (The typical male Alorese superego is "of necessity" weak.) Fantan, a third, has "the strongest character formation, devoid of inhibitions toward women." Fantan "differs from the other men . . . as much as a city slicker differs from a farmer." (The basic personality structure "for males," as the analyst defines it, is extremely inhibited in regard to heterosexuality: "the approach to the woman is filled with shyness and anxiety.") Malelaka is likewise difficult to evaluate. The analyst says, "His life history is in every way typical." This is remarkable, because Malelaka was a notorious prophet who attempted to launch a religious revival. On the other hand, he is said to be similar to Rilpada, another seer, who in turn was described as "atypical." And to complicate things still further, the analyst says that "characters such as Mangma, Rilpada, and Fantan can be found in any society."

The microcosmic metaphor is generally invoked in the cultural deductive method, which involves subjecting ethnological description to psychological analysis. In this method, the anthropologist's, historian's, or folklorist's accounts of myth and legend, religious ritual, economic relations, and so forth, are "interpreted" according to some schema, usually psychoanalytic, which treats these behaviors as if they were the neurotic productions of a single individual. This has been the particular interest of those culturological psychoanalysts who deduce from the cultural materials, with the help of psychoanalytic theory, the "meaning" of various institutions to the individual member of the society. Criticism of this procedure has sometimes been savage, since the interpretations themselves at times seem to be arbitrary, if not far-fetched, and demonstration that they are validly attributable to all, or even more than a few members, of the society is invariably lacking. *Ad hominem* argument may even displace rational discussion between antagonists in such discussions!

Rational criticisms of the microcosmic metaphor would seem

to fall into three categories: (1) that the metaphor implies a false equivalence between concepts on different levels of abstraction (for example, a personality is no more an embodiment of the culture than a baby is an embodiment of the birth rate) ; (2) that the metaphor is simplistic (there is far greater variability in personal characteristics than can be accounted for by the formulas) ; (3) that there is no reason to suppose that social organization requires a high degree of personal conformity to universalistic norms (for example, the relations between males and females depend not on mutual conformity to one role, but on a complementarity of different roles) .

Rational defenses of the microcosmic position have, however, been vigorous. Most of its proponents admit freely that every individual, even in the most uniformitarian society, is somewhat different from every other, as a result of the interplay of various genetic factors and the accidents of experience. But this diversity, as it is described, reminds one of the "diversity" of houses in a new development: the paint is of different colors, and the roof line rotates from house to house through a ninety-degree arc, but the floor plans are all the same. In other words, the dynamically important features are assumed to be the ones that are shared. Thus despite lip service to individual variations, the notion of "statistical" distribution is still resisted. Margaret Mead, for instance, has insisted that descriptions of individual characteristics and of cultural setting be so precise that perfect covariation is obtainable between them. "Any member of a group, provided that his position within that group is properly specified, is a perfect sample of the group-wide pattern on which he is acting as an informant. . . . Any cultural statement must be made in such a way that the addition of another class of informants previously unrepresented will not change the nature of the statement in *a way which has not been allowed for in the original statement.*"[3] But assertions that one component is a "perfect sample" of a pattern, once the component's relations to the other components have been specified, means no more than saying that one bead is a perfect sample of a wampum belt, if one already has the wam-

3. Mead, *op. cit.*, p. 648.

pum belt in one's hand. The question of distribution has simply been begged by sampling other informants to specify the "sample" informant's "position."

While the "cultural sampling" defense is logically weak, it is related to another proposition that has merit of its own, independent of its status in this argument (in which it is both a strong and a weak defense). This defense is the notion of "pattern" itself. "Pattern" has at least two senses in culture-and-personality writing: one in which it is a synchronic complex common to diverse representations, and another in which it is a diachronic complex common to diverse sequences. A pattern is, of course, a class of phenomena susceptible of many subclasses, which in themselves are of interest; but its identity as a recognizable class cannot be questioned merely because it contains subclasses. The strength of the pattern concept, as a defense of the microcosmic view, is that the existence of a pattern cannot be properly denied, merely by insistence on differentiating and counting the frequencies of its subclass. Its weakness is the weakness of the old comparative method: the analyst, only too easily, can take a piece from here, a shred from there, and relate them intuitively, in a pattern whose locus rests undefined. The old cultural evolutionists, as has often been said, would take a custom from this tribe, and a legend from that, and by patiently fitting together such bits and pieces, would construct a culture pattern (a "stage" of cultural evolution) that may never have existed anywhere, and certainly was not a part of the heritage of all known cultures. The pattern analysts in culture-and-personality are prone to take a childhood memory from this informant, a neurotic phobia from that, the theme from a movie, and the history of an international incident and, by skillful maneuvering of the pieces, produce a "pattern" that is discoverable in no one individual but is attributable to all. The deficiency in this procedure springs not from any lack of comprehensiveness of the observations on which it is based, nor from any lack of reliability in the processes of combining elements to form patterns, but in the *non sequitur* by which such a pattern is ascribed to uninvestigated (and sometimes, as in the Alorese case, even to investigated) individuals en masse.

There exists a parallel tradition, stemming from Sapir[4] and Hallowell[5] more than from Mead and Roheim, which partially avoids the pitfalls of the microcosmic metaphor by giving more emphasis to the uniqueness of the individual. Edward Sapir was impressed by the fact that individual informants gave different information and that no one informant knew the whole culture. "Two Crows denies this," meant, for Sapir, that Two Crows "had" a different culture, and probably a correspondingly different personality, from the other informant.[6] Melford Spiro[7] similarly has emphasized the uniqueness of private family and individual cultures, each as the product of a particular history of social interaction of the individuals being considered. But the logical consequence of this line of reasoning is another impasse: even though individual differences are more fully recognized, culture again becomes merely the subjective microcosm of personality, a distinction between the two is a "false dichotomy," and we are back where we started, with culture and personality paired off as equivalent constructs.

An alternative is the organizational theory. According to this theory, no population, within a stated cultural boundary, can be *assumed* to be uniform with respect to any variable or pattern. (For example, it cannot be *assumed* that males and females share the same values, the same role cognitions, the same emotional structure.) In every instance, a distribution will be found to characterize the sample. Personality is not assumed to be an internalization of the culture, and culture is not conceptualized as a constant environment, or projection, of all members of the society. Both personality descriptions and cultural descriptions are considered to be intuitive or formal abstractions by an observer from mazeway descriptions of individuals. Individual personality constructs are generalizations about one individual's mazeway over time; cultural constructs are generalizations and

4. Mandelbaum (ed.), *Selected Writings of Edward Sapir.*

5. *Culture and Experience.*

6. "Why Cultural Anthropology Needs the Psychiatrist," in Mandelbaum (ed.), *op. cit.,* p. 569–577.

7. "Culture and Personality: The Natural History of a False Dichotomy."

syntheses of behavior that are shared by, and/or produced by, groups. Modal personality and national character are abstractions from personality and cultural data, respectively. There is no finite list of categories that define personality, nor any specified number or proportion of individuals who must share behavior for it to be called "culture." Descriptions of culture will include statements of relations between behavior patterns that no informant has given or is able to give: cultural descriptions need not be "psychologically real"[8] to the informant.

The consequences for theory and for empirical study of taking the microcosmic or the organizational viewpoint are large, and it is this fact which makes discussion of the problem important. If the microcosmic view is adopted, then research is not necessary to demonstrate that covariation between personality and culture is exact (given constant "genetic factors") ; this is regarded as true by definition. The problem becomes essentially one of child development: *how* does the child come to "embody" his culture? Hence many of those who take the microcosmic view are preeminently interested in child training, education, and so forth. If the organizational view is adopted, however, then (as we have suggested in the Introduction) the problem of greater interest is the processes by which individually diverse organisms work to maintain, increase, or restore quantity of organization within their own psychological systems and within sociocultural and physical systems of which they are components. Child development remains a significant problem but is no longer to be considered as the only focal one. Statements about "the ———" and his cultural and personal characteristics may still be made, but they are now understood as conveniently brief expressions for more cumbersome formulations specifying subgroup membership and relative frequency.

HUMAN NATURE

There are two sets of elementary principles on which studies of personality distributions tend, tacitly, to rest: the general psycho-

8. Wallace and Atkins, "The Meaning of Kinship Terms."

logical properties of any organism capable of culture; and the psychological characteristics that men share by virtue of species membership. The second set includes the first but is not identical with it. Cultural nature would seem to require nothing peculiarly human, simply the capacity (1) to perceive stimuli; (2) to learn and remember (and to imagine, for fantasy here is being conceived as the process of reorganizing memory); (3) to discriminate between perception and memory-imagination (otherwise memory-fantasy equals perception and the organism hallucinates); (4) to attend selectively; (5) to calculate the meanings (including affective value) of perceived and remembered stimuli; (6) to respond overtly to stimuli. Cultural nature certainly does not require anything uniquely human and could be displayed by other animals on earth, the inhabitants of other planets, and conceivably even computers.

Human nature, however, implies a mixture of psychological propensities shared by all members of our species, derived by evolution from other species and to some degree shared with them, and also such features as may be unique to ourselves yet shared by all of us. The definition of human nature is peculiarly apt to be a frontier of ideological combat, for the scientific issues are readily transformed into political ones. Is man by nature competitive, aggressive, a hunter, a killer? Or is man naturally warm, loving, and open, and only corrupted and alienated by the unnatural excrescences of competitive cultures? Is he territorial, ethnocentric, nationalistic? Is he by nature inclined to some sort of biparental family structure? Is he naturally acquisitive, greedy, selfish? Does he by nature construct social systems based on dominance and submission? Is he naturally subject to Oedipal conflict? Is man the only "symboling" animal? Are men genetically more capable than women of forming the emotional bonds necessary to group organization? Does he naturally respond to mobilization signals, dispose himself into the primate marching order, and go to war? Is there a pan-cultural "language" of nonverbal communication (for example, in facial expressions of emotion)? Such questions are both posed and to some extent answered by data on infrahuman primate and other animal behavior as gathered by behavioral primatologists and ethologists[9] and by observations on the universal culture pattern. But because the answers to some of these questions can so readily be used to rationalize political positions, and preferences for one or another type of culture, it is uncomfortably apparent that interpretation is easily swayed by moral conviction. The optimistic and culturological Marxist humanism of Wilhelm Reich and Herbert Marcuse is politically as well as scientifically opposed to the cautious conservatism of the evolutionist and ethnological writings of Robert Ardrey and Desmond Morris.[10] Indeed, popular presentations of their material quite explicitly draws attention to the political and social and ideological implications of the findings and the sometimes impassioned use, or rejection, of such findings by usually sober academicians suggests that the role of ideologist, intellectual, and politician is in human nature very difficult to combine with the role of objective scholar and scientist, when the subject matter is the same for both roles.

The conception of human nature on which studies in culture and personality rests is, on the cognitive side, really a conception of cultural nature: man is a creature who uses symbols, in large part in linguistic forms, to organize his thought and to communicate. Where affect comes in, however—where values, attitudes, and motives come into play—there is a problem. Some psychoanalytic model of personality as a structure of compromises among conflicting instinctual inclinations, culturally derived motives, and realistic or moralistic restraints is perhaps most commonly employed. The Marxist humanists have made the synthesis of Freud and Marx a principal intellectual task; and the ethologists, echoing Freud, seek the origin of the darker motives in man's lustful, violent primate past. But each such model is apt to evoke challenge of some of its elementary conceptions. If it presupposes a natural instinct of aggression, it may be attacked on the ground that hostility is a product of our own sick society's

9. DeVore (ed.), *Primate Behavior: Field Studies of Monkeys and Apes,* and Lorenz, *On Aggression.*

10. Lorenz, *op. cit.;* Ardrey, *African Genesis* and *The Territorial Imperative.*

mistreatment of the young, or of the poor, or of minority groups. If it presupposes that full psychosexual maturation requires instinctual renunciation, it may be criticized as arbitrarily imputing Western European morality to mankind as a whole. Such difficulties are often the consequence of what are in the largest sense political issues; but unhappily they call for unambiguous empirical answers that are not immediately available.

It does not seem possible at present to make very satisfying generalizations about human nature, at least of the kind suggested above. But before going on to distributional questions, where it is happily unnecessary to insist on universally valid characterizations, let us suggest, if only for the sake of stimulating reflection and perhaps argument, some possible characteristics of human nature (apart from the general features of cultural nature) that conventional theories of personality do not seem adequately to take into account. These features center in the issue of primate dominance-and-submission propensities and their relationship to other motives, particularly sexuality, identity or self-esteem, family, territoriality and acquisitiveness, and aggression and hostility.

One of the difficulties of the classic psychoanalytic approach, and one to the resolution of which Freud devoted much attention, was that by making the libidinal instincts (that is, sexual instincts in the largest sense) and their vicissitudes the core of human nature, it became difficult to account for various kinds of aggression that were not directly attributable to libidinal urges. Freud postulated a "death instinct," but this somewhat far-fetched metaphysical motion has not commanded the confidence that other parts of Freud's psychology have gained. Efforts by his followers to deal with the problem have produced the frustration-aggression hypothesis, which interprets aggression as a consequence of the frustration of libidinal drives, and have contributed to the development of ego psychology, which takes up such matters as realistic strivings for mastery of the environment and for the development of an identity that embodies self-respect.

Rather than construe the issue as a polarity between life instincts and death instincts, with all the consequent problems of relating the two, let us begin with the trite observations that in the larger primates below man, individuals form strong attachments to one another and to groups, including the community, and that loss of skin contact in infants, and personal attachments and group membership in adults, is likely to be fatal. In these organizations, dominance is a function of age (adults dominating infants), of gender (males dominating females), and of strength and aggressiveness within male and female groups. It is also apparently linked to sexuality, and the rituals expressive of dominance-and-submission are, in fact, often simulations of sexual approach and of copulation, both heterosexually and homosexually. Normally, a primate troop manages to get along with minimal real fighting because the members are sorted out into a stable dominance order such that each member of a pair of animals, on confrontation, knows and accepts his relative position. Serious challenges to this order, chiefly as a result of the maturation, in-migration, changing alliances, and senescence of individuals, take the form of actual fighting or "agonistic" (threatening) displays. Accidental or trivial challenges elicit irritable responses, but ready ritual submission generally aborts a developing conflict. All animals know, and are capable of relating to others in, both dominant and submissive roles, depending on the circumstances; and dominance is not pressed to the point where any animal is excluded from food, sex, reproduction, or group membership; indeed, male group solidarity may flourish where hierarchy is clear. Social play, in which existing dominance stuctures are suspended in nonescalating agonistic competition, occurs primarily among the young. Mother-son incest is minimized because it requires behavior that complicates an age-based dominance relationship. Species differ in regard to territoriality and acquisitiveness, but it cannot be said that preoccupation with territoriality and property is a universal primate trait. Destructive aggression between groups is rare or nonexistent. Nor are the lower primates primary carnivores and hunters of other species, although the larger species can and do hunt on occasion.

If one were to use these data as the baseline, then, one would postulate the following fundamental (and very old) pattern for human nature: men are creatures who live most comfortably in small troops and profoundly fear rejection by their group; whose sexual impulses are closely connected with dominance-and-submission impulses in both sexes; who sort themselves out into established dominance hierarchies; who are irritably sensitive to challenges to dominance and respond to such challenges with agonistic displays, but who also are capable of switching to a comfortable and passive submission; who can form close personal attachments to mothers, to children, to leaders, to friends, and to sexual consorts, and who as children enjoy playing at games in which dominance roles alternate.

Now let us suppose that our protohuman creature has a relatively large and perhaps especially efficient brain, enjoys a prolonged infancy and childhood, walks on two feet with hands free, and has fine stereoscopic color vision, and as a result of the superiority of this biological equipment, invents wood, stone, and bone tools, controls fire, develops language, becomes a professional hunter, specializes occupationally, and in the end produces a kind of culture we can call human. What kind of problems of psychodynamics will his desire to maintain this economically advantageous mode of life entail for him?

One obvious problem will be a tendency to find innumerable new and technically inconvenient ways in which dominance can be both exercised and challenged. And along with this, because of the old tie between dominance and sex, will go a sexualizing of these new opportunities for dominance and submission. This tendency will be a problem because the technology, the language, and the specialization of labor will increasingly necessitate the modification of a sexually oriented dominance hierarchy based on simple physical fighting and agonistic display. Hence there will have to be elaborate rules for the compartmentalization of dominance into areas of authority and responsibility based on many criteria of competence, not just irritability and physical strength; a partial separation of dominance from sexuality, by such devices as incest taboos in kinship structures, by taboos on nepotism, and (with an eye to the efficiency of large male organizations) by taboos on or at least careful management of homosexuality; and a prohibition of dominance relations in certain contexts. Many of the creatures will spend much of their time mechanically carrying out instrumental tasks without a satisfying sense of either dominance or submission. Many will feel that they deserve to be dominant but are not permitted to be; many will feel inadequate to maintain the dominance required of them. All this will become a source of innumerable potential frustrations and anxieties that will be the more pervasive the more complex the technology and the social system becomes; fear of loss of social acceptance and of self-acceptability may become chronic. The psychoanalytically described mechanisms of defense, and their institutionalized counterparts in religious belief and ritual, in play, and in the arts, develop to relieve some of this chronic fear; what cannot be handled in these structurally stable compromises produces the symptomatic expressions of anxiety, delusion, "regressive" displays of agonistic and sexual behavior, and all the rest of the disorders we lump together as mental illness, meaningless violence, unreasonable exploitation, and senseless war.

The nuclear problems, for this kind of primate nature, then become first, one of constantly minimizing fear by separating areas of experience and by responding to challenge not with impulsive dominant or submissive actions but on the basis of socially sanctioned calculation, and second, differentiating between dominance-submission relationships that may include explicit sexual aspects and those that may not, irrespective of provocations and solicitations, opportunities and impulses.

Issues of territorality and property are of importance primarily because they can be coded in terms of dominance and submission and thereby attached spuriously to displaced agonistic impulses; yet these issues lead to war, to exploitation, and to intergroup antagonism. Furthermore, in this context, it becomes the individual's identity dynamics, involving his image of himself in the dominance (and therefore group) situation, rather than his appetite dynamics, which is of primary concern in character development and, when necessary, in psychiatric treatment, both because of their importance in themselves and because the person's problems in the dominance area automatically interfere with the related (in a "wired-in" way) libidinal dynamics. Furthermore, in situations of group social exploitation, peculiarly pretentious and sometimes destructive displays of agonistic behavior by the exploited, and of insult and repression by the exploiters, recurrently plague the larger social systems.[11]

SYNCHRONIC DISTRIBUTIONS

Synchronic distributional studies of personality attempt to answer the questions: at a given point in time, what is the frequency distribution of certain personal characteristics in a certain class of persons? "Class of person" is defined by the possession, by *all* the persons in the class, of some property in common: a type of culture (for example, "peasant culture," "poverty culture," "colonial culture"), a nationality ("Japanese"), a race ("Mongoloid"), a region ("the southern United States"), an age group ("persons over sixty-five"), a civilization ("Western culture"), a culture area ("the Plains Indians"), a social class ("the bourgeoisie"), an ethnic group ("second generation Italian-Americans"), a religion ("conservative Judaism"), an economic status ("families with an average yearly income of less than $2,000"), an occupation ("waiters"), a sex ("female"), a tribe ("the Ojibwa"), a community ("Plainville, U.S.A."), or, in fact, any one or combination of an indefinitely large number of possible properties. Many of these class-defining properties are noncultural (for example, "age"), but since all are likely to be related to variation in cultural systems, they are met with in culture-and-personality studies.

The panel of personal characteristics used in culture-and-personality studies is as large as the panel of classes. The psychology of personality has yielded many systems, concepts, and measurement devices. These various schemata, as we indicated in the Introduction, do not claim exclusive validity; rather, they are relevant and appropriate to different practical purposes and operational situations. But all have in common, at least, a connotation of concern with that structure of relatively abstract values, and their means of achievement, that is maintained by an

11. See Wallace, "Anthropological Contributions to the Theory of Personality" for further discussion of "what kind of people are people."

individual over a protracted time. We may classify them with respect to the technique of investigation (projective test, depth interview, galvanic skin response, free association, questionnaire, and so forth), or analytical schema (authoritarian versus democratic, introversion versus extroversion, the psychoanalytic dynamic characterology, and so forth). Within anthropology, perhaps the most commonly employed analytical frames have been the following: genius (as of a culture or civilization), world view, ethos, themes, values, national character, basic personality structure, and modal personality structure. Technically, some of these are largely constructed by abstraction from individual personality descriptions, and others by deduction from cultural descriptions. Some emphasize cognitive positions (beliefs); others, affective orientation (emotional tone) and motivation. Now let us briefly discuss each analytical frame separately.

"Genius"

Most abstract and least affective in content is a set of psychological characteristics, usually inferred from cultural data, that may, for want of a better term (Bateson's term "eidos" has not become widely used), be labeled "genius," in the sense connoted by such expressions as "the genius of Greek civilization." It is probably in psycholinguistics, following the tradition set by Sapir and Whorf, that the theory behind this approach is most rigorously developed; but Kroeber, Spengler, Toynbee, and other philosophers of history have been concerned to capture its essential theme. The genius of a people has both a continuous and an evolutionary aspect. Its continuity is provided by the constant presence, throughout an extended historical process, of a definite frame of reference that provides certain primitive categories into which experience can be coded, and defines the kinds of relationships that conceivably can exist between such categories. Thus it functions (in theory at least) as a set of parameters or rules governing mental operations. In this sense, genius can be compared to the primitive predicates, operators, and axioms of a logical calculus; once established, only certain propositional functions can be constructed; indeed, only a finite number of these functions is possible. In its evolutionary sense, the genius of a people is the plot or program that is displayed in its history: the unfolding, over centuries or millennia, of the inner potentialities of the primitive cultural axioms. Here again, the comparison to a logical calculus is apt, for the plot of a culture unfolds in a way comparable to the gradual unfolding, in logical and mathematical discovery and proof, of new theorems, each of which serves as the basis for further cumulative synthesis. Genius is like a geometry, being expressible both in its primitive axiomatics and in the historical process of theorem development. Ultimately, of course, an end may be reached, when the genius has fulfilled its destiny, and a phase of sterility ending in "death" supervenes.

Thus the concept of genius often has both a mystical, fatalistic quality, best expressed by philosophers of history such as Spengler, and a hard and logical quality, voiced by psycholinguists such as Whorf, by culturologists such as Kroeber and White, and by historians of science, particularly Thomas Kuhn[12] who uses a concept of "paradigm" in science analogous to that of genius in culture. It is both the "soul" of the superorganic and the phonemics, lexicon, and syntax of culture, depending on the use to which the concept is being put.

Examples of descriptions of genius, in its continuous and evolutionary aspects, will make the concept clear. Whorf, for instance, describes certain features of the genius of the Hopi in his intensive examination of the Hopi language:

After long and careful study and analysis, the Hopi language is seen to contain no words, grammatical forms, constructions or expressions that refer directly to what we call "time," or to past, present, or future, or to enduring or lasting, or to motion as kinematic rather than dynamic (i.e., as a continuous translation in space and time rather than as an exhibition of dynamic effort in a certain process), or that even refer to space in such a way as to exclude that element of extension or existence that we call "time," and so by implication leave a residue that could be referred to as "time." Hence, the Hopi language contains no reference to "time," either explicit or implicit.

12. *The Structure of Scientific Revolutions.*

At the same time, the Hopi language is capable of accounting for and describing correctly, in a pragmatic or operational sense, all observable phenomena of the universe. . . . Just as it is possible to have any number of geometries other than the Euclidean which give an equally perfect account of space configurations, so it is possible to have descriptions of the universe, all equally valid, that do not contain our familiar contrasts of time and space. The relativity viewpoint of modern physics is one such view, conceived in mathematical terms, and the Hopi Weltanschauung is another and quite different one, nonmathematical and linguistic. . . .[13]

This analysis of Whorf's, and comparable exercises by other psycholinguists, was explicitly recognized by Whorf as an approach to understanding psychological processes. As Whorf put it:

linguistics is essentially the quest of MEANING. It may seem to the outsider to be inordinately absorbed in recording hairsplitting distinctions of sound, performing phonetic gymnastics, and writing complex grammars which only grammarians read. But the simple fact is that its real concern is to light up the thick darkness of the language, and thereby of much of the thought, the culture, and the outlook upon life of a given community, with the light of this "golden something," as I have heard it called, this transmuting principle of meaning. As I have tried to show, this amounts to far more than learning to speak and understand the language as the practical language teacher conceives these ends. The investigator of culture should hold an ideal of linguistics as that of a heuristic approach to problems of psychology which hitherto he may have shrunk from considering—a glass through which, when correctly focused, will appear the TRUE SHAPES of many of those forces which hitherto have been to him but the inscrutable blank of invisible and bodiless thought.[14]

From this point of view, therefore, linguistics becomes a method for investigating what may be termed the semantic geometry of culture. It may be doubted whether structural linguistics per se is fully equipped to conduct such investigations; but such further,

13. *Language, Thought, and Reality*, pp. 57–58.
14. *Ibid.*, p. 73.

semantically directed, procedures as are offered by componential analysis, in combination with lexical and grammatical analysis *à la* Whorf, can make rigorous investigation possible.

In the evolutionary sense, genius is the program of development of a logical system: the successive working out of the theorems, as it were, which are implied by the axioms of the semantic geometry. Kroeber, in his study *Configurations of Culture Growth,* in his outline of native North American culture areas,[15] and in various other places, has pointed out that the histories of cultures display a characteristic sequence of rise, climax, and fatigue. He suggests that this sequence is the program of the working out of the "logical possibilities" of particular "styles" or "patterns." The analysis of the development of Greek mathematics is typical:

We have seen that Greek science and mathematics came in a four-century spurt and then stood still. The Greeks never did achieve much in simple arithmetic, probably partly because their method of writing quantities—by letter symbols denoting certain specific numbers instead of by position numerals—made ordinary computations of any size difficult. Even less was accomplished by them in algebra, of which the imperfect rudiments began—or first appear to our view—some four hundred years after Greek general mathematical progress had stopped. The branch of mathematics the Greeks did wholly originate and develop was geometry—plane, solid, and spherical. Here they substantially "exhausted the pattern," fulfilled its possibilities, and left nothing for others to discover. Now geometry is a special way of doing mathematics—with a compass and rule and nothing more, the Greeks insisted. It visualizes properties and relations; it can be pictured, as algebra and arithmetic cannot be. Although already truly abstract, geometry easily retains the most concrete aspect of all branches of mathematics. This geometric approach was the Greek "style" in mathematics. One part of the style was the Greek emphasis on proportion, which can also be diagramed; and the Greek avoidance, where possible, of all but integral numbers, which can be handled like visible and tangible blocks; and the avoidance also of negative quantities and irrational fractions, which cannot be handled

15. *Cultural and Natural Areas of Native North America.*

in this way. On the positive side, again, the Greeks pushed on from their geometry into conic sections—dealing with plane cuts across cones, resulting in curves such as ellipses, parabolas, hyperbolas. This is a branch of mathematics which we still call by the original name of "conic sections," although we mostly express its concepts algebraically now. The further limitations of the mathematical style of the Greeks are shown by their failure to develop anything at all in the field of logarithms, analytical geometry, calculus, or the concept of function. What they could do with their geometrical and whole-numbered manner of style, they achieved. Other mathematical possibilities, like these mentioned, were simply left to be realized by other peoples and times—chiefly by western Europeans in the last three or four centuries.[16]

Kroeber's type of analysis applies equally well to other categories of culture and, indeed, to the "style" (or genius) of whole civilizations.

In sum, then, we can define the "genius" of a population as a paradigm—a set of highly generalized primitive concepts and axioms that serve as the frame of reference for a whole society (or, at least, a large portion thereof). These axioms may, themselves, not be consciously recognized by their holders and, in general, may be abstracted from cultural or psychological data. They imply the program of possible cultural evolution and thus set limits on possible cultural development by the population that entertains them.

World View

Still predominantly cognitive, but more concrete in reference to observable things, is world view. The concept of world view has been most effectively developed by Robert Redfield and others associated with him. It primarily refers to cognitive content, some of which may be affectively neutral, and is derived by abstraction from ethnographic description. Redfield defines world view as that outlook upon the universe which is characteristic of a people:

16. *Anthropology*, pp. 330–331.

"World view" differs from culture, ethos, mode of thought, and national character. It is the picture the members of a society have of the properties and characters upon their stage of action. While "national character" refers to the way these people look to the outsider looking in on them, "world view" refers to the way the world looks to that people looking out. Of all that is connoted by "culture," "world view" attends especially to the way a man, in a particular society, sees himself in relation to all else. It is the properties of existence as distinguished from and related to the self. It is, in short, a man's idea of the universe. It is that organization of ideas which answers to a man the questions: Where am I? Among what do I move? What are my relations to these things?[17]

But Redfield does not really mean *any* existential belief; he is referring to broad classes of such beliefs. Thus it is very similar to the concept of "implicit dominant ontology," which refers to the major assumptions about the existential nature of the world that are held by a population, to "cosmology," which may be conceived as a systematized world view, and to what has more recently come to be called the "symbol system." Redfield regards some categories of world view as psychic universals: belief in a division of things into those that are self and those that are nonself; in a division of the latter into human, nonhuman but material, and supernatural; in distinctions between earth and sky, day and night, birth and death, and so forth. Among the multitude of world views that the anthropologist may observe, Redfield pays particular attention to one kind: the primitive world view, said to be characterized by three major assertions: (1) that the distinction between the self and that which the self confronts is blurred, so that man tends to see himself as united with nature, rather than standing apart from it; (2) that man participates in maintaining this unitary system of man-in-nature, rather than dominates or changes it; (3) that the universe is morally significant, because all of nature is animate and hence man's relationship with nature, like all social relationships, must be moral.

17. "The Primitive World View," p. 30.

Other scholars, of course, have dealt with comparable concepts in contrasting primitive and civilized, folk and urban, provincial and cosmopolitan, and so forth. When Cassirer[18] describes the "mythopoeic personality" of the primitive; when Hallowell[19] discusses time and space orientation among the Ojibwa; when Wallis, Löwith, and Bury[20] consider various concepts of eschatology and progress; when Weber[21] analyzes the Protestant ethic; when Mannheim[22] discusses ideologies and utopias; when Foster[23] describes the "image of limited good" in peasant societies, each is dealing with world view.

Mention of Mannheim must turn the reader's attention to the traditional interest of Continental sociologists in the sociology of knowledge. The essential theme of Mannheim's work is thoroughly at home in anthropological theory: that the whole fabric of institutions of a society must be intimately related to the dominant system of existential belief, which, in turn, not merely rationalizes, but springs naturally from the exigencies of functional organization. Thus a world view is not merely a philosophical by-product of each culture, like a shadow, but the very skeleton of concrete cognitive assumptions on which the flesh of customary behavior is hung. World view, accordingly, may be expressed, more or less systematically in cosmology, philosophy, ethics, religious ritual, scientific belief, and so on, but it is implicit in almost every act. In Parsonian terms, it constitutes the set of cognitive orientations of the members of a society.[24]

Values, Ethos, and Themes

Something of value is something that an organism will work to experience. "Values" as such, however, as abstract entities, are

18. *Language and Myth.*

19. *Culture and Experience.*

20. *Culture and Progress, Meaning in History,* and *The Idea of Progress.*

21. *The Protestant Ethic and the Spirit of Capitalism.*

22. *Ideology and Utopia.*

23. "Peasant Society and the Image of Limited Good."

24. Parsons and Shils (eds.), *Toward a General Theory of Action.*

rather difficult to define. In one sort of economic usage, "the value" of anything is, in a sense, an intangible property added to a raw, primitive material by a producer who performs work upon it and by a consumer who performs work to obtain it. The measure of this added value is a function of both the producer's and the consumer's work. In psychological, sociological, and anthropological usage, the "value" of a thing or a state of affairs is, somewhat comparably, its positive or negative valence, that is, its relative potency as a goal ("reward," "punishment," "pleasure," "pain," and so on) toward which, or away from which, the organism strives. An object that has acquired psychological value is said to have been "cathected." The "value" of a long life, or food pellets, or sexual satisfaction, or membership in a prestigeful group, or whatever, can be stated as a quantity, or at least as a rank order, on a scale from minus-x through zero to plus-y. But "a value," in the sense of the term used by psychologists, anthropologists, and sociologists, means more than the cathexis figuratively clinging, like a static charge of positive or negative electricity, to some object. First of all, "a value" refers not merely to the cathectic "charge," but also to that which bears the "charge"—the mental image, or the object itself, that is the goal ("consummatory values") and, sometimes, even to behavioral gambits that the organism may employ to approach or avoid it ("instrumental values"). Second, because "values" in the latter sense are closely related to ontology, empirical descriptions of "values" tend to include descriptions of genius and world view.[25] Finally, in anthropological usage, "the values" of a people, or a culture, are not really any and all object-cathexes, but only those that the anthropologist can show to be widely shared, to be considered "desirable," as well as merely "desired," and to pervade many different cultural categories: in a word, they are abstractions or logical types of very high order.

The concept of values sometimes appeals to social anthropologists who, for one reason or another, do not feel comfortable with personality psychology. In particular, as criticism of the uniformitarian implications of some national character studies

25. Cf. Rapoport, *Changing Navaho Religious Values.*

has mounted, the concept of values has provided a kind of substitute. "Personality" may be variable, but are not the "values" of a people shared? And are not "values" somehow more impersonal, more structural, more clearly relevant to culture? Do not certain "values" organize the diversity of personalities in society?

The most extensive use of the concept of values by anthropologists has been made in Harvard University's Comparative Study of Values in Five Cultures (Navaho, Zuni, Mormon, Texan, and Spanish-American).[26] The Study works with broad values, such as "the harmony of the universe" (a positively valued state of affairs among the Navaho) and "individual independence" (a positively valued state among the Texans). A similar tradition has been maintained in the development of the Parsonian calculus, also at Harvard, but the Parsonian schema has emphasized the classification of these already broad abstractions into a componential taxonomy of value types. (For instance, a society's central values may be simply classified as "universalistic-achievement," or "particularistic-ascription," in character).[27] This kind of typology has a certain usefulness as a heuristic device; its justification as an analytical tool we shall discuss later.

The term "ethos" denotes one particular kind of "object" to which value is apt to be commonly attached by members of a society. That "object" is style of emotional experience, or as Honigmann puts it, "the emotional quality of socially patterned behavior."[28] The best-known example of the description of ethos is Ruth Benedict's famous *Patterns of Culture* (in which the word "pattern" is used to denote what we here call "ethos"). She contrasts two types of ethos, the Dionysian and the Apollonian:

The desire of the Dionysian, in personal experience or in ritual, is to press through it toward a certain psychological state, to achieve excess. The closest analogy to the emotions he seeks is drunkenness, and he values the illuminations of frenzy. With

26. Cf. Parsons and Shils (eds.), *op. cit.*
27. Vogt and Albert, *People of Rimrock.*
28. *Culture and Personality.*

Blake, he believes, "the path of excess leads to the palace of
wisdom." The Apollonian distrusts all this, and has often little
idea of the nature of such experiences. He finds means to outlaw
them from his conscious life. He "knows but one law, measure in
the Hellenic sense." He keeps the middle of the road, stays within
the known map, does not meddle with disruptive psychological
states. In Nietzsche's fine phrase, even in the exaltation of the
dance he "remains what he is, and retains his civic name."[29]

Other writers have dealt with such culturally valued and dis-
valued emotional states under a variety of terms: thus, for
instance, Jane Belo[30] has alluded to the Balinese "temper"; Otto
Klineberg[31] has reviewed attitudes toward emotion expressed in
Chinese literature; Osgood[32] and his followers have used this
semantic differential to compare the profiles of affective connotation associated with concepts in various cultures.

The concept of "themes" in culture, as developed by, among
others, Morris Opler,[33] is also a value-oriented concept. The
themes of a culture are a finite list (a dozen, let us say) of propositions about what constitutes the good life, about what are the
valid and enduring goals of a human existence, shared by the
members of a group. In restricted form, thematic analysis has
been extensively used in the study of literary productions: novels,
plays, movies, myths, and artificial productions, such as the
Thematic Apperception Test. Such themes describe, essentially,
the familiar plots of a culture: those goals, positive and negative,
together with their methods of achievement and avoidance, that
are publicly recognized and intelligible to the audience.[34] One
can discern in the popular American "Western," whether short
story, novel, movie, or television play, one theme: the proposition
that good men, hard to find in this chaotic and lawless world,

29. P. 72.

30. "The Balinese Temper."

31. "Emotional Expression in Chinese Literature."

32. *The Measurement of Meaning.*

33. "Themes as Dynamic Forces in Culture."

34. Mead and Metraux (eds.), *The Study of Culture at a Distance.*

must be moralistic heroes who fight and fight tirelessly against great odds to bring order to the community, but are sure to triumph and to receive sexual love and public approbation, if not material reward, if they do. This theme is also dominant in the "tough" genre of crime stories, where the "private eyes" are typically disillusioned idealists, lacking faith in the power structure of their society, who nonetheless do the right thing for their wronged clients. The Western and private-eye themes are different from the late nineteenth-century English "mystery," whose heroes emphasized the virtue of cleverness in logical deduction, rather than of well-intentioned brutality, accepted the rightness of the power structure, and tirelessly and politely worked to maintain order in an already well-ordered community. All three differ from the theme of the seventeenth-century English drama whose heroes are not concerned with the welfare of society, but with the gratification of private appetites in a community that is recognized to be hypocritical, corrupt, and exploitative.

One of the most productive of these lines of study has been David McClelland's "achievement motivation" research.[35] Noticing that American TAT subjects differed in the frequency with which their stories contained themes of competition with a standard of excellence, he hypothesized that such a generalized value (or personality variable) should be correlated both with patterns of socialization and with such features of national culture as industrial development. In studies of Americans, a substantial correlation between *maternal* encouragement of the child's independence strivings and a highly individualistic kind of achievement motivation has been found; and America is certainly a prime exemplar of industrial prowess. Predicted relationships among socialization, achievement motivation, and economic enterprise have been reported in other cultures. In Nigeria, for instance, the entrepreneurial success of the Ibo in comparison with the Hausa has been attributed to a difference in their conception of the means of "status mobility," the Hausa emphasizing

---

35. McClelland, *The Achieving Society;* LeVine, *Dreams and Deeds: Achievement Motivation in Nigeria;* De Vos, "Achievement and Innovation in Culture and Personality."

clientage and the Ibo personal initiative. But as DeVos has pointed out, the American situation, in which need for achievement is inversely related to need for affiliation, is not necessarily the universal psychological precondition for economic success. In Japan, achievement motivation has been closely tied to affiliation drives: the individual works hard and responsibly to advance the interests of the family, the company, and the state, with which he identifies himself. And this pattern of motivation has worked very well in Japan.

Another, rather similar, approach has been developed by Francis L. K. Hsu in his studies of social structure and personality in China, the United States, India, and Japan.[36] Hsu suggests that in each society, one of a limited number of kin relationships is dominant. Each such relationship has certain inevitable attributes and these provide a kind of model of all human relationships and thus directly mold other institutions and values. In the United States, the dominant kin relationship is husband-wife. This relationship, among other things, is based on free choice and mutual satisfaction; and Hsu sees in the American propensity for joining "clubs" of all sorts an outgrowth of the dominance of the husband-wife relationship. In traditional China, by contrast, the dominant relationship is father-son, which is ascriptive and permanent, and he suggests that in consequence the Chinese tend to be clan rather than club oriented. Hsu's basic argument does not depend on particular cases but on the general proposition that a certain central institution (the dominant kin relationship) is mirrored throughout the culture and in the personality. The varieties of the dominant kin relationship, then, in his system play the role which the several vicissitudes of the Oedipus conflict play in classical psychoanalytic theory: they provide the essential image of human relations, of which the actual institutions are but topological transformations.

Fundamentally, all the approaches that emphasize values— value studies, ethos, themes—postulate, in the mazeway of the individual, the existence of certain semantic parameters. One or

36. "The Effect of Dominant Kinship Relationships on Kin and Non-Kin Behavior: A Hypothesis"; *Caste, Clan, and Club*.

the other of these parameters gives connotation to virtually all experience but does not necessarily enter into the *explicit* definition of anything. They are the emotional counterparts of the semantic geometry and of the world view of a people. Every motive can theoretically be classified under the heading of one or another value or theme, but the identity of these values is apt to emerge only after extensive coding and supercoding of the data of culture and of individual behavior.

National Character and Basic Personality

The description of the national character of a people is apt to include statements about genius, world view, and values. What distinguishes national character as a concept is, first, its usual restriction to the citizens of modern, political organized states; and, second and more important, its emphasis upon the articulation of a large number of components into a structure or pattern. (Pattern, in this sense, is not quite the same as Benedict's meaning. Benedict's "patterns" were, essentially, simple emotional elements found in most of the units of a cultural structure, comparable to the chromosomes found in most of the cells of a body. But the "pattern" of a national character structure is a set of intricate dynamic interrelationships among different aspects of a personality or character.) The kind of phenomenon to which national character refers is the same as that denoted by the phrase "basic personality." But basic personality is applicable to any culturally bounded group, whether tribe, nation, or culture area; and it has tended to connote a more thoroughgoing use of the psychoanalytic theory of personality. It is inconvenient to have to change terms according to political form, however, and awkward to use the adjective "national" to refer to any and all social groups. So, in this section, we shall use the term "basic personality," in order to have one phrase, whether the group be a small primitive tribe, a modern state, a culture area, or a whole civilization. We also disavow partiality to any particular theoretical schema. Basic personality, as we shall use the term, implies neither a particular type of social organization nor a particular theory of personality; it merely refers to a structure of articulated personality characteristics and processes attributable, nonstatistically, to almost all members of some culturally bounded population.

In method, the basic personality approach primarily rests on the cultural deductive principle; that is, the analyst first prepares an ethnographic description and then infers, from the ethnographic data, the intrapsychic structures of the members of the society.[37] He feels able to do this because he is equipped with a complex, often psychoanalytic, theory that states equivalences between behavior (or experience) and motivation. Thus knowledge of how children are toilet-trained, or how the dead are mourned, implies some knowledge of, respectively, consequent and antecedent motivational structures; this knowledge increases with the complexity of the description of the context of action. Generally the maintenance system of the culture—the essential economic institutions and the kinship, political, educational structures dependent thereon—is considered to be responsible for determining the nature of the basic personality structure. Furthermore, this theory requires the basic personality analyst to discriminate between peripheral and nuclear motives: nuclear motives are both "basic" to psychodynamic structure and "universal" in the society. The relationship of nuclear motives is, generally speaking, considered to form a conflict-structure, with motives (and values) being paired off against one another, dialectically, with overt behavior representing some sort of compromise synthesis. The basic motivational structure is assumed to be learned, usually in infancy and early childhood; later experience, however, and especially stressful experience, may lead to the development, or use, of various institutionalized mechanisms such as religious belief and ritual ("the projective system"). These defend the essential integrity of the structure by giving indirect gratification to the subordinate but rebellious motives. The general form of the conflict structure is often described in

37. Mead, *op cit.,* p. 648; Wallace, "Individual Differences and Cultural Uniformities."

terms of an ideal public personality, in order to emulate which the individual must sacrifice important private motives or even physiological needs; this sacrifice in turn requires some socially harmless and more or less disguised outlets, particularly in religious belief and ritual and in play. Spiro, among others, has provided an elegant formulation of this analytical model under the rubric of "teleological functionalism."[38]

An example of basic personality theory is Geoffrey Gorer's controversial swaddling hypothesis. Gorer, in discussing the Great Russians, suggested that Russian culture institutionalized extreme discipline and authoritarianism in human relations but allowed periods of orgiastic license for creature indulgence and for destructiveness. This seemed to imply (by the cultural deductive method) a type of personality in which the ego feels a need for strong external restraints in order to satisfy the value placed on discipline and order, and to control the rebellious desire for freedom from restraint. This conflict structure in Gorer's theory, was established in the infant (but was reinforced in many other later experiences) by the experience of prolonged tight swaddling, with occasional intervals of release during which the child kicked violently, while nurses watched anxiously, fearful lest the child injure himself in his freedom.[39] As Mead points out, much of the criticism of Gorer's hypothesis is misdirected: Gorer did *not* say that Russians are incapable of freedom because they are swaddled as infants.[40] Given the assumption that a common conflict structure exists in all Great Russians and that it is both the psychological equivalent of certain adult institutions and the product of certain series of infantile experiences, the hypothesis is rational. The appropriate criticism, if any, must apply to the assumptions.

This appropriate criticism is essentially that which applies to microcosmic theories in general. What is the evidence that all

---

38. "Ghosts, Ifaluk, and Teleological Functionalism."

39. Gorer and Rickman, *The People of Great Russia;* Mead and Metraux (eds.), *op. cit.*

40. Mead, *op. cit.*, p. 644.

Great Russians do experience this conflict structure, that their adult institutions are the cultural equivalents of this uniform conflict structure, that their infantile experience is uniform, and that their infantile experience determines their adult personalities? Such questions anticipate further discussion; for the moment we defer their consideration and go on to the closely related concept of modal personality.

Modal Personality Structure

Basic personality is a nonstatistical concept, emphasizing the importance of pattern and attempting to dispose of questions of frequency by excluding "deviants" and "peripheral" traits, thus leaving a core structure that is supposedly common to all members of a group. The corresponding statistical construct is modal personality. Properly speaking, "modal" refers to that value of a variable which is most frequent in a distribution: it is conceptually, and often empirically, distinct from other measures of central tendency, such as the mean (average) and the median. But for simplicity's sake, in this section we shall use "modal personality" loosely to denote any method that characterizes the personality typical of a culturally bounded population by the central tendency of a defined frequency distribution.

Cultural descriptions rarely are phrased in such a way that statistical distributions of personal characteristics can be deduced from them. Hence modal personality must, in most cases, be constructed from data other than an ethnographic report. Such data are most easily gathered by giving psychological tests to a sample of a culturally defined population; other devices, such as recording dreams, taking life histories, and recording the frequency of certain behaviors, are sometimes used, but they are more tedious and consequently more difficult to apply to adequately large numbers of people. Modal personality has come to be associated with the various projective techniques: the Rorschach Test, the Thematic Apperception Test (both in its original form and in the various cultural modifications), the Stewart Emotional Response Test, and a number of others. There exists a considerable literature now on the cross-cultural use of projective techniques.[41]

The peculiar weakness of the modal personality concept is complementary to the weakness of the basic personality concept. Basic personality has difficulty dealing with questions of frequency; modal personality has difficulty dealing with questions of structure and pattern. As we have seen, the basic personality theory uses the relationship of conflict to bind motives into elaborate homeostatic systems that are transformed over time, shifting and moving according to the pressures put upon them. Modal personality description can do as little as stating the central tendency of a frequency distribution of values of one variable and must content itself at best with stating the frequency of certain combinations of values on several variables. For instance, Wallace was able to state that the modal type of personality, defined on twenty-one dimensions of observation in a certain Indian population, was shared by only 37 percent of the sample tested.[42] Such combinations, whether identified by simple techniques of correlation and association, or by factor analysis, or by the modal group technique described, in themselves do not constitute a dynamic structure; they are essentially taxonomic structures. The dynamic structure (for example, the conflict structure) represented by a particular combination of values (for example, a Rorschach profile) must be deduced from a formal interpretive code. Furthermore, many modal personality studies are vulnerable to statistical criticism of sample design, of choice of statistic, and of the justification of inference. A further corollary weakness of the statistical approach is that the method requires extreme selectivity. The richness of human experience is not savored, for the choice of a statistical tool usually means that only a few dimensions of behavior can be tapped and that these must be integrated into aridly abstract types.

Nevertheless, a statistical approach has the great virtue of mak-

41. Cf. Henry and Spiro, "Psychological Techniques: Projective Tests in Field Work," and Lindzey, *Projective Techniques in Cross-Cultural Research.*

42. *The Modal Personality Structure of the Tuscarora Indians, As Revealed by the Rorschach Test.*

ing it possible (despite the common error of treating central tendencies as if they represented all the individual instances) to recognize the diversity of human characteristics within culturally bounded groups like tribes, nations, sex, age, status, class groups, and so on. It is upon the notion of the organization of diversities, as well as the reproduction of uniformity, that a progressive science of human behavior must base itself.

DIACHRONIC DISTRIBUTIONS

Child Development

The most conventional time sequence in culture-and-personality is the transformation of a cohort of infants into socialized adults. The assumption usually made here is that the transformation of any cohort is accomplished by its manipulation at the hands of a preceding cohort that has undergone the same transformation. Gorer has stated it clearly:

It is on the basis of social continuity that the assumption is made that in any given society (or portion of society, where the society is large enough to be differentiated by regions or classes or a combination of both) the observable adults shared experiences and vicissitudes of childhood similar to those which observable infants and children are now undergoing; and further, that observable infants and children will grow up to have shared predispositions and characters similar to those of the observable adults. This assumption of *recapitulation* would seem to be the basic assumption of the study of national character, and is the assumption that divides the study of national character from the study of individual psychology.[43]

This model of continuous intergenerational transformation, since it makes of each cohort a replica of its adult predecessor, is logically comparable to models of genetic copying in biological reproduction. The mechanism, in genetics, is the gene, which

43. In Mead and Metraux, *op. cit.*, p. 63.

carries genetic information to each cell of the maturing organism, instructing it how to respond to various circumstances. National character, in Gorer's sense, is the analogue of genetic structure in the geneticist's sense: it is assumed to be constant for each "cell" in the social organism, and to carry the information that determines the response of that "cell" to its environment. It is this analogy that rationalizes Mead's assertion, which has already been mentioned with some disapproval earlier in this chapter:

Any member of a group, provided that his position within that group is properly specified, is a perfect sample of the group-wide pattern on which he is acting as an informant. So a twenty-one-year-old boy born of Chinese-American parents in a small upstate New York town who has just graduated *summa cum laude* from Harvard and a tenth-generation Boston-born deaf mute of United Kingdom stock are equally perfect examples of American national character, *provided that their individual characteristics are taken fully into account.*[44]

Mead is asserting that the differences between the Chinese-American and the Boston-born deaf mute are of the same order as the differences between a neurone in a person's brain and an epithelial cell in the same person's finger: each is (in the analogy) a perfect mature expression of the same genetic structure developing under different circumstances. A result of phrasing the problem of temporal sequence in this genetic form is that two socialization processes may be considered. One is the process by which the "genotype"—the cultural character and the basic personality —is transmitted from one generation to the next; the other is the process by which individuals are "phenotypically" differentiated from one another, as the result of differential experience, in order to play different social roles.

Anthropologists always have been interested in the techniques used in the education (or "enculturation" or "socialization") of the young in a given sociocultural system. In part, this interest is inseparable from the task of general ethnography. For instance, it has long been recognized that much of the ritual impedimenta

44. Mead, *op. cit.,* p. 648.

of society is devoted to the task of accomplishing, with maximum speed, the social and psychological transformation of individuals. Many *rites de passage* explicitly aim at effecting in individuals certain changes in motivation, appropriate to the newly assumed social roles that are publicly proclaimed by the ritual. Ceremonies at puberty ("initiation rites"), at marriage, at entrance into organizations, at bereavement, and so on, have the dual function of notifying society of the change in role and of instilling in the participants the values and beliefs that will make performance of the new role congenial. A few anthropologists have been interested in the sequential structure of conditioning processes whose role transitions are discontinuous. They have suggested, for instance, that without such ritual conditioning the individual pays a "great psychic cost."[45] But it is not known, in general, how effective *rites de passage* of various kinds are, under various circumstances, in accomplishing the motivational transformation of the individual. It has been suggested that ritual dissociation facilitates learning in *rites de passage*, but there is little empirical information available.[46] Similarly, although a few anthropologists have interested themselves in primitive methods of "formal" education,[47] an analysis of the efficiency of these procedures is lacking.

Studies emphasizing developmental processes within the "family" (which, of course, is not the same thing from one society to the next) largely have been guided by culturally modified psychoanalytic hypotheses. John Whiting's group at Harvard, in their cross-cultural survey of child-rearing practices and various cultural variables, seeks statistically reliable correlations between developmental experience and adult institutionalized behavior.[48] The same group has also pursued more intensive case studies based on their own field work.[49] Mead and her associates, in their less statistically organized studies, have described patiently how the multiple and unfolding experience of the child

45. Benedict, "Continuities and Discontinuities in Cultural Conditioning."
46. Wallace, *Religion: An Anthropological View*, pp. 236–242.
47. For example, Pettitt, *Primitive Education in North America*.
48. Whiting and Child, *Child Training and Personality*.
49. See Whiting, *Six Cultures: Studies of Child Rearing*, and Whiting, Child, and Lambert, *Field Guide for a Study of Socialization*.

gradually induces an adult who plays (more or less) the same culturally standardized role as his parents did before him. In this kind of work, as we have pointed out earlier, the facts of individual diversity and of culture change are held constant conceptually; the system is treated as if uniformity, synchronically and diachronically, were the rule.[50] Despite the consequent deficiencies, which we have already labored to disclose, an impressive consequence of such studies of age patterning is the demonstration of the fact of multiple imprinting of a relatively small number of broad themes or values, each with its special phrasing for various age, sex, and other conditions, by the immensely complex sequential pattern of experiences to which the growing person is subjected in any organized society. This process may not be as reliable as is believed, but the *kind* of process is well authenticated. As Mead eloquently observes:

simultaneity of impact is carried not only by the behavior of each individual with whom the child comes in contact, but is also mediated by ritual, drama, and the arts. The shape of a pot, the design on the temple door, the pattern of the courtyard, the form of the bed, the grave posts or the funeral urn, the dancer's headdress and the clown's mask, are again reinforcements and whole statements of the same pattern which the child is experiencing serially.[51]

It is worth remarking that, despite the ceremonial deference shown to academic psychology's learning theories in anthropological research, the kind of learning that goes on in patterning by multiple imprinting is not adequately described by formal learning theory. Consequently, efforts[52] to use learning theory to analyze the socialization process, or language learning, do not evoke the more complex psychological reality that Mead's poetic language calls forth. Possibly, information processing approaches and models of learning by "imprinting," which follows the "law

50. Mead, "The Implications of Culture Change for Personality Development."
51. *Ibid.,* p. 634.
52. Like that of Whiting's, reported in *Becoming a Kwoma.*

of effort,"[53] will prove to be more useful to anthropologists in analyzing the enculturation process than current reinforcement theory, which emphasizes the "law of effect."

In an effort to rehabilitate the notion of individual differences, Wallace formulated a probabilistic statement of the relation between cultural learning and personality development:

the probability of any definable sequence of formative events is equal to the probability of the emergence of a given type of personality, and the total number of individuals possessing that type of personality will be the product of that probability and the size of the population.[54]

But Wallace's formulation, like Sapir's and Spiro's cited earlier, still leaves unresolved the basic problem of all these procedures: the reliability of the processes *as they are operationally defined.*

Most treatments of child development processes seem to imply either that development is a very reliable process which can be predicted from a knowledge of cultural milieu and family situation, or that it is a very unreliable process. The proponents of reliability include most of, if not all, the child development workers in culture-and-personality. But some disquieting reports exist in the psychological and sociological literature that, taken at face value, suggest that cherished assumptions about supposedly invariant relations between infantile experience and adult personality are not verifiable by rigorous investigation.[55] Proponents of reliability may point out, in defense, that rigorous studies which attempt to "control" all but a few factors simply abolish the phenomenon under investigation. The solution of this problem can be found only by abandoning the expectation that *any* study will in the near future be able to demonstrate near-perfect reliability for developmental processes, not because the processes are not lawful, but because they are so complex and so protracted that empirical observation cannot record a

53. Cf. Hess, "Imprinting."

54. "Individual Differences and Cultural Uniformities," p. 748.

55. Orlansky, "Infant Care and Personality"; Sewell, "Infant-Training and the Personality of the Child."

sufficient number of relevant dimensions. This, however, is the standard situation at any scientific frontier. Progress now can be made by discovering empirically what the limits of confidence are in predictions of personality development. Such limits presumably will vary, both with the complexity and identity of the particular aspect of the developmental process being predicted, and with the number and identity of independent variables on which the prediction is based. Cross-cultural research into the differential reliability of developmental disciplines will pay handsome dividends, both in practical knowledge and in advancing knowledge of culture and personality as related systems.

Intergenerational Change in Group Character

The replication-of-uniformity approach does not, in itself, allow for intergenerational change; it simply assumes that the *same* pattern is transmitted from generation to generation. Students of culture-and-personality do, nevertheless, recognize that group character changes over time (although, it has been suggested, basic personality is apt to lag behind cultural change). The mechanism for an intergenerational change in replication theory must be a variation in the manner in which a new cohort is treated by the older generation. What processes can induce such change in adult behavior? Some of the answers are extremely cautious. Mead, for instance, in her review of the theoretical position of workers in the field of national character, merely observed apropos of culture change:

Each culture may be expected to change concomitantly with impinging events which were hitherto outside the system—an invasion from a hitherto unknown people, an earthquake, an epidemic arising outside the society, and so on . . .[56]

She also nods in passing to the concept of cultures as "historically patterned systems" and notes that "each member of each generation, from infancy to old age, contributes to the . . . reinterpre-

56. "National Character," p. 647.

tation of the cultural forms." Conversely, ill-advised adventures in culture change may collapse when they collide with the national character of a people.[57] Such relations between intergenerational changes in personality and cultural events outside the maturational cycle are, presumably, mediated by the child development process itself. Economic and technological changes, for instance, that occur as the result of rational ("peripheral") motives or of coercive environmental changes, may set in motion other changes that ultimately bring about alterations in child-rearing practices. Thus intergenerational change in character can come about via cultural changes that first affect *post*infantile experience. David Riesman, for instance,[58] sees a general relationship between demographic condition, economic process, family structure, and personality structure. In almost all such studies, personality is conceived as the dependent variable and economic change (or migration) as the independent, with socialization practices as an intervening variable, dependent on economic change (or migration). Changes in basic personality, furthermore, are usually granted to be very slow and to become noticeable only after efforts to restrain or channel culture change have failed and after the basic personality has suffered gross and painful distortion under stress.

A correlation between the level of acculturation of individual members of a community and various personality features has often been remarked. It has also been observed that different parts of culture change or are replaced at different rates, sometimes without apparent regard to their usefulness. After a perceptive study of a Mandan-Hidatsa reservation community, Bruner[59] suggested that the crucial variable in these processes may be the infant and early childhood experience. Those institutions most readily discarded in culture change are those learned relatively late in the person's life (such as religious ritual and age-grade societies); those most resistant to change are learned

57. *Ibid.*, p. 647.

58. *The Lonely Crowd: A Study of the Changing American Character.*

59. "Cultural Transmission and Cultural Change" and "Primary Group Experience and the Processes of Acculturation."

early in life (such as kinship terminology and certain basic values). Change in the areas of culture that are learned early in life—at least in the community he studied—required the presence of a different parental model in the child's early experience. This model was an intermarrying white person. Without early intimate association with a white parent, no major interruption in the replication of the basic personality was possible, at least within a few generations, because geographical and social separation precluded any other identification with whites in the child's early life. This suggests, more generally, that the personality structures of various minority groups are not easily changed in the direction of the reformers' by intensifying formal education and by economic and political reconstruction. Intermarriage may be required since this alone can bring the parental model into contact with the child. Failing this measure, one could expect the continuation of plural cultures and plural personality structures.

Cultural changes that increase the heterogeneity of the society, such as acculturation and urbanization, often are believed to pose a serious threat to both personality and social integration.[60] The notion that heterogeneous cultures, split into incongruous fragments, must inevitably produce conflict-ridden personalities, is a corollary of the common-motive thesis, which defines integration as a function of homogeneity. From the organization-of-diversity standpoint, however, culture change is not necessarily traumatic; indeed, it is to be regarded as the natural condition of man. If we regard most "living" cultures as heterogeneous (and all modern nations are culturally pluralistic to an extreme degree) and in constant, relatively rapid change (rapid change, incidentally, does not necessarily imply either change in material artifacts or rapid cumulative evolution), we note first that heterogeneity and change by definition no longer imply psychological and cultural disorganization. The causes of such disorganization must be sought elsewhere. The fundamental problem again becomes the organization of diversity rather than the replication of uniformity.

60. Cf. Mead, "The Implications of Culture Change for Personality Development"; Beaglehole, "Cultural Complexity and Psychological Problems."

Now it is possible that when the culture is "heterogeneous" and rapidly changing, there will be a wider variety of personality types produced than in the homogeneous, slowly changing culture. Each of these types may be as consistent internally as any type produced in a stable homogeneous culture. The problem of such a complex society will not be that all of its members have split personalities, but rather that the problems of sociocultural organization may exceed the capacities of its members. Under the latter eventuality, many individuals secondarily may experience privation and frustration and come to suffer from psychosomatic and neurotic complaints; but these will be the consequence of failure of the system to answer the wants of certain of its members. In particular, the traditionally disadvantaged subgroups in a society—for example, ethnic or religious minorities, native populations under foreign domination, and the lower economic classes—may suffer high incidences of discomfort and illness. This is not directly because of the heterogeneity of the society, but because of the particular disadvantages from which they happen to suffer disproportionately, such as inadequate nutrition, contempt, epidemic illness, physical abuse, and (as we shall discuss in more detail in the following chapter) the shock of cultural loss.

Current studies of disadvantaged populations emphasize the extent to which social segregation, poverty, overcrowding, and the presence of pervasive bureaucratic structures that are both paternalistic and antagonistic (such as some school systems, police forces, and welfare agencies) can communicate even to very young children so intense a sense of being of no value to the larger society, let alone to parents, that self-esteem and cognitive and emotional development are grossly thwarted. (There is also evidence that malnutrition associated with extreme poverty may produce irreversible marginal brain damage in infants.) But similar processes can also occur in affluent groups where the very ease of material existence for children and youth, and their rigid exclusion from the serious work of the world, lead also to a sense of being of little worth and to a desperate search for self-respect. The established milieu, which conveys no sense of personal value, is rejected and the person seeks self-respect by participation in noble revolutionary causes.

The insults to identity mounted by poverty and affluence both seem to drive the individual back to phylogenetically primitive modes of adaptation: to a dependence upon simple agonistic displays for self-validation and to reliance upon the material and emotional support of small-band organizations, such as gangs, communes, and militant or conspiratorial groups. To the extent that increasing population pressure may exacerbate these problems of socialization, such disorders—and also the revitalization movements they will prompt—can be expected to multiply.

chapter five
THE PSYCHOLOGY OF
CULTURE CHANGE

In this chapter we shall take up in more detail the subject of how psychological processes affect, and are affected by, changes in culture. The reader should keep in mind, throughout the discussion, the conceptual distinction between affective and cognitive components of motivation. Derivative from this distinction is a corollary: the distinction between emotions and values. And the reader must keep in mind that two sorts of values are inherent in any motivational structure: consummatory values ("wants") and instrumental values ("needs").

INNOVATION: THE PROCESS
OF INVENTION AND DISCOVERY

There is an old adage to the effect that "there is nothing new under the sun." This piece of folk wisdom is quoted when some innovation is discovered to have had a prototype in an ancient or exotic community; it is intended as a reproach to the pride of latter-day innovators. But behind the seeming paradox (for we "know" that innovations occur) lie two significant problems.

The first is that some societies—in particular, the ancient Near Eastern societies from which our own culture has largely been derived—have defined apparent innovations not as "new," but merely as stages in a repetitive cosmic cycle. In such a view, a "new" technological device or a "revolutionary" social transformation is no more an innovation than is the coming of spring or the eruption of a baby's first tooth; such changes in state are merely stages in a recurrent process. Thus our modern notion of an innovation as a *new identity* is, to a degree, culturally determined, and our very willingness to think of innovations is a habit of thought distinctive of ourselves.

The second problem, foreshadowed by the first, is the philosophical problem of identity. What are the criteria by which we do, or should, decide that two perceptual experiences were stimulated by the same phenomenon? When are we, or should we be, content to say that a thing no longer exists, or that a new thing has come into existence? The answers to these questions are important not merely as observations on the psychological processes of innovation itself; they also will affect the manner in which innovation is investigated.

Homer Barnett, the author of the most extensive anthropological treatise on the subject of innovation,[1] devotes a large part of his volume to the philosophical analysis of identity and to the psychological processes by which it is recognized. Barnett takes issue with those older psychologists who claim that the organization of perception is dependent on the formal properties of the *thing* observed. In pointing out that much of perception is determined by the past experience of the perceiver, he is in the more contemporary perceptual psychologist's tradition; and, incidentally, in conformity with the viewpoint expressed by Hallowell[2] concerning the dependence of perception on culturally predictable experience. This quasi-independence of perception from the "objective" reality of nature makes possible two mental phenomena: first, the ability of the perceiver to say that two sensibly different experiences involve the "same thing" ("sameness" being determined by constancy of configuration, by continuity over time in space, or by various other criteria) ; second, the possibility of two perceivers, or the same observer at different times, perceiving the "same" object differently, depending on differences in their own perceptual equipment and experience. The former ability makes possible learning and cultural continuity; but the latter makes possible culture change. "The mental interaction between what is and what was, in fact, does provide the only basis for a recombination of natural events; that is, for innovation, the uniquely mental contribution to newness."[3]

1. *Innovation: The Basis of Cultural Change.*
2. *Culture and Experience.*
3. *Innovation: The Basis of Cultural Change,* p. 448.

Barnett goes on to analyze the logical structure of innovation in such a way as to avoid, in part, the dilemma of developmentalism versus discontinuity. Innovation is conceived as entirely a mental process and its substance as not "things" but "mental configurations" (that is, "any unified pattern[s] of experience"). Every innovation (or discovery) is essentially a recombination of two or more mental configurations. The innovator does three things to these configurations: (1) he analyzes each of them, discriminating their component elements and considering the relations among them; (2) he matches them, identifying certain elements of one with certain elements of another, in the context provided by the particular configurations; (3) he recombines the configurations, substituting the identified elements and recognizing changes in the mutual relations among the several elements. The process may be very simply exemplified in the following paradigm, in which verbal statements are taken as the prototype and stimulus and their recombination as the innovative idea (innovative, that is, in the context of these statements) :

Stage 1 (Analysis)
    Prototype: "Submarines, with a submarine shape, move
            slowly in relation to their length."
    Stimulus: "Fish, with a fish shape, swim fast in relation
            to their length."
Stage 2 (Identification)
    Identify "fish" with "submarine."
    Identify "swim" with "move."
    Identify "fish shape" with "submarine shape."
Stage 3 (Recombination)
    Substitute "fish shape" for "submarine shape" in prototype statement.
    Substitute "fast" for "slowly" in prototype statement.
    Innovative statement: "Submarines, with a fish shape,
                    move fast in relation to their
                    length."

The innovative statement (a valid one, incidentally) is a new configuration, and a new *Gestalt,* with all sorts of implications for submarine design, naval strategy, and so forth; but, as Barnett argues, no element or relation is uniquely new, since the morphemes and syntax were both provided by the prior statements.

The "recombination of configurations" thesis has the virtue of answering the question of where the pieces come from, and thereby aligns the analysis of the innovative process with the study of other natural processes, in which the "new" state of any system is a function of the "old." But while this eliminates the problem of discontinuity, it exacerbates the complementary problem of continuity. Every innovation, and thus all culture change, must be considered to be a recombination of previously existing configurations. This makes any evolutionary sequence in culture comparable to the development of the logical implications of a set of axiomatic propositions and suggests that a "beginning" must exist where one could find certain primitive configurations from which all subsequent recombinations have been derived. This, however, is precisely Adolph Bastian's notion of *Elementargedanken,* which has proved to be an inadequate foundation for studies of cultural evolution and also for inquiries into the nature of the psychic unity of man.[4] A further implication of the recombination thesis is that there exists a finite, even if very large, number of possible configurations, the magnitude of this number being determined by the size of the original set of elements and relations. This, in turn, requires the deduction that there is a finite number of possible cultures.

The partial inadequacy of the recombination thesis, however, lies not in any necessary fallacy of the assertion that every innovation is a recombination of pre-existing mental configurations (even though the implications of this position are so far-reaching as to be untestable and hence metaphysical). It lies, rather, in the inadequacy of the position to state the conditions under which a particular innovation will occur; that is, to predict which of several possible recombinations will be made, by whom, and when. Predictions of this sort involve considerations of personal motivation, idiosyncratic experience, cultural and situational milieu, and general cognitive process.

4. Cf. Wallace, "The Psychic Unity of Human Groups."

Motivational theories of innovative behavior are of two kinds: (1) "positive" theories, which attempt to account for the creative act; (2) "negative" theories, which attempt to account for non-innovative conservatism. These theories vary widely with respect to their level of generality, some applying to all organisms that can learn, and others applying only to specific subgroups in particular human societies (for example, to professional inventors in twentieth-century America). Perhaps the most generalized positive motivation theory is that which postulates an instinct or drive, characteristic of all organisms, to explore, to play, to experience and satisfy "curiosity," to enjoy aesthetic pleasure, to reduce the "cognitive dissonance" between imagination and reality.[5] Wallace has formulated his postulate in terms of organization theory:

[The] Principle of Maximal Organization . . . asserts that an organism acts in such a way as to maximize, under existing conditions, and to the extent of its capacity, the amount of organization in the dynamic system represented in its mazeway; that is to say, it works to increase both the complexity and the orderliness of its experience.[6]

When circumstances are such that a particular innovative recombination will maximize the organization quantity in a given mazeway, and the physiological milieu is adequate to support the cognitive task, then that innovation will be produced.[7] Such a recombination will not, however, occur unless the necessary prototypical and stimulus configurations are already present.

Another body of theory takes up the problem of the processes by which the prototype and stimulus configurations necessary for a particular innovation are assembled in a mazeway. White,[8]

5. Linton, *The Study of Man,* p. 90; Festinger, *A Theory of Cognitive Dissonance.*

6. "The Psychic Unity of Human Groups," p. 157.

7. Cf. Wallace, "Mazeway Resynthesis: A Bio-Cultural Theory of Religious Inspiration" and "Stress and Rapid Personality Changes."

8. *The Science of Culture.*

Kroeber,[9] and many others (including a number of historians and sociologists), disputing the popular impression that genius spontaneously creates a cultural something out of an idiosyncratic nothing, have presented evidence to show that particular innovations are apt to be independently and almost simultaneously produced by many individuals in a given type of cultural milieu. Such instances of simultaneous invention suggest strongly that culture, as it evolves, "provides" many individuals with the prototype and stimulus configurations necessary to a given innovation, and that only certain innovations are possible in any given cultural milieu.

What can one say about the psychological properties, including the motivations, of the innovators? First of all, it is virtually necessary to assume, as Barnett does, and as organization theory implies, that all persons occasionally innovate within the limits imposed by their own culture, local situation, and individual abilities. Some innovation occurs by chance and by cognitive error. Furthermore, societies may be congenial or uncongenial to innovation, depending on the cognitive process by which the innovation was accomplished. For instance, seventeenth-century Iroquois culture highly encouraged religious (ritual and mythological), political, and even economic innovation if the cognitive modality was hallucinatory.[10] In our own society, scientific, technological, religious, and artistic innovation is readily rewarded, irrespective of the cognitive modality by which it is achieved, but political and economic innovation is far less so, and has virtually no chance of success if the cognitive modality of discovery is known to be hallucinatory. If one approaches the matter of motivation from the standpoint of reinforcement learning theory, one would expect that each member of society will "learn" to innovate in precisely those cultural areas in which innovation is apt to be rewarded by the society (or, at least, his part of it). These are the areas, to use Melville Herskovits' phrase, of "cultural focus."[11] In such areas, the drive for maximal organization

9. *Configurations of Culture Growth.*

10. Wallace, "Dreams and the Wishes of the Soul."

11. *Man and His Works,* p. 637.

is most apt to find satisfaction. But it would be a mistake to carry such a faith in the cultural conformity of innovation too far, for here we are dealing as much or more with the criteria of acceptance as with the process of innovation. As we have suggested, innovation may reap rewards other than those society offers. Creativity is notoriously difficult either to command or to suppress. Innovation, indeed, seems to be produced by a most extraordinarily heterogeneous population, under the most remarkably varied circumstances, and for such highly diversified conscious purposes that one suspects that innovation per se as a mental process is almost independent of motivation; in itself innovation is an "instinctive" propensity of the human organism, activated under the merest provocation of desire for richer or more orderly experience. It is more likely that motivational processes of the kind connoted by the term "personality" will govern *response* to innovation (including the innovator's own response) .

RESPONSE TO INNOVATION:
ACCEPTANCE, USE, AND REJECTION

Anthropologists traditionally have maintained interest in those psychological processes which determine whether a proposed innovation will be accepted or rejected for use by the innovator himself, by other members of his society, and (in diffusion and acculturation situations) by members of other societies. In such situations, typically, the innovation is conceived as being any configuration that is matched with a prototype maintained by the change, such as an inventor, a trader, a religious or political reformer, a war prisoner, or a spouse from an alien cultural setting. Such an offered innovation may be conceived as a stimulus configuration that is matched with a prototype maintained by the recipient. Acceptance of the innovation will result, usually, in its modification in order that it may fit into the larger cultural *Gestalt,* but for the sake of simplicity we shall speak of "acceptance" without mentioning the modification process explicitly. The members of the community consider the innovation, accept or reject it, and finally (if it is accepted) use it. (Obviously, we are not here considering such micro-innovations as are involved in linguistic drift, which do not seem to involve rational evaluation.) These processes need not be deliberate or even conscious: the only necessary assumption is that the innovation must pass through a sort of screen, which evaluates it as a "new thing," before any substantial use can be made of it.

The acculturation situation generally conforms well to the model described above: a "donor" culture "presents" a "new" cultural configuration to the "recipient" culture. The members of this culture then subject the new configuration to various tests and, sooner or later, accept or reject it. The mechanisms involved, however poorly understood, have come to be of major practical importance in the modern world as, both internally and externally, the various national governments anxiously strive to induce potential allies, as well as their own people, to undertake new patterns of culture.

One kind of determinant is the so-called psychological screen that modal personality structure interposes between presentation and acceptance. This screen sorts presented innovations into two groups: (1) those which are compatible with some structure of motives common in the society; (2) those which are not. The motivational structure connoted in this process exists on a high level of abstraction, consisting of broad values implicit in ethos, national character, or modal personality structure, such as the desirability of material wealth, need for achievement, the relative importance of kinship and community obligations, the definition of masculinity, or the significance of punctuality.[12] Any single affectively weighted category of this kind can be used to classify a large number of particular innovations that would seem to be immediately relevant to more limited contexts. Thus these values function as constant parameters of choice in a culture, giving connotation to most phenomena, however disparate their individual definitions. It may be noted that the psychologist Osgood's semantic testing device (the "semantic differential")[13]

---

12. Cf. Wallace, "Some Psychological Determinants of Culture Change in an Iroquoian Community," and Linton, "The Change from Dry to Wet Rice Culture in Tanala-Betsileo."

13. *The Measurement of Meaning.*

is eminently suited for use in assessing the function of such broad values in giving connotative values to a variety of existential phenomena, including innovative proposals.

If an innovation succeeds in passing the screen of general values, however, it faces still other tests. (The reader will note, of course, that the order of these discrimination processes is chosen for heuristic purposes and does not necessarily exist in nature.) Certain of these other obstacles to acceptance constitute together the major part of the concern of "applied" and "action" anthropology. Their general character is "functional": that is, the criterion of acceptability is the conviction, on the part of potential recipients, that the innovation will, in sum, contribute more importantly to the satisfaction of a network of wants and needs than to their frustration. Once an innovation acquires such a cultural meaning, it has itself the status of a felt need. It is necessary to point out, of course, that the donor's conception of the wants and needs of the recipients is not necessarily the same as the recipient's own conception. There now exists a sizable body of literature in applied anthropology, describing and analyzing situations wherein potential recipients refused to accept innovations that donors expected them to embrace warmly. The error of the donor generally lies in neglecting to assess the relevant negative functions of the proposed innovation; that is, in incorrectly identifying the institutionalized motives that the innovation would actually tend to frustrate.[14]

A further obstacle to the acceptance of innovations, in most recipient societies, is the existence of groups with different vested interests, grievances, or ambitions. American anthropology, because of its tendency (abetted in part by the earlier culture-and-personality school) to concentrate attention on behavioral homogeneity, even in complex societies, has had some difficulty in coming to grips with intrasocietal groups. British and French social anthropology, with its emphasis on the interaction between social entities, such as kin groups, corporations, and the like, has sometimes seemed to Americans to neglect "psychological" proc-

14. Cf. Goodenough, *Cooperation in Change;* Paul (ed.), *Health, Culture, and Community: Case Studies of Public Reactions to Health Programs;* Mead, *Cultural Patterns and Technical Change;* Spicer, *Human Problems in Technological Change.*

esses. Continental scholarship goes even farther: building on a century's tradition of intense interest in the conflict of interest groups, particularly the social classes, the European social scientist seems to be living in a world of mystically abstract intergroup dynamics, wherein social classes collide, plot, and counterplot, like vast shadows on a giant screen. But it is of the utmost importance to the theory of culture and personality that anthropologists incorporate, and use, British and European insights into the dynamic role of group loyalties, identifications, and interests in determining the course of culture change. The fact that systematic group differentials, with respect to acculturation, can be shown to exist, even within small societies[15] is, of course, an important first step. It is also useful to point out, as applied anthropology has frequently done, that the vested interests of one individual or group may be jeopardized by an innovation that promotes the welfare of another; the consequence is apt to be rejection by one, acceptance by the other, and mutually destructive conflict between the two (sometimes displaced onto the donor). But the issues go beyond this commonly observed polarization of a society into more, or less, vigorously "pro" and "anti" factions with respect to any proposed innovation. The major point is that many societies, especially the more complex ones, are apt to maintain for considerable periods of time *two* major constellations of interest groups, irrespective of any innovation proffered from without. These two groups are termed by Karl Mannheim (a sociologist whose method of analysis is essentially anthropological) the proponents of *ideology* and the proponents of *utopia*. Ideology is the conservative world view, which rationalizes, expresses, and supports the existing sociocultural system with which some members of the society are content. Utopia, on the other hand, is the revolutionary world view, which rationalizes, expresses, and supports efforts to transform the existing sociocultural system in order to bring greater satisfaction to the discontented. In their mutual struggle, according to the traditional view of Mannheim's school, a synthesis of the two

15. Cf. Spindler, *Sociocultural and Psychological Processes in Menominee Acculturation.*

world views will emerge to become the ideology of the dominant class in the next phase of the dialectical process.[16]

The importance for acculturation theory of such intrasocietal struggles between ideology and utopia is that the response of the utopian mentality to a proposed innovation will *not* be based on considerations of its functional suitability in the existing sociocultural system. Thus the "utopian" response will differ from the conservative response not merely by virtue of the different present behavioral systems of the two groups, but also by virtue of their different temporal orientation. The utopian's functional calculus will demand estimates of the innovation's utility in breaking up the existing system (that is, on its negative value for his opponents) and on its virtue in the better world of the future. A useful innovation adroitly calculated to fit into an existing system with minimal disturbance may, paradoxically, be repudiated by the utopian faction, precisely because of its excellent adaptation to the current status quo. Another consequence of factionalism is that innovations, entirely apart from rationally calculated estimates of their functional value, may become symbols of social group membership. If that group membership is positively regarded, the innovation may be valued entirely out of proportion to its "intrinsic" worth; conversely, if its acceptance connotes identification with an "enemy" or "inferior" group, the individual who accepts it must abandon, or be abandoned by, the group to which he belongs. The individual's self-image and self-esteem are heavily dependent on his conception of his acceptability to the reference group with which he identifies himself; therefore, otherwise unimpeachable innovations, whose acceptance implies identification with a negatively valued donor, may find acceptance difficult.

Having discussed various characteristics of the recipients, which affect the likelihood of acceptance or rejection of an innovation, we must now turn our attention to another group of factors. These factors are the various kinds and degrees of pressure that the donor may apply to the recipient, in the course of presentation, in order to ensure that the recipient accepts, or rejects, the

16. Cf. Mannheim, *Ideology and Utopia*.

innovation. It is rarely the case that the donor is indifferent to the recipient's response; usually, the donor has interests of his own that will be served by the recipient's acceptance or rejection of a given innovation. These donor interests are, as a group, extremely heterogeneous, ranging from honest concern for the welfare of the recipient society, through enlightened self-interest, to purely selfish purposes of an economic, military, or political character. Commonly, various donor motives are mixed, either in the same person or among various representatives of the donor. Furthermore, one donor may be concerned about ensuring rejection of another donor's "gifts": Quaker missionaries to the American Indians, for instance, worked hard to persuade their charges to reject such proffered innovations as whiskey, while they promoted the acceptance of the plow, the spinning wheel, and the loom.

The techniques employed by the donor generally involve presenting the innovation to the recipient under conditions suggesting that acceptance will be rewarding and noncompliance will be frustrating. In crude form, this means that the recipient either is openly bribed or threatened. In more subtle approaches, the donor's interests may be disguised and the reinforcement paradigm presented in such a way that the rewards do not appear to entail the sacrifice of other interests and the threats do not openly refer to any punitive action of the donor, but merely to an unwanted course of events. These events are inevitable under the circumstances and are irrespective of the donor's interests. American applied anthropology, as Goodenough[17] emphasizes, is concerned with noncoercive "cooperation in change," which is often more effective. But an ethical preference for the noncoercive methods of free choice, of education and mutual aid, should not blind the theoretician to the fact that coercive methods frequently are employed by most societies, including our own, when methods of persuasion fail, because of the compelling motive that lies behind the donor's presentation. The history of religious wars, of political revolutions, of class, caste, and ethnic conflicts, of missionary enterprises, of public health and civil rights controversies,

17. *Cooperation in Change.*

and of many other intergroup tensions, all testify to the readiness with which donor groups use more or less severely coercive measures to induce the acceptance of innovations, when recipient acceptance is viewed by the donor as necessary for the satisfaction of his own wants or as a moral imperative.

The methods of coercion may be viewed as standing on a continuum of severity, from minimal to most severe. At the minimal pole, of course, stands the limiting case: presentation with indifference. Here the innovation may not have been intentionally presented at all; the recipient group has free choice to accept or to reject; response will be entirely determined by the values and the functional meaning of the innovation itself to the recipient society. Next stand the methods of peaceful example— persuasion, negotiation, and cooperation—analyzed by Goodenough at length. Here, the donor carefully attempts to develop a mutually beneficial relationship in change, in which the interests and motives of both parties are well satisfied on a long-term basis. A certain amount of peaceful argument and education may be offered by the donor, but no threat is implied or intended. More severe is the deliberate use of threat. Here, the formula is, in effect, "Accept (or reject) this innovation or you will be prevented from satisfying some want." Hellfire-and-damnation preachers, political overlords, and even friends and allies are apt to turn to this technique when less easy methods fail. This is also the device frequently employed by commercial advertisers attempting to induce a target group to accept its product: non-buyers are threatened with loss of friends, job, health, and sexual satisfaction, if they fail to buy the proffered soap, deodorant, toothpaste, liquor, hairdressing, perfume, or whatnot. Equally direct is the use of mass suggestion by entrapping the target population in a milieu in which they cannot escape the monotonous reiteration, in multiple channels and by multiple spokesmen, of the presentation. Such suggestion is notoriously effective in inducing mass acceptance of behaviors that, under circumstances of free choice, the component individuals would reject unhesitatingly. Finally, and most severe of all, is the use of techniques, such as physical torture and exhaustion, that produce in the target a psychophysiological state wherein acceptance of innovation becomes almost automatic. Stansfeld Sargant[18] sees in this process of conversion or "brain-washing" the operation of Pavlov's "paradoxical" and "ultraparadoxical" modes of conditioning.

It is evident, in view of the considerations presented above, that prediction of group acceptance or rejection of an innovation, once presented, will be determined by the balance of a number of complexly interrelated psychological valences, negative and positive, in the individual mazeways of the group's members. The individual must, whether deliberately or not, calculate the sum of the organizational decrements and increments that either acceptance or rejection will bring. If the sum total of all decrements and increments is positive, then the innovation will be accepted. The values involved in such a calculation will, in the last analysis, be personal (even though their distribution in the society may be a cultural fact), and their evaluation by an outside observer will consequently be difficult. Nevertheless, knowledge of the screen of values imposed by ethos, national character, or modal personality; of the functional structure of the present psychologically real culture of the population; of the vectors of nativism and utopianism; and of the nature of the coercion (if any) employed in presentation, will make it possible to form a useful estimate of the likelihood of group acceptance. Group acceptance or rejection, however, may be less than uniform, because of the differential interests in the innovation of the several subgroups. Consequently, a long process of intrasocietal interaction, with one subgroup attempting to influence others, is apt to ensue, with each separate stage repeating the process described above.

TYPES OF CULTURE CHANGE PROCESS

Anthropologists tend to consider culture change either over very long periods of time (macro-temporal change), or over very brief periods of time (micro-temporal change). Macro-temporal proc-

---

18. *Battle for the Mind.*

esses are frequently labeled cultural evolution and diffusion; micro-temporal processes go by such rubrics as innovation, acculturation, and nativistic movement.

Macro-Temporal Processes

Studies of macro-temporal processes of culture change, covering hundreds or thousands of years, are generally based on the assumption that "human nature," whatever that is, must be treated as a constant parameter of cultural function and thus, for all practical purposes, may be ignored. The four major models share a common impersonality that is rarely broken by considerations, such as those of Eiseley[19] and Angel[20] of the human organism as a variable factor.

The Oscillation Model. Culturally organized societies sometimes have been compared to organisms with a predisposing heredity and an evocative environment that pass through various stages of coming-into-being, maturation, maturity, senescence, and death. Various accidents along this path are treated as education, reproduction, trauma, illness, recovery, and so forth. While this historiographic use, like others, of the organismic analogy is vulnerable to criticism, nevertheless the model has inspired a number of scholars to undertake or interpret empirical studies, and thus it may be said to satisfy the minimal requirement of a good scientific model: to inspire research. The life-cycle model has particularly appealed to those humanistically inclined anthropologists, historians, and philosophers who have reflected on the rise, climax, and fall of the classic high civilizations; but, in principle, it is applicable to any society. The model typically implies a more or less complex oscillation of indices of cultural organization. Indeed, it is the notion of a more or less regular oscillation in level of cultural organization, over larger or smaller stretches of time, that is the important feature of this model; the

19. *Darwin's Century: Evolution and the Men Who Discovered It.*
20. "Physical and Psychological Factors in Culture Growth."

organismic analogy is merely a vehicle for the communication of
the oscillation idea.

   The Partial-Ordering Evolution Model.   Nineteenth-century
ethnologists believed that a very large proportion of the data of
ethnography could be arranged in partial orderings that would
represent one evolutionary series. The term "unilinear evolution," applied to their theories, is derived from an implication of
the partial-ordering model: that, in order for any society to
change from one state to another, it must pass successively
through all the intervening points in the scale of states. In such
a model, societies in state i must have passed through states 1, 2,
..., i-2, i-1, in that order. In this sense, their evolution has been
unilinear. Thus Tylor wrote:

On the whole it appears that wherever there are found elaborate
arts, abstruse knowledge, complex institutions, these are the results
of gradual development from an earlier, simpler, and ruder life.
No stage of civilization comes into existence spontaneously, but
grows or is developed out of the stage before it. This is the great
principle which every scholar must lay firm hold of, if he intends
to understand either the world he lives in or the history of the
past. . . . Human life may be roughly classed into three great
stages, Savage, Barbaric, Civilized . . . So far as the evidence goes,
it seems that civilization has actually grown up in the world in
these three stages . . .[21]

Tylor, in more detailed discussion, points out the barbaric and
savage lineage not merely of civilization in general, but of such
specific civilized societies as Victorian England and ancient Egypt
and Babylonia. Although later, more relativistic anthropologists
have realized that far fewer cultural elements scale, and that many
scale only under particular values of various parameters, such as
ecological and culture area, the central notion of evolution, as
a partial ordering correlated with time, has continued to receive
recognition. In the more recent investigations of White and his

21. *Anthropology*, pp. 20, 23–25.

colleagues,[22] significant qualifications of the unilinear viewpoint have been undertaken that meet many of the criticisms leveled at "evolutionism" in the past. A distinction is made between "special" evolution (the history of phylogenetic sequences) and "general" evolution (the partial ordering of first occurrences of major cultural innovations). The partial ordering of events in general evolution does not necessarily correspond to a partial ordering of events in any but *one* phylogenetic sequence; also, one phylogenetic sequence, because of the effectiveness of cultural diffusion, need not be (and in fact has not been) located within the boundaries of one social or geographical entity.

The Stochastic Evolution Model. Implicit in the concept of partial ordering is the notion that a system in a given state i can change to one, and only one, next state j. This restriction makes the partial-ordering model perfectly predictive with respect to direction of change (though not with respect to whether or not change will occur). In some problems, however, it is not possible to justify such a rigid schema; one may wish only to state the probabilities of the system moving into alternative states j_1, j_2, ..., j_m, once it is in state i. Such probabilistic processes are exemplified by the evolution of kinship systems, as treated by George Murdock,[23] and they can be conceptualized (although anthropologists do not conventionally do so) as the evolution of periodic and aperiodic stochastic (particularly Markov) processes. A stochastic process is a set of events so related that the probability of any one event occurring next in series is conditional upon the identity of the preceding event or events. Murdock demonstrates empirically, first of all, that certain significant statistical associations exist among the categories of social structure; that is, some features of kinship entail others. Father's brother's daughter, for instance, tends to be referred to by the same term as wife's brother's wife in societies with exogamous moieties but by a different term in societies without exogamous moieties. But these

22. See particularly Sahlins and Service (eds.), *Evolution and Culture.*
23. *Social Structure.*

static associations are paralleled by dynamic associations in the form of rules stating the order in which three dimensions of social structure—rule of residence, type of descent, and type of kinship terminology—change, and stating the transition probabilities among the values on these dimensions. Furthermore, Murdock implicitly assumes that the rules are constant over long periods of time and thus that the process is "stationary." This, in turn, implies, via the ergodic hypothesis, that no matter what were the original frequencies of various types of social organization, these types gradually will assume a fairly fixed relative frequency among human cultures. The ergodic hypothesis asserts that, once a set of rules has been established, whatever the initial distribution of states, the universe of events more or less quickly (quickness depending on the rules of the statistical process and on the frequency of events of change) will approach a single asymptotic equilibrium distribution of states. One may, of course, question whether the "rules" that define the process are constant over any extended span of time; but, even with only temporary constancy of rule, the theory implies that great changes in the distribution of types of social organization may occur, on a worldwide scale, within a relatively brief span of time.

The Age-Area Diffusion Model.   The diffusion of cultural content, with or without modification, from one society to another when viewed on the grand scale sometimes can be conveniently conceptualized after the so-called age-area model. With respect to any trait, and often with respect to complexes, the data may be arranged on a map with a center of diffusion surrounded (in theory at least) by roughly concentric lines representing the limits of spread of the trait in question at successive time periods. It is apparent that the resulting concentric distribution is ordered (again, in fact, partially ordered) in such a way that the relative antiquity of the trait in an area is perfectly correlated with its rank order of geographic distance from the center of distribution.

This technique has been widely used in the analysis of data distributions by physical anthropologists, archeologists, and ethnologists, for the reconstruction of extended historical processes and for the analysis of intergroup relations (as, for instance, in folk-urban differentials). At the present time, however, it is considerably less popular than evolutionary, directly historical, or micro-temporal models, because of the difficulty of analyzing the processes involved in the "diffusion" itself from purely carto-graphic syntheses.[24]

Micro-Temporal Processes

The use of personalistic constructs is more convenient in stud-ies of change processes covering relatively brief spans of time, of the order of a few generations or less. Rather than attempt a complex typology, we shall consider only three categories: moving equilibrium processes, paradigm development processes, and re-vitalization processes. These three types are relevant here because they can be derived from the psychological considerations pre-viously introduced.

Moving Equilibrium Processes. A culture, under certain con-ditions, during a period of time can be said to be an open system in a state of stable but moving equilibrium: that is, it maintains a boundary, accepts inputs and produces outputs at approxi-mately equal rates, and changes continuously but gradually in internal structure. The inputs, in this case, are accepted innova-tions, acquired by invention, acculturation, or diffusion; the outputs, abandoned elements of culture. The quantity of organi-zation of the system (the product of its complexity and its order-liness) remains relatively constant, or increases or decreases slowly.

Culture change during moving equilibrium has several charac-teristics, some of which we have discussed earlier in this chapter. First of all, the course of change appears as a chainlike series of acceptances and abandonments. The rate may be relatively fast or slow, and the changes themselves large or small; but the transformation of structure is accomplished by an orderly piece-by-piece replacement and realignment of parts. Because of the

24. See Hodgen, *Change and History*, pp. 116–121 for a critical discussion of the diffusion and age-area models.

phenomenon of psychological screening and because of the structure of functional interests, there will be differentials in the
susceptibility of various areas of culture to change. This will give
rise to the phenomena of relatively frequent change within areas
of so-called cultural focus, and of relatively infrequent change
within areas of cultural lag. Furthermore, because of the existence of differential interest groups, in any society responses to
any given proposed innovation will differ. Very commonly, with
respect to any given innovation, there will be a rejection and an
acceptance faction. Those who generally favor innovations in
"lag" areas of culture will be characterized as the radicals (uto-
pians); those who resist innovation even in "focus" areas will
be characterized as conservatives. Manifestly, the more complex
the culture, the higher the likelihood of systematic intrasocietal
differentials in attitude toward proposed innovations, even under
equilibrium conditions, and the more difficult the accomplish-
ment of general acceptance of changes. These difficulties, in turn,
can be considered to be the root problem of political organization in rapidly changing complex societies. Some sort of constitutional democratic political process and some sort of coordinated
executive planning are both necessary to solve this problem:
constitutional democratic process in order to ensure adequate
communication, public confidence, and an acceptable balance of
advantages and disadvantages for the various interest groups; and
coordinated executive planning in order to prevent extreme and
uncontrollable oscillations, unanticipated functional blockages,
and undue slowness or randomness of change.

Paradigm Development Processes. In an earlier section we
referred to that aspect of national character which has been called
"genius" (as in the phrase, "the Greeks had a genius for geometry"). Implicit in such notions, and in the related concepts of
"cultural climax,"[25] of sets of thematic transformations,[26] and of
the unfolding of the potentialities of a civilization[27] is the idea

25. Kroeber, *Cultural and Natural Areas of Native North America.*
26. Lévi-Strauss, "The Structural Study of Myth."
27. See, for example, Kroeber, *Configurations of Culture Growth.*

that much of the process of culture change consists of the development of the implications of a paradigm of assumptions. In the history of science, Kuhn[28] has given some aspects of this notion elegant expression but the formulation can be extended far more broadly, to such grand events as the Neolithic, Urban, and Industrial Revolutions, and to innumerable smaller processes of technical, social, and ideological change.

The core of the paradigm development process is the working out of the implications of a set of broad rules for how to go about solving a type of problem or accomplishing a general purpose. The process of working out can ideally be conceptualized as a self-contained, purposeful, orderly piece of thinking, usually by several generations of specialists who build on each others' work. Once launched, unless it is stopped by catastrophe, this process follows its own inner logic and is apt to be notably indifferent and even irrelevant to change going on in other cultural domains. A convenient example is the development of Greek geometry. Basing itself on a widespread Near Eastern acquaintance with practical geometric problems encountered in surveying, architecture, and perhaps sculpture, a paradigm was formulated during the fourth century B.C. that determined the further development of Greek mathematics, defining both its potentialities and its limitations. The paradigm involved the assumption that an abstract mathematics could be based on the use of the syllogism and constructions by straight-edge, compass, and pencil, which would reveal invariant relations among the measurable features of triangular, rectangular, cubic, spherical, cylindrical, and conical forms. There was no advanced algebra and no arithmetic that would require a place-numeral system. With these limitations in mind, Euclid summarized the paradigm as it had been developed by the end of the fourth century in his ten axioms. The development of new theorems and their proof, and the application of the products of the mathematical development to problems in astronomy and engineering, continued for several centuries until there was virtually nothing left to work out. The program had been completed and practically nothing new was added to geometry

28. *The Structure of Scientific Revolutions.*

as such until the parallel postulate was challenged by Riemann, Lobachevsky, and Bolgai in the nineteenth century. Further applications of Greek geometry—such as "the calculus"—became possible when algebraic methods were applied to the analysis of geometric forms.

It is apparent that the evolution of the technical core of Greek geometry can most profitably be analyzed as a self-contained cognitive process involving several generations of a small group of specialists whose thinking about geometry (but not necessarily their thinking on other subjects) proceeded with necessary and magnificent indifference to the various tumultuous social and cultural changes going on around them. But spinning off from this technical core, of course, were various implications for the solution of practical problems, which had some consequences for such enterprises as architecture, navigation, and weaponry, and these in turn entailed various social and cultural consequences both for their contemporaries and for their cultural descendants in Western Europe and ultimately the whole world.

The relationship of the core development to other processes of change is more readily apparent in the history of the Industrial Revolution. In this case, the paradigm was based on the assumption that sources of power, such as falling water and the wind, and eventually the steam engine and other energy resources, could be harnessed in mills to fine and intricate machinery for performing manufacturing work that hitherto had required skilled hands. (Since Roman times, existing mills had been used only for gross tasks such as sawing lumber, forging iron, and grinding grain.) A series of English and American inventions beginning in 1733 with the flying shuttle and culminating in the cotton gin in 1793 made possible the further development of large water-powered factories filled with numbers of such machines that were tended and supervised by persons who functioned not as craftsmen but as machine operators. Simultaneously, new sources of power, particularly the steam engine, were being developed, and the agricultural revolution, which depended on the rational improvement of livestock and vegetable species by controlled breeding, and on the more efficient utilization of land by individually managed estates, was displacing the peasantry and thereby making available a larger supply of labor for work at the mills.

The technical core of the paradigmatic development in this case is, of course, the successive generations of machine design specialists who worked out the problems of power transmission (gears, shafts, and pulleys), toolmaking, control, maintenance, and so forth. But the social and cultural consequences of this paradigm development are equally conspicuous. One can divide them into two groups: first, the development of adequate technical and social adaptations to solve the problems of promoting agricultural and industrial development, of keeping the machines going, and of distributing their products and, eventually, of taking care of the operatives and of the rest of the society affected by the machines; and second, the creation of a new ideology which, for all parties concerned, would rationalize, justify, and explain both the core paradigm process and the instrumental adaptations that this process was eliciting. An example of a social adaptation to the requirements of technology was the series of notorious Enclosure Acts by which the English peasantry were driven by Parliament off their fields and commons to make room for the great English agricultural estates of the nineteenth century. The proletariat thus created migrated in part to America and in part to the English mill sites where they gained employment. The economic and social hardships of the mill hands and their families in turn later prompted the passage of legislation regulating factory hours and other matters; and systematic conflict of interest between owners and managers, on the one hand, and laborers on the other eventually produced effective labor unions and a legally regulated system of negotiation involving the rights to organize, protest, and strike for better wages and working conditions without risk of punishment or discharge. A rationalization of the industrial system in turn was quickly undertaken, along two contrasting lines: first by Malthus, Ricardo, and the classical economists, who postulated maximum progress under laissez-faire market conditions, and soon after by Marx, who deplored the suffering entailed by the changes in industry and agriculture and looked forward to a classless society that would ensure social justice, but who did not for a moment conceive that the industrial paradigm would not continue to develop.

As one observes the evolution of such core paradigms, and of the adaptations and rationalizations that they generate, one cannot help but be impressed by their nonnormative and essentially unpredictable quality. In a sense, the development of the technical core is radically unpredictable, even though it is implied in the initial assumptions of the paradigm, because the prediction, if given in any detail, is not so much an anticipation of that which will occur in the future as it is the event itself. To predict in detail is to invent; the prediction becomes the event predicted. Furthermore, the adaptations and rationalizations are not so much invocations of tradition, although they are of necessity colored by the existing culture, as ad hoc innovations made in an attempt to realize anticipated advantages to be obtained from applications of the evolving paradigm. Thus it is more valid to think of the whole process as cognitive, as information-processing and problem-solving, as creative discovery, invention, and policy-making, than as some sort of mechanical interaction of simple social and cultural forces whose resultant is readily calculated in advance from the basic paradigmatic formula.

Revitalization Processes. Implicit in the foregoing discussion was the assumption that, even during periods of stable moving equilibrium, the sociocultural system is subject to mild but measurable oscillations in degree of organization. From time to time, however, most societies undergo more violent fluctuations in this regard. Such fluctuation is of peculiar importance in culture change because it often culminates in relatively sudden change in cultural *Gestalt*. We refer, here, to revitalization movements, which we define as deliberate, organized attempts by some members of a society to construct a more satisfying culture by rapid acceptance of a pattern of multiple innovations.[29]

The severe disorganization of a sociocultural system may be caused by the impact of any one or combination of a variety of forces that push the system beyond the limits of equilibrium.

29. See Wallace, "Revitalization Movements"; Mead, *New Lives for Old.*

Some of these forces are: climatic or faunal changes, which destroy the economic basis of its existence; epidemic disease, which grossly alters the population structure; wars, which exhaust the society's resources of manpower or result in defeat or invasion; internal conflict among interest groups, which results in extreme disadvantage for at least one group; and, very commonly, a position of perceived subordination and inferiority with respect to an adjacent society. The latter, by the use of more or less coercion (or even no coercion at all, as in situations where the mere example set by the dominant society raises too-high levels of aspiration), brings about uncoordinated cultural changes. Under conditions of disorganization, the system, from the standpoint of at least some of its members, is unable to make possible the reliable satisfaction of certain values that are held to be essential to continued well-being and self-respect. The mazeway of a culturally disillusioned person, accordingly, is an image of a world that is unpredictable, or barren in its simplicity, or both, and is apt to contain severe identity conflicts. His mood (depending on the precise nature of the disorganization) will be one of panic-stricken anxiety, shame, guilt, depression, or apathy.

An example of the kind of disorganization to which we refer is given by the two thousand or so Seneca Indians of New York at the close of the eighteenth century. Among these people, a supreme value attached to the conception of the absolutely free and autonomous individual, unconstrained by and indifferent to his own and alien others' pain and hardship. This individual was capable of free indulgence of emotional impulses but, in crisis, freely subordinated his own wishes to the needs of his community. Among the men, especially, this ego-ideal was central in personality organization. Men defined the roles of hunting, of warfare, and of statesmanship as the conditions of achievement of this value; thus the stereotypes of "the good hunter," "the brave warrior," and "the forest statesman" were the images of masculine success. But the forty-three years from 1754, when the French and Indian War began, to 1797, when the Seneca sold their last hunting grounds and became largely confined to tiny, isolated reservations, brought with them changes in their situation that made achievement of these ideals virtually impossible. The good hunter could no longer hunt: the game was scarce, and it was almost suicidally dangerous to stray far from the reservation among the numerous hostile white men. The brave warrior could no longer fight, being undersupplied, abandoned by his allies, and his women and children threatened by growing military might of the United States. The forest statesman was an object of contempt, and this disillusionment was perhaps more shattering than the rest. The Iroquois chiefs, for nearly a century, had been able to play off British and French, then Americans and British, against one another, extorting supplies and guarantees of territorial immunity from both sides. They had maintained an extensive system of alliances and hegemonies among surrounding tribal groups. Suddenly they were shorn of their power. White men no longer spoke of the League of the Iroquois with respect; their western Indian dependents and allies regarded them as cowards for having made peace with the Americans.

The initial Seneca response to the progress of sociocultural disorganization was quasi-pathological: many became drunkards; the fear of witches increased; squabbling factions were unable to achieve a common policy. But a revitalization movement developed in 1799, based on the religious revelations reported by one of the disillusioned forest statesmen, one Handsome Lake, who preached a code of patterned religious and cultural reform. The drinking of whiskey was proscribed; witchcraft was to be stamped out; various outmoded rituals and prevalent sins were to be abandoned. In addition, various syncretic cultural reforms, amounting to a reorientation of the socioeconomic system, were to be undertaken, including the adoption of agriculture (hitherto a feminine calling) by the men, and the focusing of kinship responsibilities within the nuclear family (rather than in the clan and lineage). The general acceptance of Handsome Lake's Code, within a few years, wrought seemingly miraculous changes. A group of sober, devout, partly literate, and technologically up-to-date farming communities suddenly replaced the demoralized slums in the wilderness.[30]

30. See Wallace, *The Death and Rebirth of the Seneca* for a detailed account of this movement.

Such dramatic transformations are, as a matter of historical fact, very common in human history, and probably have been the medium of as much culture change as the slower equilibrium processes. Furthermore, because they compress into such a short space of time such extensive changes in pattern, they are somewhat easier to record than the quiet serial changes during periods of equilibrium. In general, revitalization processes share a common process structure that can be conceptualized as a pattern of temporally overlapping, but functionally distinct, stages:

I. *Steady State.* This is a period of moving equilibrium of the kind discussed in the preceding section. Culture change occurs during the steady state, but is of the relatively slow and chainlike kind. Stress levels vary among interest groups, and there is some oscillation in organization level, but disorganization and stress remain within limits tolerable to most individuals. Occasional incidents of intolerable stress may stimulate a limited "correction" of the system, but some incidence of individual ill-health and criminality are accepted as a price society must pay.

II. *The Period of Increased Individual Stress.* The sociocultural system is being "pushed" progressively out of equilibrium by the forces described earlier: climatic and biotic change, epidemic disease, war and conquest, social subordination, acculturation, internally generated decay, and so forth. Increasingly large numbers of individuals are placed under what is to them intolerable stress by the failure of the system to accommodate the satisfaction of their needs. Anomie and disillusionment become widespread, as the culture is perceived to be disorganized and inadequate; crime and illness increase sharply in frequency as individualistic asocial responses. But the situation is still generally defined as one of fluctuation within the steady state.

III. *The Period of Cultural Distortion.* Some members of the society attempt, piecemeal and ineffectively, to restore personal equilibrium by adopting socially disfunctional expedients. Alcoholism, venality in public officials, the "black market," breaches of sexual and kinship mores, hoarding, gambling for gain, "scapegoating," and similar behaviors that, in the preceding period, were still defined as individual deviancies, in effect become institutionalized efforts to circumvent the evil effects of "the system." Interest groups, losing confidence in the advantages of maintaining mutually acceptable interrelationships, may resort to violence in order to coerce others into unilaterally advantageous behavior. Because of the malcoordination of cultural changes during this period, they are rarely able to reduce the impact of the forces that have pushed the society out of equilibrium, and in fact lead to a continuous decline in organization.

IV. *The Period of Revitalization.* Once severe cultural distortion has occurred, the society can with difficulty return to steady state without the institution of a revitalization process. Without revitalization, indeed, the society is apt to disintegrate as a system: the population will either die off, splinter into autonomous groups, or be absorbed into another, more ·stable, society. Revitalization depends on the successful completion of the following functions:

1. Formulation of a code. An individual, or a group of individuals, constructs a new, utopian image of sociocultural organization. This model is a blueprint of an ideal society or "goal culture." Contrasted with the goal culture is the existing culture, which is presented as inadequate or evil in certain respects. Connecting the existing culture and the goal culture is a transfer culture: a system of operations that, if faithfully carried out, will transform the existing culture into the goal culture. Failure to institute the transfer operations will, according to the code, result in either the perpetuation of the existing misery or the ultimate destruction of the society (if not of the whole world). Not infrequently in primitive societies the code, or the core of it, is formulated by one individual in the course of a hallucinatory revelation; such prophetic experiences are apt to launch religiously oriented movements, since the source of the revelation is apt to be regarded as a supernatural being. Nonhallucinatory formulations usually are found in politically oriented movements. In either case, the formulation of the code constitutes a reformulation of the author's own mazeway and often brings to him a

renewed confidence in the future and a remission of the complaints he experienced before. It may be suggested that such mazeway resynthesis processes are merely extreme forms of the reorganizing dream processes that seem to be associated with REM (rapid-eye-movement) sleep, which are necessary to normal health.

2. Communication. The formulators of the code preach the code to other people in an evangelistic spirit. The aim of the communication is to make converts. The code is offered as the means of spiritual salvation for the individual and of cultural salvation for the society. Promises of benefit to the target population need not be immediate or materialistic, for the basis of the code's appeal is the attractiveness of identification with a more highly organized system, with all that this implies in the way of self-respect. Indeed, in view of the extensiveness of the changes in values often implicit in such codes, appeal to currently held values would often be pointless. Religious codes offer spiritual salvation, identification with God, elect status; political codes offer honor, fame, the respect of society for sacrifices made in its interest. But refusal to accept the code is usually defined as placing the listener in immediate spiritual, as well as material, peril with respect to his existing values. In small societies, the target population may be the entire community; but in more complex societies, the message may be aimed only at certain groups deemed eligible for participation in the transfer and goal cultures.

3. Organization. The code attracts converts. The motivations that are satisfied by conversion, and the psychodynamics of the conversion experience itself, are likely to be highly diverse, ranging from the mazeway resynthesis characteristic of the prophet, and the hysterical conviction of the "true believer," to the calculating expediency of the opportunist. As the group of converts expands, it differentiates into two parts: a set of disciples and a set of mass followers. The disciples increasingly become the executive organization, responsible for administering the evangelistic program, protecting the formulator, combatting heresy, and so on. In this role, the disciples increasingly become full-time specialists in the work of the movement. The tri-cornered relationship between the formulators, the disciples, and the mass followers is

given an authoritarian structure, even without the formalities of older organizations, by the charismatic quality of the formulator's image. The formulator is regarded as a man to whom, from a supernatural being or from some other source of wisdom unavailable to the mass, a superior knowledge and authority has been vouchsafed that justifies his claim to unquestioned belief and obedience from his followers.

In the modern world, with the advantages of rapid transportation and ready communication, the simple charismatic model of cult organization is not always adequate to describe many social and religious movements. In such programs as Pentecostalism, Black Power, and the New Left, there is typically a considerable number of local or special issue groups loosely joined in what Luther Gerlach has called an "acephalous, segmentary, reticulate organization."[31] Each segment may be, in effect, a separate revitalization organization of the simple kind described above; the individual groups differ in details of code, in emotional style, in appeal to different social classes; and, since the movement as a whole has no single leader, it is relatively immune to repression, the collapse of one or several segments in no way invalidating the whole. This type of movement organization is singularly well adapted to predatory expansion; but it may eventually fall under the domination of one cult or party (as was the case, for instance, in Germany when the SS took over the fragmented Nazi party, which in turn was heir to a large number of nationalist groups, and as is the case when a Communist party apparatus assumes control of a revolutionary popular front).

4. Adaptation.   Because the movement is a revolutionary organization (however benevolent and humane the ultimate values to which it subscribes), it threatens the interests of any group that obtains advantage, or believes it obtains advantage, from maintaining or only moderately reforming the status quo. Furthermore, the code is never complete; new inadequacies are constantly being found in the existing culture, and new inconsistencies, predicative failures, and ambiguities discovered in

31. "Five Factors Crucial to the Growth and Spread of a Modern Religious Movement."

the code itself (some of the latter being pointed out by the opposition). The response of the code formulators and disciples is to rework the code, and, if necessary, to defend the movement by political and diplomatic maneuver, and, ultimately, by force. The general tendency is for codes to harden gradually, and for the tone of the movement to become increasingly nativistic and hostile both toward nonparticipating fellow members of society, who will ultimately be defined as "traitors," and toward "national enemies."

True revolutions, as distinguished from mere coups d'état, which change personnel without changing the structure, require that the revitalization movement of which they are the instrument add to its code a morality sanctioning subversion or even violence. The leadership must also be sophisticated in its knowledge of how to mobilize an increasingly large part of the population to their side, and of how to interfere with the mobilization of the population by the establishment. The student of such processes can do no better than to turn to the works of contemporary practitioners such as Che Guevara and Mao Tse Tung for authoritative explications and examples of the revolutionary aspect of revitalization.

5. Cultural transformation. If the movement is able to capture both the adherence of a substantial proportion of a local population and, in complex societies, of the functionally crucial apparatus (such as power and communications networks, water supply, transport systems, and military establishment), the transfer culture and, in some cases, the goal culture itself, can be put into operation. The revitalization, if successful, will be attended by the drastic decline of the quasi-pathological individual symptoms of anomie and by the disappearance of the cultural distortions. For such a revitalization to be accomplished, however, the movement must be able to maintain its boundaries from outside invasion, must be able to obtain internal social conformity without destructive coercion, and must have a successful economic system.

6. Routinization. If the preceding functions are satisfactorily completed, the functional reasons for the movement's existence as an innovative force disappear. The transfer culture, if not the

goal culture, is operating of necessity with the participation of a large proportion of the community. Although the movement's leaders may resist the realization of the fact, the movement's function shifts from the role of innovation to the role of maintenance. If the movement was heavily religious in orientation, its legacy is a cult or church that preserves and reworks the code, and maintains, through ritual and myth, the public awareness of the history and values that brought forth the new culture. If the movement was primarily political, its organization is routinized into various stable decision-making, and morale-and-order-maintaining functions (such as administrative offices, police, and military bodies). Charisma can, to a degree, be routinized, but its intensity diminishes as its functional necessity becomes, with increasing obviousness, outmoded.

V. *The New Steady State.* With the routinization of the movement, a new steady state may be said to exist. Steady-state processes of culture change continue; many of them are in areas where the movement has made further change likely. In particular, changes in the value structure of the culture may lay the basis for long-continuing changes (such as the train of economic and technological consequences of the dissemination of the Protestant ethic after the Protestant Reformation). Thus in addition to the changes that the movement accomplishes during its active phase, it may control the direction of the subsequent equilibrium processes by shifting the values that define the cultural focus. The record of the movement itself, over time, gradually is subject to distortion, and eventually is enshrined in myths and rituals which elevate the events that occurred, and persons who acted, into quasi- or literally divine status.

Two psychological mechanisms seem to be of peculiar importance in the revitalization process: mazeway resynthesis[32] and hysterical conversion. The resynthesis is most dramatically exemplified in the career of the prophet who formulates a new religious code during a hallucinatory trance. Typically, such persons,

---

32. Wallace, "Mazeway Resynthesis: A Bio-Cultural Theory of Religious Inspiration" and "Stress and Rapid Personality Changes."

after suffering increasing depreciation of self-esteem as the result of their inadequacy to achieve the culturally ideal standards, reach a point of either physical or drug-induced exhaustion, during which a resynthesis of values and beliefs occurs. The resynthesis is, like other innovations, a recombination of preexisting configurations; the uniqueness of this particular process is the suddenness of conviction, the trancelike state of the subject, and the emotionally central nature of the subject matter. There is some reason to suspect that such dramatic resyntheses depend on a special biochemical milieu, accompanying the "stage of exhaustion" of the stress (in Selye's sense) syndrome, or on a similar milieu induced by drugs. But comparable resyntheses are, of course, sometimes accomplished more slowly, without the catalytic aid of extreme stress or drugs. This kind of resynthesis produces, apparently, a permanent alteration of mazeway: the new stable cognitive configuration, is, as it were, constructed out of the materials of earlier configurations, which, once rearranged, cannot readily reassemble into the older forms.

The hysterical conversion is more typical of the mass follower who is repeatedly subjected to suggestion by a charismatic leader and an excited crowd. The convert of this type may, during conversion display various dissociative behaviors (rage, speaking in tongues, rolling on the ground, weeping, and so on). After conversion, his overt behavior may be in complete conformity with the code to which he has been exposed. But his behavior has changed not because of a radical resynthesis, but because of the adoption under suggestion of an additional social personality which temporarily replaces, but does not destroy, the earlier. He remains, in a sense, a case of multiple personality and is liable, if removed from reinforcing symbols, to lapse into an earlier social personality. The participant in the lynch mob or in the camp meeting revival is a familiar example of this type of convert. But persons can be maintained in this state of hysterical conversion for months or years, if the "trance" is continuously maintained by the symbolic environment (flags, statues, portraits, songs, and so on) and continuous suggestions (speeches, rallies, and so on). The most familiar contemporary example is the German under Hitler who participated in the Nazi genocide program, but reverted to *Gemütlichkeit* when the war ended. The difference between the resynthesized person and the converted one does not lie in the nature of the codes to which they subscribe (they may be the same), but in the blandness and readiness of the hysterical convert to revert, as compared to the almost paranoid intensity and stability of the resynthesized prophet. A successful movement, by virtue of its ability to maintain suggestion continuously for years, is able to hold the hysterical convert indefinitely, or even to work a real resynthesis by repeatedly forcing him, after hysterical conversion, to reexamine his older values and beliefs and to work through to a valid resynthesis, sometimes under considerable stress. The Chinese Communists, for instance, apparently have become disillusioned by hysterical conversions and have used various techniques, some coercive and some not, but all commonly lumped together as "brain-washing" in Western literature, to induce valid resynthesis. The aim of these communist techniques, like those of the established religions, is, literally, to produce a "new man."

It is impossible to exaggerate the importance of these two psychological processes for culture change, for they make possible the rapid substitution of a new cultural *Gestalt* for an old, and thus the rapid cultural transformation of whole populations. Without this mechanism, the cultural transformation of the 600,000,000 people of China by the Communists could not have occurred; nor the Communist-led revitalization and expansion of the USSR; nor the American Revolution; nor the Protestant Reformation; nor the rise and spread of Christianity, Mohammedanism, and Buddhism. In the written historical record, revitalization movements begin with Ikhnaton's ultimately disastrous attempt to establish a new, monotheistic religion in Egypt; they are found, continent by continent, in the history of all human societies, occurring with frequency proportional to the pressures to which the society is subjected. For small tribal societies, in chronically extreme situations, movements may develop every ten or fifteen years; in stable complex cultures, the rate of a society-wide movement may be one every two or three hundred years.

In view of the frequency and geographical diversity of revitalization movements, it can be expected that their content will be extremely varied, corresponding to the diversity of situational contexts and cultural backgrounds in which they develop. Major culture areas are, over extended periods of time, associated with particular types: New Guinea and Melanesia, during the latter part of the nineteenth and the twentieth centuries, have been the home of the well-known "cargo cults." The most prominent feature of these cults is the expectation that the ancestors soon will arrive in a steamship, bearing a cargo of the white man's goods, and will lead a nativistic revolution culminating in the ejection of European masters. The Indians of the eastern half of South America for centuries after the conquest set off on migrations for the *terre sans mal* where a utopian way of life, free of Spaniards and Portuguese, would be found; North American Indians of the eighteenth and nineteenth centuries were prone to revivalistic movements such as the Ghost Dance, whose adherents believed that appropriate ritual and the abandonment of the sins of the white man would bring a return of the golden age before contact; South Africa has been the home of the hundreds of small, enthusiastic, separatist churches that have broken free of the missionary organizations. As might be expected, a congruence evidently exists between the cultural *Anlage* and the content of movement, which, together with processes of direct and stimulus diffusion, accounts for the tendency for movements to fall into areal types.[33]

CULTURAL ABANDONMENT, CULTURAL STABILITY, AND THE REACTION TO CULTURAL LOSS

In the earlier discussions of innovation, we did not explicitly deal with the process of cultural abandonment. While much of innovation is cumulative, in the sense that new configurations are added to an existing stock, there is usually a correlative process of deletion: as new content is added, old content is abandoned. Where express dissatisfaction with the old configuration is the motive for innovation, the two processes are often so closely

33. See Burridge, *Mambu: A Melanesian Millenium.*

associated that the relationship is not seen as problematical. Thus, for instance, in urban areas the introduction of the electric light is associated with the abandonment of oil lamps. But from time to time, the anthropologist is confronted with cases of the abandonment by a society of culture traits, or even major *Gestalten,* without the acceptance of any visibly superior substitute. He is also confronted with many circumstances in which his ingenuity in functional analysis is stretched to its limits—sometimes, beyond these limits—to account for the refusal of people to abandon components of their cultural system that, from a theoretical viewpoint, ought to have been abandoned. Cultures appear to possess a stability that is difficult to account for by simple psychological principles such as the law of effect. Finally, since the development of serious interest in the psychology of acculturation, the anthropologist has been interested in the apparently psychopathological responses of people to unplanned and unintended cultural loss. Indeed, as we remarked in the previous chapter, a part of culture-and-personality theory has been explicitly concerned with the damaging "impact" of culture change on personality structure.

The classic cases of cultural abandonment would seem to be those inexplicable periods of decline that afflict great civilizations, such as the Roman Empire, Greece, and Imperial Spain. It is difficult to account for such phenomena by functional arguments without postulating a lesion of some component, whose failure sets in motion a train of functionally inevitable disasters that result in the ultimate collapse of the system. But where to find the lesion? Here speculative historians have a free field to adduce anything, from a decline in hay production to the equality of women to lead poisoning to inbreeding, as the source of the lesion. Such particularistic speculations, however, are often no more convincing than metaphysical appeals to the law of entropy or the theory of cycles. Nor, in such cases, is it always possible to find some overwhelming external interference of the kind that we have suggested, as the precipitants of a pre-revitalization slump in organization. One is left, in fact, with the suspicion (already voiced in the discussion of the "genius" of cultures) that not all functioning sociocultural systems are in stable equilibrium, but rather that some—and these are the ones we are now discussing—are in a state of gradually increasing oscillation, or are following an exponential curve in regard to some crucial parameter; their demise is the inevitable consequence of the uninterrupted operation of their own internal laws. This consideration leads us to suspect that not merely whole civilizations, but also—and perhaps more typically—particular institutions and customs are governed by processual laws that make their obsolescence and abandonment inevitable. Still other subsystems, particularly economic ones, may be governed by processual principles that make their operation cyclical; for example, the trading stamp industry in the United States which, within any one state, is characterized by a cycle from legalization, through partial acceptance, to universal acceptance (at which point it becomes merely an expense without advantage to any storekeeper), to prohibition, to legalization again.

But from the psychological standpoint, the critical issue is the determination of the point in the process of increasing disfunction at which the group jettisons the disfunctional cultural equipment. In a general way, it may be suggested that the jettison point will lie somewhere *beyond* the point at which the average individual member of the group recognizes that maintenance of the institution will cost him more than any alternative in the near future. The actual jettisoning will probably occur, beyond this point, after respected community agencies publicly propose abandonment. An example of the process in the anthropological literature is given by the abandonment of taboos in Hawaii, by the forsaking of burdensome religious rituals among Mayan descendants in Guatemala, by the grateful acceptance of the *pax colonialis* among head-hunters in New Guinea, and by the relinquishment of torture among the eighteenth-century Iroquois. The emotional cost of cultural abandonment, however, even in the presence of an immediately recognizable functional substitute, is remarkably high. It is suspected that this high psychological cost of abandonment itself, rather than continued reinforcement, is responsible for some of the remarkable phenomena of cultural stability. Let us therefore examine the nature of these costs of abandonment.

The most dramatic demonstration of the psychological need to maintain the image of cultural continuity is provided by behavioral responses to the impact of disasters. Immediately following a sudden, unexpected impact (such as a tornado or atomic explosion) that wreaks extensive physical damage and kills or injures many people, many survivors, both injured and uninjured, experience what has been called the "disaster syndrome." This is a behavior sequence that may last for minutes, hours, or days, depending on individual circumstances. In the first stage, the individual is described as being "dazed," "stunned," "apathetic," "passive," "aimless." He is (literally) apt to be insensitive to pain, to be almost completely unaware, consciously, of his own injuries or of the seriousness of the injuries of others, and to ignore the extent of the visible damage. First-stage victims will do trivial things, such as sweeping off the doorstep of a flattened house, or will leave seriously injured kinfolk in order to chat with neighbors. In the second stage, the individual is no longer dazed, but he becomes pathetically eager for support and reassurance that known persons, structures, and institutions have survived. Personal loss is minimized; concern is for reassurance that the community is intact. Persons in this stage can be easily led and formed into work teams, but they are not effective in leadership. In the third stage, a mildly euphoric altruism obtains: the individual enthusiastically participates in group activity, designed to restore and rehabilitate the community. Observers remark on the high morale and selfless dedication to be seen on all sides. Finally, as the euphoria wears off, there is full awareness of the long-term effects of personal and community loss. Complaint and criticism against public agencies, bickering with neighbors, and dismay over the personal cost of the disaster attain full consciousness. This syndrome has been repeatedly identified in the aftermath of both natural and wartime disasters[34] and in the responses of target groups in cultural crises.[35]

34. Wallace, *Tornado in Worcester: An Exploratory Study of Individual and Community Behavior in an Extreme Situation;* Wolfenstein, *Disaster: A Psychological Essay.*

35. Reina, "Political Crisis and Revitalization: The Guatemalan Case."

The theoretical importance of the disaster syndrome lies in the fact that large physical disasters present an almost laboratory-pure situation of cultural loss. Individuals, one moment secure in their status as members of an ongoing community with an effective culture, are shorn of much of the tangible evidence of that culture. An initial fantasy, reported by some survivors of the Worcester tornado, was that it was the end of the world. Such an impression should not appear bizarre to an anthropologist, for, in a sense, this impression is valid: even though the physical destruction is not complete, the damage in casualties, and in material loss, inevitably must shatter the existing *Gestalt* by virtue of the principle of functional interdependence.

The deprivation of data that confirm to the individual his psychological set, his "mazeway," arouses shattering anxiety and is followed by denial: the individual virtually blots out awareness of injury and loss. Related phenomena would seem to be the "denial" of anxiety-provoking sensory isolation by means of hallucination in the well-known psychological experiments; the sequences of disturbance and denial, elicited by perceptual disconfirmation—"cognitive dissonance"—as analyzed by psychologists;[36] the refusal to admit death in the mourning process; and, in general, neurotic fears of abandoning a nongratifying response. The psychological principle behind all these manifestations is fundamental to any theory of cultural stability and culture change; it may be expressed as a Principle of Conservation of Cognitive Structure: (1) the individual will not abandon *any* particular conception of reality (including, therefore, his culturally standard conceptions), even in the face of direct evidence of its current inutility, without having had an opportunity to construct a new mazeway, with or without substitute conceptions, in which the invalid conception is not a functionally necessary component; (2) initial confrontation of the individual with evidence of inutility will arouse an anxiety-and-denial syndrome, and this anxiety-and-denial response may continue for a considerable period of time; (3) it is easier for the individual to abandon a conception if substitutes are offered and models of

36. Festinger, *A Theory of Cognitive Dissonance.*

new mazeways are presented, than if the abandonment must be made "blind," in response to awareness of the inutility of the concept.[37] A corollary of this principle is the "dilemma of immobility": rather than face the anxiety of cultural abandonment, individuals will cling for years to a disordered sociocultural system, in which events do not follow reliably upon their supposed antecedents.

A similar dilemma is particularly poignant in acculturation situations where an acceptable alternative cultural system exists, which the group would willingly accept, even at the cost of giving up shreds of the older culture, but which cannot be adopted because of active interference by a "prejudiced" and discriminatory and dominant society. Often, in such situations, insult is added to injury by the dominant group expressing severe contempt for the disorderly nature of the subordinate group, even while it may prevent the exchange for something better. The emotional dilemma of the individual who is entrapped in such a situation is productive of severe anxiety and, secondarily, of quasi-pathological defenses. He is caught, on the one hand, between shame at, and lack of confidence in, his "own" truncated disorderly system, and, on the other, fear that if he abandons parts of this admittedly inadequate culture, he will merely restrict himself to an existence that is no more orderly than it was before and is considerably smaller. Evidence of the personality damage resulting from chronically corrosive situations of this type is one of the standard features of the culture-and-personality literature. Hallowell's data on the Ojibwa personality under (retarded) acculturation are perhaps the best known. In a series of papers comparing the relatively unacculturated Ojibwa of the Lake Winnipeg region with the more acculturated people of northern Wisconsin,[38] he found, in both Rorschach records and general behavioral data, evidence that the partly acculturated Ojibwa personality was a "regressive" (that is, quasi-pathological) version of the unacculturated personality. In view of the economic uncer-

---

37. Cf. Wallace, "Mazeway Disintegration: The Individual's Perception of Socio-Cultural Disorganization"; Conant, *On Understanding Science*.

38. *Culture and Experience.*

tainty of Wisconsin Ojibwa life, the relatively low social status, and the presence of the standard dilemma of immobility—unreliability of existing culture, unavailability of an acceptable substitute—this evidence of personality damage is not unexpected. Similar findings were reported by Abram Kardiner and Lionel Ovesey[39] on the American Negro, for whom the problems of cultural and ethnic identification assume major significance, even in individual psychodynamics. The "marginal man," indeed, is an ideal type constructed to label persons caught precisely in the vortex of such dilemmas, unable to forsake the old culture, yet, because of experience in the new, unable to be happy in it either.

The resolution of such "dilemmas of immobility" can, it would seem, normally come about via any combination of three processes: (1) revitalization; (2) assimilation; (3) nativism or nationalism. We have already discussed revitalization at some length as a deliberate syncretic cultural reorganization within a definably bounded social group. Assimilation and nativism (or nationalism), without revitalization (although revitalization movements may be nativistic or nationalistic), are most apt to occur in the subordinate society in an acculturation situation. In assimilation, the subordinate group attempts to abandon its existing inadequate culture by entering into the society of the dominant group and accepting its culture almost *in toto* (retaining only token vestiges of their distinctive culture traits). Pure nationalism, with no effort at revitalization,[40] is often military in character and is motivated by a desire to rid the group of the presence of members of the dominant group who are the source of constant shame-producing reminders of cultural inferiority, as well as of practical interference. An example of this is the so-called Black Hawk War, in Illinois and Wisconsin, in 1832. A band of displaced and humiliated Sac, Fox, and Kickapoo, under the warrior Black Hawk, attempted to retain their settlements on ceded land, east of the Mississippi, in the face of eviction orders. Their actions were interpreted by the United States as a military attack and the group of about one thousand men, women, and children virtually

39. *The Mark of Oppression.*
40. Ames, "Reaction to Stress: A Comparative Study of Nativism."

was exterminated. But much nativism and nationalism is not military in character; it takes the form of stubborn ideological denial of cultural inadequacy, with withdrawal and deliberate insularity as, for instance, in religious groups such as the Amish and Hutterites.

chapter six
CULTURE AND
MENTAL ILLNESS

We shall now consider the relationship between the culture of a society and the forms and frequencies of the mental diseases suffered by the members of that society.

It is necessary to begin this chapter with a caution. The anthropological student of mental illness must beware of gross semantic chasms that lie hidden beneath the seemingly objective and scientific surface of psychiatry, clinical psychology, and affiliated fields, including his own. Even the relationship between the meanings of the terms "mental health" and "mental disease" is a trap for the unwary, for, as Marie Jahoda[1] points out, for many writers "mental health"does not mean merely an absence of "mental disease," nor "mental disease" merely the reciprocal absence of "mental health." Many persons belong in a vaguely bounded middle category, characterized neither by positive mental health nor by definite mental illness. It is the questionable size and composition of this middle category that produces part of the semantic difficulty, for each authority sets the boundaries at different points on the scale.

For the anthropologist, who must consider mental health and mental illness in exotic non-Western cultures and in cross-cultural comparison, the semantic ambiguities of Western science are compounded by the diversity with which human cultures conceive of, and respond to, illness, and by the variety of the forms of illness themselves. "Hysteria," "possession," and "schizoid," for instance, are terms used by anthropologists in contexts where their significance, as labels for psychiatric disorder, is questionable, to say the least. Despite equivalence of process, that which is regarded as "illness" in one society may be regarded as merely one aspect of the normal and healthy life in another. The same apodictic disorder of experience, such as

1. *Current Concepts of Positive Mental Health.*

alcoholism or drug intoxication, or hallucination, may be given a variety of interpretations by the subject, depending on his culture, his personal history, and the situation at the moment.[2] The anthropologist's well-intentioned effort, both to apply the concepts of Western science as descriptive categories and to reflect the psychological reality of the native world, thus frequently entangles him in semantic conflicts.

Efforts to resolve these conflicts have inspired a small body of anthropological literature, devoted to the elaboration of cross-culturally valid definitions of mental illnesses and of the concept of mental illness itself.[3] Treatment and hospitalization are obviously invalid criteria, because only a few societies in the ethnographer's universe have institutionalized the Western psychiatric concepts and have mental hospitals. The anthropological definitions, therefore, generally center about some notion of behavioral deviance or abnormality as the universal sign of mental illness. Such a definition may refer to statistical distribution as the locus of the abnormal, or it may emphasize nonconformity with appropriate behavioral pattern, rather than rarity, as the criterion of abnormality. The advantage of such a definition lies in the fact that it does not beg questions of symptomatology, etiology, or prognosis, and in effect utilizes the social diagnosis of the society itself as the measure of behavioral normality. The disadvantage of such a definition is that it tends to ignore (or to cover only by speculation) the phenomenology of the individual's private motives, beliefs, and feelings of anxiety, sorrow, conflict, and so forth.

TYPES OF MENTAL ILLNESS

Despite the aforementioned uncertainty as to the proper abstract definition of mental illness, and despite the eloquent pleas of

2. See Wallace, "Cultural Determinants of Response to Hallucinatory Experience," and MacAndrew and Edgerton, *Drunken Comportment: A Social Explanation.*

3. See Benedict and Jacks, "Mental Illness in Primitive Societies"; Devereux, "Normal and Abnormal: The Key Problem of Psychiatric Anthropology"; Wegrocki, "A Critique of Cultural and Statistical Concepts of Abnormality"; Opler, *Culture, Psychiatry, and Human Values;* Linton, *Culture and Mental Disorders;* Murphy and Leighton, *Approaches to Cross-Cultural Psychiatry;* Plog and Edgerton, *Changing Perspectives in Mental Illness.*

"dynamic" psychiatrists to abjure the "static" categories of mere "descriptive" psychiatry, it is of fundamental importance to describe and name classes of psychopathological phenomena, according to some rational schema, in order to plan treatment and to define an orderly research program. European and American psychiatrists have, in clinical practice during the past half century, developed a working descriptive typology of mental diseases that is serviceable, if not logically elegant. The grosser categories of this typology, after a few culturally specific allusions are pruned away, are usable by the anthropologist for cross-cultural purposes. The schema that follows is based on the *Diagnostic and Statistical Manual: Mental Disorders* of the American Psychiatric Association, which was published in 1952 after a careful analysis of clinical and research practice, and revised in 1968. Because of the importance of identifying the range of the phenomena with which the anthropologist interested in culture and mental illness must deal, we shall present the overall typology in some detail.

Two main categories of mental disease are recognized in the *Manual*: (1) the organic brain syndromes, a group of disorders caused by or associated with impairment of brain tissue function; (2) disorders not attributable to organic conditions and presumably of psychogenic origin or without clearly defined physical cause or structural change in the brain. The respective symptomatologies overlap almost completely: hallucinations, delusions, disorientation, impoverishment of memory, impaired reality testing, and a long list of other behavioral disturbances occur in both the organic and the functional categories. Indeed, it may be difficult to assign a given case confidently to one category or the other, without extensive laboratory and psychological testing. The differentiation essentially is based on the principle that, where an organic disturbance of brain tissue is *known* to be the precipitating factor, the disease is classified as a disorder of brain function; where no such organic disturbance is *known* to be responsible, the illness is classified as "psychogenic" or "functional." A given case may be classified under both categories (for instance, a mental defective who is also psychotic).

All of the organic brain disorders are characterized by a basic common syndrome, consisting of:

1. impairment of orientation in time and space
2. impairment of memory
3. impairment of all intellectual functions (comprehension, calculation, knowledge, learning, and so on)
4. impairment of judgment
5. instability and shallowness of affect

Frequently, hallucinations, delusions, and various behavior disturbances are displayed by the organic disorder. They are divided further into two main groups: (1) psychoses associated with organic brain syndromes; and (2) nonpsychotic organic brain syndromes. Some cases of mental retardation are also attributable to organic conditions; others are assignable to environmental circumstances, such as "psychosocial deprivation."

The acute organic brain syndromes are produced by intracranial infections (encephalitis, meningitis, abscess, and so on); by systemic infection (pneumonia, typhoid fever, acute rheumatic fever); by drug or poison intoxication (barbiturates, opiates, hormones, lead, gases, and so on); by alcoholic intoxication (acute drunkenness and delirium tremens); by severe physical injury (accident, gunshot, surgery); by circulatory disturbance (cerebral embolism, arterial hypertension, and so on); by metabolic disturbance (as in uremia, diabetes, hyperthyroidism, vitamin deficiency, and so on); by intracranial neoplasm (tumors), and by various diseases of unknown or uncertain cause. Other chronic syndromes may be the product of congenital cranial anomaly, producing some degree of mental deficiency (as in congenital spastic paraplegia, Mongolism, prenatal maternal infectious disease, birth trauma, and so on); of syphilis of central nervous system; of cerebral arteriosclerosis; of senile brain disease; of various disturbances of metabolism, growth, or nutrition (pellagra and other vitamin deficiency diseases, various endocrine disorders, and so on); of diseases of unknown cause (multiple sclerosis, Pick's disease, Huntington's chorea), and of any of the determinants of the acute brain disorders, if the disorder is later found to be chronic.

The remainder of the known mental disorders thus are placed in a residual category of noncongenital disorders in which no known physical impairment of brain tissue function has been demonstrated as yet and in which, in some instances, the origin may be "psychogenic" or "psychosocial." Most of the theoretical and research activity of social scientists has been devoted to this large residual category, with the conspicuous exception of mental deficiency.[4] This residual category is divided into several sub-categories: psychoses; neuroses; personality disorders; psycho-physiologic disorders; transient situational personality disorders; and behavior disorders of childhood and early adolescence.

The psychoses in general are characterized by personality disintegration, impairment of intellectual functions, and social failure. This characterization, of course, is very close to the characterization of the brain syndromes, and the differential diagnosis is based on the absence of evidence of brain tissue disfunction more than on clear-cut behavioral distinctions. As before, hallucinations, delusions, and disorganized overt behavior may be present. The psychoses are further divided into the major categories: the schizophrenias (formerly denoted by the term "dementia praecox"); affective psychoses, including involutional melancholia (depressions, primarily in women, during menopause) and manic-depressive conditions (oscillating manic-depressive reactions and relatively stable depressive or manic reactions); and pure paranoid states (which are extremely rare). It has been suggested that another category, the "hysterical psychoses," be reintroduced into respectable usage to take account of transient but extremely agitated conditions such as some of the more exotic ethnic psychoses, including amok and piblokto.[5]

The neuroses, characterized by chronic anxiety and periodic or constant "maladjustment," but lacking the gross personality, intellectual, and social impairments of the psychoses, are classified under eight major headings: anxiety neurosis (formerly called "anxiety state"); hysteria, including dissociative reactions such as depersonalization, dissociated personality, stupor, fugue, amnesia, dream state, somnambulism, and so on, and also con-

4. Sarason and Gladwin, *Psychological and Cultural Problems in Mental Subnormality: A Review of Research*.

5. Hollender and Hirsh, "Hysterical Psychosis."

version reactions such as anesthesia, paralysis, tremor, and so on; phobias (fear of syphilis, dirt, closed places, high places, open places, animals, and so on); obsessive compulsive neurosis (touching, counting, ceremonials, handwashing, recurring thoughts, and so on); depressive neurosis (of less malignant severity than in the psychoses); neurasthenia; depersonalization syndrome; and hypochondria. The psychophysiologic category excludes the conversion hysterias and refers to a wide panorama of conditions affecting single organ systems: skin diseases, anorexia, loss of weight, certain menstrual and endocrine disturbances, hypertension, cramps, certain asthmatic conditions, and so forth. The etiology is in all cases emotional.

The remainder are classified as personality disorders, transient situational personality disorders, and childhood behavior disorders. These include such categories as "inadequate" personality, schizoid personality, cyclothymic personality, paranoid personality, explosive personality, passive-aggressive personality, compulsive personality, and antisocial personality (essentially the old "psychopathic personality"). Alcoholic and drug addictions and sexual deviations are also classified as personality disorders. The "transient" disorders include "gross stress reactions" (reversible psychopathology, of almost any symptomatic variety, precipitated by severe physical or emotional stress, such as combat or disaster) and equally various "adjustment reactions," temporarily mimicking all sorts of more serious chronic disturbances, characteristic of various age groups (for example, "low morale" in adults, sleeping difficulties in infants, truancy in children). In our view, this melange of unwanted behaviors, together with outright criminality, are "diseases" only to the extent that all behavior, including that which is socially undesirable, is determined by forces beyond the control of the individual. Hence in this chapter we shall not devote our attention to categories such as alcoholism, suicide, crime, and drug addiction, which may or may not be culturally defined as delinquencies and may or may not be symptoms of diseases that fall under other categories, such as schizophrenia or depression. Their relevance to theories of mental illness is a subject that goes beyond the scope of this chapter.

THEORIES OF THE "CAUSES"
OF MENTAL ILLNESS

The discerning reader will already have recognized some of the implications of a point made in the preceding section: that the disorders involving physical impairment of brain tissue are distinguished not by their symptomatology, but by the fact that an organic deficiency is known to be the (or a) cause (in the sense of a preceding complex of circumstances sufficient to bring about the onset of the disorder). In a broad sense, then, "theory" is not necessary to account for these disorders; *the* cause, in most instances, is known, and the *kind* of cause is assumed to be physical in all instances. The research and clinical problem is simply to identify the specific physical lesion or deficiency responsible for a given disorder.

The remainder (which constitute the second category) of the mental disorders are the subject of endless theorizing, considerable research, and not very much positive knowledge with regard to either etiology or treatment. The aim of scientific research must be to determine the necessary and sufficient conditions under which a class of phenomena occurs. But neuropsychiatric science is far from being able to state these conditions for *any* of the "functional" (that is, not definitely known to be organic) mental disorders. Two major schools of thought at present still contend (with minimal mutual lip service) with respect to etiological and therapeutic theories: the biochemical and the psychosocial. The biochemical school primarily orients itself to the psychoses and concerns itself with identifying those currently unknown anomalies of body chemistry (in protein fractions and minerals in blood, spinal fluid, endocrine secretions, neural tissue, and so on) that are responsible for psychosis, and with discovering the appropriate physical therapies for correcting such anomalies. Thus the biochemical school, in effect, expects to bring the psychoses over into the category of organically determined, and perhaps in some instances genetically determined mental disorders. With the recent discovery that anxiety can be precipitated by purely chemical means—a sodium lactate infusion[6]—as well as reduced by drugs, it appears that a biochemical complicity in the neuroses may also be established. The psychosocial school embraces the various psychoanalytic disciplines, social, experimental, and clinical psychology, and (for the most part) sociology and anthropology. While this school is heterogeneous, it shares a common faith that it is in some distortion of the subject's social learning experience and current social situation that his psychopathology originates. Theories vary, however, with respect to the locus of the responsible distortion: psychoanalytic and social anthropological theories tend to emphasize early experience, particularly the parents' relationship to the child; sociologic theories tend to emphasize ecological and social class factors, and so on. With respect to cultural anthropology's participation in the scientific investigation of mental illness, the most glaring weakness until recently has been the bland assumption that "mental disorder" (a few outstanding organic and nutritional complaints apart) is caused solely by disorders in social, cultural, and psychological processes. This bland assumption in part was based on failure to consider seriously the fact that the various known organic impairments can and do regularly produce symptomatologies practically indistinguishable from the whole gamut of "functional" symptomatologies, ranging from psychosis to the transient situational reactions. It was also in part based on neglect of the existing evidence for genetic and biochemical complicity in the development of the supposedly "psychogenic" or "functional" psychoses. Since cultural anthropologists generally are consulted by, and read the works of, those psychiatrists and psychologists who are committed to the psychosocial tradition, this bias was not corrected from outside the field and stunted the development of cultural anthropological research in this important area.

In view of its importance for the theoretical orientation of students of anthropology, a brief outline is here given of a theory that attempts to relate biochemical and psychosocial processes in mental disease. Of all the psychoses, the schizophrenic syn-

6. Pitts, "The Biochemistry of Anxiety."

drome is probably the most common. It is the writer's opinion that this psychosis is precipitated and maintained by a biochemical disorder or disorders for which hereditary predisposition is common. Biochemical disorder reduces the "semantic capacity" of the individual below the level necessary for adequate cultural participation. From the microcosmic viewpoint, this critical level is the boundary between normalcy and deviancy; from the organization viewpoint, it is the degree of diversity that the individual must be able to maintain in a state of relative orderliness, acceptable to self and others. Such a semantic decrement is experienced by the victim as a condition of relative meaninglessness or, as the psychiatrist puts it, as "feelings of unreality" and "lack of affect." These experiences of desemantication may, or may not, be accompanied by other disturbing phenomena, such as hallucination and hypochondriacal sensations. From the initial desemantication flows, inevitably, a set of consequences: a deterioration of the victim's existing personality structure; the development of increasingly desperate and generally inadequate "psychotic" defenses, intended to forestall social extrusion; and, eventually, social extrusion in some form or other. This theory recognizes that cultural differences will be reflected in the symptomatic content and the prevalence of the syndrome in various populations, but it relies upon the concept of the cultural capacity of the individual to relate biochemical and psychosocial processes in the individual case.[7]

CURRENT CONCEPTIONS OF THE RELATIONS OF CULTURE AND MENTAL ILLNESS

Current conceptions of the relationship of culture to mental illness may be conveniently classified under four headings: cultural epidemiology, culture as providing the pathogenic process, culture as providing the therapeutic process, and culture itself as affected by mental disorder.

7. Cf. Wallace, "The Bio-Cultural Theory of Schizophrenia."

Cultural Epidemiology

The epidemiology of mental disease considers the distribution of mental disorders of various kinds over a number of variables, only one of which is culture; others are sex, age, migration history, social class, education, morbidity in other disease categories, nutritional level, ecological zone, and so on. Most of these other categories are, however, not independent of culture and, consequently, are definitely relevant to culturally oriented inquiries.

From the days of the earliest systematic ethnological fieldwork, up to the present time, anthropologists have been interested in the fact that the symptoms of mental disorder vary, depending on the cultural context of the victim. Sometimes the patterning of these symptoms is so unlike Western clinical portraits as to suggest that a new mental disease has been discovered. Familiar examples may be cited; amok and latah in Southeast Asia; piblokto among Eskimo, and imitative arctic hysteria among northern Siberian peoples; the windigo psychosis among northeastern Algonkian forest hunters. Even within Western society, as Marvin Opler has demonstrated, the nature of the symptoms typically exhibited by members of such ethnic groups as Irish and Italians, in New York City, is sharply different: Irish male schizophrenics tend to be quiet and withdrawn, and their Italian counterparts tend to be noisy and aggressive.[8] These differences do not, however, justify the imputation of a different disease category. Windigo psychosis, with its common pattern of somatic delusions, ideas of reference, supernatural persecution complex, and "cannibalistic panic," is a precise image of paranoid schizophrenia, as observed in Western man, except that the overt ideas of persecution or influence of Western man are apt to be oriented toward different supernatural beings or even toward other human beings (such as "the men in the Kremlin" or "the FBI"), and to emphasize sex rather than food (the cannibalistic panic being replaced by the homosexual panic). Most such "ethnic psychoses," which

8. Opler and Singer, "Contrasting Patterns of Fantasy and Mobility in Irish and Italian Schizophrenics."

reflect in their behavior the specific cultural content of the victim's society, are simply local varieties of a common disease process to which human beings are vulnerable. In this light, then, all mental disorders must be considered to reflect, in symptomatic content, the victim's past and present cultural environment.

Similarly, cultures differ somewhat in the severity of the evaluation they make of wrong acts and may choose to explain such acts in various ways ranging from simple irresponsibility to criminality to mental illness. Thus almost all cultures define some kinds and occasions of incest as wrong; but the definition of incest, as well as the degree of concern displayed, vary markedly, and it may or may not be regarded as a symptom of mental illness. Homosexuality is variously viewed, depending on the culture, as a natural expression of human sexuality, as a sin against divine law, as a crime against nature, as an amusing idiosyncrasy, or as an illness in itself. The intensity of concern about symptoms may have some relation to type of social organization and level of cultural evolution. In simple societies where kinship groupings provide the main dimensions of social structure, incest as locally defined may be regarded as particularly threatening to the welfare of the group because it may lead to fighting and to the upsetting of established dominance-and-submission relationships whose security is viewed as essential. In societies maintaining extensive male-dominated bureaucracies managing complex technologies, both nepotism and homosexuality within the organization, and sometimes even kinship and sex outside, may be regarded as extremely dangerous because they threaten to substitute kinship and sexual attachments, with their attendant potentialities for favoritism, jealousy, and quarreling, for a principle of authority and of reward for merit based on technical competence and loyalty to the group as a whole.

Culture as Pathogenic Influence

If we conclude that the major categories of mental disorder are universal types of human affliction, even though cultural differences are responsible for conspicuous local differences in the content of symptomatology, we must still ask whether cultural differences are associated with differences in the frequency of illness in the major, and universal, diagnostic classifications. Despite semantic difficulties, and notwithstanding the scattered nature of the material, two general conclusions concerning cultural epidemiology can be made: (1) culturally differentiated populations do vary measurably in the incidence (the number of persons who contract a disease during a specified period of time, usually taken as a year) of one or another of the various disease entities, a fact which suggests that, whatever the etiological factors are, in part they are culturally determined; and (2) culturally differentiated populations do vary measurably in the prevalence (the number of persons who suffer from a disease during a specified period of time) of one or another of the various disease categories. These generalizations suggest strongly that, whatever the therapeutic and chronicity factors are, their incidence and prevalence in part are culturally determined.

Epidemiological inquiries essentially are based on demographic and social survey statistics. Clinical observation, however, is the source of the data and intuitions that point to the role of culture as a pathogenic influence. Such a putative influence is considered to be direct when the very structure of human relations, and the beliefs and values commonly held in a society, are conceived to be necessarily productive of psychological conflict and anxiety in individuals who participate in the organization. The influence may be considered as indirect when the mere participation in the sociocultural organization is not, in itself, considered sufficient to elicit psychopathology.

Culture as Indirect Pathogenic Influence

Let us consider the indirect pathogenic influence first. A particularly clear example of such an influence is given by studies of the mental disorders accompanying *trypanosomiasis* ("sleeping sickness"), a general bacterial infection transmitted to man by the bite of the infected tsetse fly. This disorder is said to be "the commonest cause of mental derangement throughout large areas of West Africa,"[9] and is difficult, if not impossible, to distinguish from schizophrenia without identification of the trypanosome microorganism in the body fluids. The symptomatic picture in "tryps" is as variable as that in "true" schizophrenia, and the same types of behavioral disorder may be found in either. But, in line with the distinction described earlier, one (tryps) is an "organic" psychosis and the other (schizophrenia) is not.

The type of tryps to which most psychiatric attention has been paid is that carried by the flies *Glossina palpalis* and *Glossina tachinoides*. These species feed principally on human blood; they breed in shady places by the edges of streams and water holes. Human beings are bitten and infected when they visit these streams and water holes to wash and to collect water. The public health measures that are effective, in a given local area, are three: (1) clearing away undergrowth at the edge of water; (2) sterilizing the blood of infected persons; (3) prevention of migration of infected persons into the "cleansed" area from adjacent endemic areas. The first requires continuous public attention and compliance in brush clearing. The second requires that infected persons, or their relatives, bring cases of tryps in the early stages for chemical treatment (before the pathological sleeping and schizophrenia-like symptoms begin, and when the illness is manifested chiefly by a miscellany of somatic complaints—aches and pains, fever, headache, amenorrhea, and so on). It is difficult, however, to recognize tryps in the early stages, because its early symptoms are difficult to distinguish from both malaria and yaws, which almost everyone in the region is apt to experience at one time or another; and the later stages are similar to syphilitic paresis. The third measure requires control of immigration, which is impossible for various economic and political reasons: ". . . the Gold Coast is surrounded by endemic areas and there is a virtually uncontrollable migration of persons across its borders, which are arbitrarily defined, so that, until tryps has been eradicated from tropical Africa as a whole, epidemics and sporadic cases are bound to occur."[10] Thus we find that the incidence

9. Tooth, *Studies in Mental Illness in the Gold Coast,* p. 1.

10. *Ibid.,* p. 2.

of tryps is affected by a host of culturally bound factors: the technology of water use, the availability of labor supply for brush clearing, awareness of the value of chemical treatment, economic pressures affecting migration, the location and significance of the political boundaries, various cultural factors that affect the incidence of yaws and malaria (because their incidence determines the "visibility" of early tryps), and so on.

Tryps is not an unusual example. Other "organic" psychoses —for instance, general paresis accompanying the tertiary stage of syphilis, and the mental disorders accompanying nutritional deficiencies—with equal obviousness are related to cultural factors via the mediation of the structure of sexual, economic, religious, domestic, and political relations, and of popular beliefs and attitudes relating to the disorder in question. Still other disorders, at present regarded as psychogenic, also may be caused by biological factors, such as nutritional and infectious disease, and thus be related indirectly rather than directly to culture.

Culture as Direct Pathogenic Influence

We have defined the "direct pathogenic influence" of culture, in respect to mental disorder, as the result of conflict-and-anxiety-producing sets of cultural forms. The reader will note that we are concerned, here, with culture as determinant not of the *content* of disorder, but of its *occurrence* and that, for the sake of simplicity of exposition, we shall not labor a point already made: that the weaknesses of the microcosmic viewpoint afflict most of the several fairly specific types of hypotheses. Most of the hypotheses that have been offered to explain the function of culture as a direct pathogenic influence are based on one variety or another of psychoanalytic theory.

1. Culture Per Se as Cause of Neurosis. Freud expressed a view, common to many a humanist, that there is an unavoidable tragedy inherent in the human condition—namely, that the practical necessity of maintaining and transmitting across generations *any* sort of culture demands the partial, but grievous, frustration of human instincts, both sexual and aggressive. Such instinctual deprivation inevitably elicits from all human beings some sort of neurotic compromise, of greater or lesser degree, ranging from such minor phenomena as slips of the tongue and selective forgetting of unpleasant experiences, to the grand symptoms of clinical neurosis. This view is embedded, of course, in larger philosophical speculations about the universality of the Oedipus complex, castration anxiety, and self-destructive tendencies. Some anthropologists, a little naïvely, object that culture is a complex device for instinctual gratification rather than for deprivation. It is certainly true that human instincts are usually gratified, when they are gratified, in a cultural medium; but it is also true that human instincts are frustrated, when they are frustrated, in a cultural medium.

2. *Culture as Content of Neurosis.* Some anthropologists[11] and anthropologically inclined psychoanalysts[12] have felt that major areas of the culture pattern of any given society may be conceived as widely shared and institutionalized neurotic, or even psychotic, symptomatology, arising out of particular instinctual deprivations imposed on the members, particularly in their childhood. ("Neurosis," in this usage, implies that various mechanisms of defense are employed in the building and maintenance of the personality structure; but since all human beings use such mechanisms, all have a "neurosis" in this generic sense.) This view does not necessarily include the doctrine that culture per se invariably produces neurosis, and some of these authors even offer recipes for nonneurotic cultures based on enlightened methods of child rearing. Usually, it is the so-called projective systems—religious belief and ritual, aspects of political relations, mythology, art, and so forth, which are believed to be related to particular systems of child rearing—to which the tag "neurotic" is applied. In incautious hands, such an approach is dangerous,

11. For example, Roheim, *The Origin and Function of Culture.*
12. For example, Kardiner, *The Individual and His Society.*

for even professedly straightforward cultural or modal personality description may imply that an entire people is "sick," as when Benedict casually describes the Kwakiutl society as "megalomaniac paranoid."[13] Such characterization of whole societies or cultures as mentally ill is rarely, if ever, defensible on scientific grounds; a society of psychotics is a contradiction in terms, and the use of a diagnostic label in national character evaluation expresses merely the author's hostility toward the subjects of his description. Sometimes, of course, psychiatric terms must be used to describe mental processes that occur in both sick and healthy persons as, for instance, the terms for defense mechanisms, such as "repression," "sublimation," and so forth. When such descriptive language is used in a modal personality statement, without the use of diagnostic labels, no harm is done, unless the naïve reader wrongly infers psychopathology whenever a piece of psychiatric jargon is employed. But the use of diagnostic labels, such as "paranoid," "psychotic," and "schizophrenic," or words implying such labels, is *never* justified when referring to an entire society, except in cases where that society has suffered a major and identifiable trauma to which an illness, definable by the group itself as a pathological state, is a general response. Another risk in this mode of analysis is the overly free imputation of unconscious purpose to account for functional relationships in culture. Clinical psychoanalytic interpretation depends heavily upon the guess that describing the consequences of an act will define its motives. In culture-and-personality analysis, the entire culture of a society is regarded as the consequence of the acts of its members. The statement that some pattern of unconscious motives creates and maintains the culture is apt to invoke an animistic teleology that, however useful in the art of psychotherapy, is not justifiable in rigorous analysis. Furthermore, it requires the use of the dubious "cultural-deductive method."[14]

In recent years, anthropologists have entered more and more aggressively into studies aimed directly at social criticism, at the

13. *Patterns of Culture*, p. 205.

14. See Ch. IV, pp. 150–151.

identification and amelioration of social problems within the Western cultures, or even at facilitating a radical transformation of the social and cultural matrix (the "system") of these cultures. The more rigorous of these studies, like the Leightons' of an economically depressed area of Newfoundland, show clearly that the prevalence of various "mental" conditions can be higher in communities rated lower in level of morale, social cohesion, and the like.[15] And in general, "lower" social classes in the United States display higher incidences of the chronic psychosis schizophrenia.[16] Oscar Lewis's intimate biographies of the culture of poverty also reveal much behavior that could be construed as not merely culturally specialized but pathological.[17] But these studies demonstrate only that in a general way poverty is associated with higher risks of serious mental illness; they do not require the conclusion that the culture as a whole, with and within which the poor population survives, is sick in any psychiatrically meaningful sense.

The charge that American culture (and, for that matter, any number of other nonprimitive, bureaucratized, urban, industrial, national cultures) is psychiatrically sick is, however, explicit in the impassioned writings of the intellectuals of the New Left, who include a number of distinguished anthropologists, and others who, although not part of the New Left, share its animosity against established institutions. Jules Henry's *Culture Against Man* is perhaps the best known piece of ethnographic writing in this genre; it develops an essentially psychiatric thesis, tracing the unhappy consequences of the Americans' family life and educational practices for their psychological development. Their materialistic fun culture, devoid of authentic human relationships, leads in his analysis to a paranoid world view that is responsible for a delusional fear of communism and a reliance on militarism both for economic and emotional stability. The similarly unfavorable diagnoses of American character and institutions generated by some of the branches of the New Left move-

15. Hughes, *et al., People of Cove and Woodlot.*
16. Hollingshead and Redlich, *Social Class and Mental Illness.*
17. *The Children of Sanchez.*

ment depend in large part upon an intellectual *rapprochement* between a Marxian theory of alienation and one or another interpretation of psychoanalysis. The analyst Wilhelm Reich, in his earlier writings, developed this line of thought[18] and Herbert Marcuse, Norman Brown, and Paul Goodman have given it a somewhat more generalized form and a popular currency. The thesis, in essence, is that with or without psychiatric symptomatology in the narrow sense, virtually all members of industrial bureaucratic societies (including both the Soviet Union and the United States) suffer from a profound deficiency in ability to interact meaningfully with other human beings, both sexually and aggressively. Instead, they preoccupy themselves with superficial materialistic values and with destructive hatreds and suspicions; indifferent to the feelings of others as they are to their own real needs, they devote the vast resources of civilization to racism, to war, and to economic exploitation, glossing over these perverse motives with a morality that is hypocritical when it is not manifestly evil.

Such gross characterizations are no better than the old vulgarities of racist stereotypes that explain the supposed laziness and violence of the Negro in terms of an inability to defer impulse gratification and invoke the principle of collective guilt to condemn all Jews as Christ-killers. The utility of such "psychiatric" diatribe in political propaganda is obvious enough; and it is certainly the function of the professional intellectual to generate the rationale for political action (a role sharply contrasting with that of the scholar and scientist). To couple political criticism with psychiatric diagnosis is, furthermore, particularly congenial in the United States, where it is conventional in the liberal community to interpret social evils as medical or educational emergencies, a proceeding that immediately invokes the administrative powers and monies of the Department of Health, Education, and Welfare, and that also conveniently permits the critic to avoid the awkwardness of overt expression of invidious "moral" judgments. But the procedure is corrupting to science

18. *Selected Writings: An Introduction to Orgonomy.*

and scholarship, for it makes the criterion political expediency rather than truth, and permits the intellectual to conceal his moral judgments behind a façade of psychiatric jargon. Within institutional psychiatry, as Thomas Szasz[19] has pointed out repeatedly, there is a tendency to say "sick" when what is meant is "bad"; and this tendency inevitably operates to the disadvantage of those least valued by the middleclass medical establishment. The same process works, alas, in the broader field, where ritualistically diagnosing "white middleclass values" as a kind of emotional plague, instead of with honest partisanship condemning them as evil, makes the establishment of the left as blind as the system it imagines it is opposing. In such literature, genocide is a recognized crime against humanity but the indiscriminate annihilation of whole political parties, social classes, occupational groups, and even nations has no label and can be conceived as justified by the principle of collective guilt; physical violence by police and the military can be defined as evidence of the sickness of the society, while similar violence by the revolutionary can be justified by the recitation of noble aims; established bureaucracies are readily diagnosed as soul-destroying even while plans proceed for new bureaucracies equally impersonal and cold.

3. Culturally Enjoined "Disorders." In many societies, religious ritual and other ceremonial protocol require individuals of certain statuses to undergo types of experiences that, in contemporary Western psychiatric tradition, often are regarded as symptomatic of mental disorder. The class of pseudo-illnesses, culturally enjoined, include such diverse phenomena as ritual dissociation (trance and possession), drug or alcohol intoxication (as, for example, in peyote), self-mortification leading to hallucination (as in the vision quest), ceremonial torture and cannibalism, and ecstatic conversion experiences. The physiological and psychological mechanisms immediately involved in the "abnormal" state in such pseudo-disorders may well be the same as those involved in symptom production in Western mental

19. "The Myth of Mental Illness."

patients. Nevertheless, the consequences of such experiences are vastly different, since a "ceremonial" neurosis or psychosis, unlike the "true" disease, is voluntarily initiated, is usually reversible, and leads neither the subject nor his associates to classify him as "abnormal" and unworthy of complete social participation. Such disorders are comparable, in our own society, to the generation of dissociated states in healthy individuals by hypnosis, or the production of hallucinations by administration of lysergic acid or sensory deprivation, or the elicitation of disorganized speech in guests at a cocktail party. The subjects of such manipulations are not, as persons, classified as mentally ill, despite the fact that, under special circumstances, they have temporarily entered states that characterize chronically some mentally ill persons.

4. Cultural Definitions of the Meaning of "Symptoms." It may be taken as axiomatic that it is the concern of all human beings to maintain an image of themselves as persons competent to attain their essential goals, including maintenance of group membership. Such a self-image in part is dependent on the individual's evaluation of his own behavior, and in part on the evaluation of this behavior that is communicated to him by others. Shame —awareness of incompetence in any sphere, whether growing from self-observation or information from others—may arouse so much anxiety as to inhibit further the person's competence. In our own society, serious mental disease is conceived and recognized by law as a generalized incompetence and (not unexpectedly) the imputation of mental disease to an individual is a commonly used metaphor of insult. It is also popularly believed to be possible to "gaslight" a perfectly healthy person into psychosis by interpreting his own behavior to him as symptomatic of serious mental illness. While "gaslighting" itself may be a mythical crime, there is no question that any social attitude which interprets a given behavior or experience as symptomatic of a generalized incompetence is a powerful creator of shame, and thus of anxiety, in those who experience or behave in the "symptomatic" way. One may expect, then, that whenever a culture defines a given item of behavior as a symptom of general incompetence, the individual so behaving will suffer from shame, which elicits anxiety. This anxiety will further tend to decrease his competence, thus precipitating a reciprocal interaction between "incompetent" behaviors and anxiety. In one society, foci of anxiety over competence may center about sexual potency or attractiveness; in another, on courage in war; in still another, on intelligence, and so on. Furthermore, those behaviors, such as hallucination, which Western societies generally interpret as symptoms of that generalized incompetence legally known as "insanity," may be less heavily stressed, or not stressed at all, in others.[20] To the extent that a society stresses failure in a given area of behavior as symptomatic of a more generalized inadequacy, and to the extent that that behavior requires minimal anxiety for successful performance, failure in such behavior probably will be repeated and will increasingly extend over other behaviors. Such reciprocal processes of shame, anxiety, and incompetent behavior are recognized today in our own mental hospitals, where patients are found to respond dramatically to almost any treatment that is carried on in an atmosphere of confidence in the ability of the patient to regain competence. Mental health associations also have worked assiduously to change popular concepts of mental disease, from the stereotype of a shameful and incurable incompetency to a respectable and curable "disease like any other." Similar contrasts in social evaluation of symptomatology, and in the amount of anxiety and deterioration consequent upon them, are worthy of study in other societies.

5. Culture Conflict and Culture Change. Anthropologists frequently have made note of the fact that primitive groups, who have been forced into situations of culture conflict and of partial, unorganized acculturation, seem prone to a higher frequency of the milder neurotic and personality trait disorders. Chronic anxiety and tension, psychosomatic complaints, alcoholism, narcotic addiction, delinquency and crime, witch fear, regressive or stunted personality development: such disorders apparently pro-

20. Cf. Wallace, "Cultural Determinants of Response to Hallucinatory Experience."

liferate under the conditions produced by culture conflict and partial acculturation. Sociologists have reported that, among migrant groups,[21] not only the incidence of such milder disorders, but also the incidence of psychosis, is measurably higher. We have discussed some of these phenomena already. Although, as usual, statistical confirmation or disconfirmation of such a hypothesis is difficult to achieve, the position that culture change is associated with mental disorder has a certain obvious plausibility. But it must not be imagined that mere change in itself is so powerful a determinant that it will elicit sharply increasing incidences of psychosis. Herbert Goldhamer and Andrew Marshall,[22] for instance, studied the trends in incidence of institutionalized psychosis in America over a hundred-year period, and found that the rate of psychosis has remained constant, despite the accelerating rate of cultural change. There is, however, one sociocultural characteristic that seems to be shared by all groups that display a markedly high general incidence of mental disorders and that is often associated with culture conflict and culture change: relatively low social status in the larger society of which the group is a part. Semiprimitive peoples, living on the shabby fringes of Western civilization, migrants in new lands, occupants of slum areas, and lower racial, ethnic, and socioeconomic classes, generally, are characterized by high incidences of both neurosis and psychosis. This suggests that a combination of physical disadvantages, such as inadequate diet, and of the reciprocal process, discussed in the preceding section, of social incompetence, shame, and anxiety, may be major factors influencing the incidence of both the psychotic and the neurotic diseases.

6. *Stresses Produced by Role and Value Conflicts Implicit in Particular Sociocultural Systems.*   Many social scientists have sought to combine epidemiological data and processual theory by the use of formulations that interpret each culture as presenting to the individual a unique spectrum of highly probable stress

21. Malzberg and Lee, *Migration and Mental Disease.*
22. *Psychosis and Civilization.*

situations; these are determined by role or value conflicts implicit in the culture. From this standpoint, a particular sociocultural system is conceived as a congeries of roles and values, with each individual during the course of his life assuming several of these roles, some of them successively and some simultaneously, and likewise addressing himself to a number of different values, depending on the occasion. Such culture conflict can be of two kinds: role incompatibility, and value incompatibility. Whenever an individual is put in a position where two incompatible roles must be played simultaneously, he experiences stress, since he cannot succeed in both. And whenever an individual, playing one role, is faced with a situation where successful performance with respect to one value entails a high likelihood of personal loss (for example, death) with respect to another, he experiences stress. Role incompatibility conflicts can be further divided into two subtypes: conflicts centering about role replacement, and conflicts centering about simultaneous roles. Role replacement means the dropping of one role for another; such events in the life cycle as birth, weaning, puberty, marriage, birth of child, retirement, and so on, frequently celebrated by *rites de passage*, are common examples of role replacement. Since role replacement entails loss of previously enjoyed rewards, the individual is apt to suffer the double stress of deprivation of past rewards and of fear of punishment if such rewards are sought again via the discontinued role. Role simultaneity conflicts are less easily noticeable, presumably because they are consciously pruned away in most societies as productive of both individual and social disturbance; at least they are avoided by scheduling role performance so as to prevent conflict, and by defining roles hierarchically, according to the relative importance of their goals. Such conflicts do, however, frequently emerge in unanticipated situations where one or another event has interfered with the normal scheduling of role behavior. This is illustrated in the role conflicts experienced by civil defense personnel during natural and man-made disasters. Another well-known category of role simultaneity conflict is provided by the phenomenon of "conflict of interest" in political organization. Value incompatibility conflicts are, again, not usually part of the ideal design of a culture, and societies attempt to forestall them by elaborate training. The classic—and an almost universal—example of value incompatibility conflicts is associated with the role of the warrior or soldier who must constantly make the choice between, in effect, being a live coward and a dead hero. Role and value conflict situations seem peculiarly apt to elicit neurotic responses; for example, in "combat fatigue" or shell shock"; in fugues, amnesias, and a variety of phobic and neurotic compromise symptoms, in which one response to the situation is repressed, often only to be allowed to return in disguised or distorted form. It may be questioned, however, whether such situations, culturally determined insofar as the content of the conflict is determined, are to be regarded as responsible for more than the superficial content of psychoses. Psychosis, in this context, is perhaps better regarded as the result of a cognitive inability to respond neurotically to a situation in which a neurotic response is the only way the "normal" individual has of avoiding a display of gross incompetence, with its consequent and crippling shame and anxiety cycle.

7. *The Communication Theory.* The external analogue of the internalized conflict theory has received emphasis recently in the work of psychiatrists, psychologists, and social scientists who seek to find in the parent-child, and especially the mother-child, relationship the etiology of schizophrenia. According to this view, the nuclear process in schizophrenia is withdrawal, both physical and psychological, from a world that has bombarded the victim with inconsistent communications—communications that demanded that he perform mutually incompatible roles or devote himself to antithetical values. The "schizophreno-genic" mother, for example, is supposedly prone to convey the two contradictory messages, by means of kinesic as well as linguistic communication, that her child simultaneously is loved and is rejected. The child may also be explicitly ordered to play the role of "love mommy," but be subtly rejected as unworthy or offensive when he does try to play this role. This viewpoint has received a variety of theoretical formulations, from Melanie Klein's and others' postulation of antithetical "good mother-bad

mother" images,[23] to attempts to construe such ambivalent mother-child relationships as a confusion of different logical types (the "double bind" hypothesis).[24] These and other narrow attempts to construct formal models of schizophrenogenic family structures and communication systems are, however, based on a somewhat sandy logical foundation. Most people, in most cultures, have to put up with a great deal of ambivalence and inconsistency in their social relationships; the "normal" response to extreme degrees of message inconsistency is neurotic rather than psychotic. Inability to cope with such poorly organized information suggests an inadequate capacity for organizing the data of experience.

More generally, however, one can see in these models and in much current experimental psychotherapy an effort to get away from the traditional psychiatric preoccupation with internal states and processes, both in theory and treatment, and out into the world of observable transactions (that is, communications). Milieu therapy within the hospital, and halfway houses in the community, and mental health clinics attempt to provide more nearly normal experience for the patient suffering from the social breakdown syndrome. Operant conditioning principles are being applied to a wide range of psychiatric patients on the tacit assumption that symptoms can be unlearned and more desirable behavior learned by direct rewards and punishments. This approach tends toward the assumption that personality is not a layered structure with overt acts appearing as surface expression of a deeper grammar of motives but is simply a concatenation of specific learned responses to specific stimuli. And there are a variety of group techniques, ranging from traditional group therapies to less controlled procedures variously labeled encounter groups, T-groups, sensitivity training, and so forth, which are being tried with patients as well as nonpatients on the theory that the essence of illness is restricted communication. By increasing the person's sensitivity and awareness of self and others, and by encouraging him to enter into honest feeling and communica-

23. Cf. Boszormenyi-Nagy and Framo (eds.), *Intensive Family Therapy.*
24. Bateson, *et al.*, "Toward a Theory of Schizophrenia."

tion, even if that is sometimes painful, it is felt that health can be enhanced. In all such approaches, the focus is on the situation here and now rather than on the past, on communicational transactions between people rather than on internal processes, and the therapist sees the psychiatric problem as located in a group rather than being housed inside a skull. Although there is something of a cultish enthusiasm associated with some of these enterprises, they add an awareness of current social and cultural reality to a field of practice that has at times tended tacitly to regard its subjects as denizens solely of the office, hospital, and laboratory. The unresolved question is whether or not such beneficial results as these therapies accomplish are narrowly bound to the relief of specific symptoms and to the specific group or situation in which the treatment occurred. If the successfully treated patient can carry a new, generalized pattern of motivation that will help him and others in areas of behavior and in social situations apart from the original therapy, then the same goal has been achieved for which the classic psychotherapies, both religious and medical, have always aimed.

8. "The Madness of Crowds."   We have already taken note of the phenomenon of culturally patterned induction of mental states that in Western psychiatric tradition are regarded as pathological. A related phenomenon is the affliction of groups of closely intercommunicating people with beliefs leading to culturally *in*appropriate acts. Examples of such events are mass panics, group delusions and illusions, mass hysterias, and mob violence. Such events depend, apparently, on two factors: first, the presence of a situational context, specifically appropriate for the particular outbreak (as, for example, a locally unavoidable threat and a limited escape route, for flight panic); second, the dissociating effect on the individual of repetitive mass suggestion in a crowd, each of whose members is suggesting to several others (as, for example, in the "chain-reaction" of mounting hostility and carelessness for legal norms in a lynch mob). Such phenomena are, in a sense, acultural: the behavior of a "mad" crowd generally violates individually held, but culturally acceptable, norms. Nevertheless, the culture may indirectly determine their incidence by providing more or fewer occasions presuited to their occurrence. Fire panics in crowded theaters and nightclubs depend, for instance, on a host of cultural factors involved in the technology of entertainment, on architecture, and fire safety regulations. But a more direct determination is provided by the character of the group itself, as it is conceived by its individual members. Disciplined, organized groups with high morale, that is with the confidence of each individual in the orderliness and mutual loyalty of his fellows, do not readily experience panic or other hysterical mass dissociations, even under extreme provocation.

Culture as Direct and Indirect Therapeutic and Preventive Influence

In this section we shall be concerned with the therapeutic and preventive measures specifically intended by members of a community to prevent or improve mental states conceived as undesirable by the victim or his community. These mental states need not be defined by the community as "illnesses" in anything like the Western psychiatric sense, although one or another of them may be in a given society; often, in primitive societies, psychiatric illnesses are interpreted according to a religious or magical theory, but the undesirability of leaving the sufferer or the community in an uncomfortable condition is not questioned. Certainly some and probably all human cultures include, as part of their traditional lore, a "theory of mind" that explains such phenomena as motivation, memory, emotion, dreams and visions, and various states that are conceived as abnormal, or at least undesirable, if continued too long. Therapeutic measures, however originated, in general would seem to be rationalized by such native theories. The Iroquois Indians, for example, used a clearly articulated type of "psychoanalytic" theory to account for dreams, obsessions, various obviously pathological behaviors, and even certain physical complaints.[25] The therapeutic devices employed in the treatment of mental disorders in any society are cultural

25. Wallace, "Dreams and the Wishes of the Soul."

artifacts like any others; thus these devices are functions not merely of the characteristics of the disease, but also of the structure and functioning of the rest of the culture.

1. Cathartic Strategies.   The efficacy of occasional or periodic release of suppressed impulses in reducing anxiety and tension is widely recognized. Most cultures provide for some sort of "recreative" catharsis on a periodic basis, encouraging the individual at these stated occasions to act out wishes whose realization would be undesirable on other occasions. Saturnalian cathartic festivals, in which large numbers of persons participate in sexual relations disallowed at other times, tend to attract attention as "orgies." But catharsis is not necessarily orgiastic, it is not necessarily sexual, and it may be either crudely direct or subtly sublimated. Thus a very wide range of behaviors of a recreational character serves the function of socially encouraged catharsis: the arts (music, drama, painting, and so on), games and sports, exercise, hobbies, "sightseeing," feasts and parties, intoxication, mourning rituals, ceremonial torture, and so on. Seasonal variations in the pace of economic activity, diurnal cycles of fatigue and vigor, rest days and vacations, and other time-scheduling frames of reference, are employed to permit cathartic acting out of wishes denied fulfillment in the work-a-day world. Such strategies may be rationalized in various ways, of course, depending on the local theory of mind: as means of limiting fatigue, as devices for gratifying the gods, as methods of satisfying the needs of the body, and so on. And their institutional locus may be correspondingly religious, or domestic, or medical, or whatever. The important common feature is the explicit provision of occasion for gratifying motives that cannot be gratified in the course of playing routine economic, military, domestic, or other socially necessary roles.

2. The Institutional Binding of Anxiety in Compromise Formations.   In the preceding section on cultural pathogenesis, it was noted that the so-called projective systems—particularly religious ritual, myth, and belief—by some were considered as the quasi-pathological products of culturally stereotyped childhood traumata. From a standpoint of "teleological functionalism,"[26] such projective systems may be regarded as devices that successfully bind the anxieties, originally produced by the traumata, to a restricted and socially acceptable sphere of expression by providing a patterned quasi-neurotic symptomatology. Thus whatever the observer's evaluation of the projective system's overall value in the general functioning of the society, it may be considered at least to have the function of preventing crippling anxiety and its expression in symptoms that might seriously interfere with the necessary performance of various economic, sexual, political, and other roles. It might be expected that interference with the routine performance of the projective systems—in culture-change situations, for example—would be productive of severe anxiety, and either would lead to outbreaks of neurotic symptomatology of kinds destructive of the social order or to the rapid development of new projective systems by religious cults. Such a relationship has been cited as one of the factors responsible for the dual phenomena of delinquency (alcoholism, violence, sexual promiscuity, and so on), and of the innumerable separatist churches among detribalized Africans who are unable to continue the practice of native ritual in labor compounds and urban ghettos.

Many primitive societies provide an additional resource for the individual who, for one reason or another, does not find relief in the available projective system. This is the process of "becoming a shaman," which is but one example of the process of mazeway resynthesis. The latter is a rather sudden reorganization—often but not necessarily via the medium of hallucinatory experience—of values, attitudes, and beliefs that "make sense" of a hitherto confusing and anxiety-provoking world. We discussed mazeway resynthesis earlier, as a source of cultural innovation, and pointed out then that its function for the individual was psychotherapeutic. The therapeutic value of such an experience, however, depends both on the resources of the individual and on the support his effort is given by the community. The culture enters into the process here, rather evidently, by impos-

---

26. Spiro, "Ghosts, Ifaluk, and Teleological Functionalism."

ing certain evaluations on the content of such experiences, as well as on their form. Some sociocultural systems embrace a wide range of mazeway resyntheses, sometimes by giving them the status of *rites de passage* (as in the vision quest), sometimes by effectively molding them (as in the process of becoming a shaman), and sometimes by holding open, as it were, a status for the religious innovator (as in the case of the Iroquois who encouraged private medicine societies based on the vision) or prophet (as in ancient Judaism). Other systems, like that of the American urban middleclass today, generally take a dim view of any sort of fervent personality transformation, especially if it is accompanied by hallucination. Thus the existing cultural milieu can act as a support or a hindrance to the mazeway resynthesis process by facilitating or suppressing the institutionalization of behavior patterns and beliefs conceived in the course of such experiences.

3. Control Strategies.   There is reason to suspect that relatively secure and confident social groups favor cathartic strategies in psychotherapy, but that insecure and disillusioned groups favor control strategies when dealing with mental disorders.[27] The reason for a tendency of disadvantaged groups to favor control therapy presumably would lie in the fact that such groups already are faced with difficulties in practical adaptation and in maintenance of orderly social life. Under such circumstances, granting persons who already contribute to social disorganization the privilege of adding additional unpredictabilities in the course of cathartic acting out in therapy simply places added burdens on the group; furthermore, the sick person in such groups may have a greater need to perceive a better organized world. Thus the condition of the society should favor the use of measures designed to press the deviant to exercise his "will" to control his disorders of behavior. Techniques for accomplishing this generally depend upon what we have earlier referred to as "hysterical conversion." Sermons depicting the terrors of hellfire, mass rallies,

27. Wallace, "The Institutionalization of Cathartic and Control Strategies in Iroquois Religious Psychotherapy."

compulsory confession and penance, "thought reform" induced by a combination of threat, confession, and indoctrination, continuous moral exhortation and encouragement, instruction conveyed symbolically in *rites de passage*—devices such as these are more effective in inducing marked "improvement" in behavior in demoralized populations than is mere threat of punishment for delinquency. Nor should it be supposed that such measures, crude though they may seem to psychiatrically sophisticated workers, are of merely superficial value. Therapeutic changes, so induced, may be remarkably stable (as in the case of the control of drunkenness among the Iroquois who joined Handsome Lake's movement). It has been argued theoretically that "superego reinforcement" is more effective than many cathartically oriented psychiatrists have recognized. In the military services, the newer "combat psychiatry," which combines brief (a day or two) periods of rest and verbal catharsis with reinforcement by suggestion of the victim's sense of responsibility, has been found to be much more successful in rehabilitating psychiatric casualties than conventional psychotherapy and psychoanalysis. A similar kind of direct therapy designed to enhance the sense of worth and awareness of reality by the use of tranquilizing drugs and open admonition is successful in getting some chronic mental patients out of state hospitals.

4. Hospital Studies. A growing number of anthropologists have taken part with sociologists and social psychologists in the investigation of various aspects of the cultural traditions and social structures of mental hospitals in England and America, with the ultimate view of discovering how the hospital milieu functions to promote or retard therapeutic progress. Some evidence now exists to suggest that the hospital's functioning, apart from the application of specific treatments (such as psychotherapy, electroshock, or drugs), can have a considerable effect on patient progress. Unhappily, such evidence is not very "hard": that is, it is rarely possible to prove that a given observed sociocultural feature of a hospital or rehabilitation unit is, to any ascertainable degree, associated with a definite mental status in patients of a definable type.[28] For instance, Henry points out that the system of "multiple subordination," characteristic of hospital social structure, maintains various chronic stresses on the nursing staff.[29] But it is not easy to show that multiple subordination is responsible for a significantly higher or lower rate of patient progress, other things being equal, in comparison with any other hypothesized system of hospital management. Furthermore, evaluation of therapy is a difficult task for the technically untrained observer. Indeed, in view of the uncertainty of the state of knowledge about the kinds of treatment processes that are "good" and "bad" for patients anyway, and in view of the multiplicity of influences to which every patient is subjected, little more can be expected at present than the somewhat random collection of data and suggestions. These are made in the hope of coming across factors which can be shown to have a major impact on particular types of patients under definable circumstances.

The Impact of Mental Illness on Culture

Up to this point we have been considering primarily the ways in which culturally standardized measures operate to cause, treat, or prevent mental disorder. Now we shall briefly examine the reciprocal effect: the ways in which mental disorder, or the fear of mental disorder, determine the nature and manner of functioning of the culture.

The fulcrum of such a causal relation is the "cost" of illness. Such costs may or may not be correctly perceived, or be consciously perceived at all, by the members of the society. Nevertheless, they are present, as interferences with the operation of institutions and, thus, as barriers between the group and the achievement of the values toward which its members strive. Some such costs are irremediable: mental illness simply functions in the societal calculus as a kind of internal waste factor. Such

28. Cf. Wallace and Rashkis, "The Relation Between Staff Consensus and Patient Disturbance on Mental Hospital Wards."

29. "The Formal Social Structure of a Psychiatric Hospital."

wastage is, in our own society, rationally calculated in terms of dollars and cents spent for medical care and of man hours lost in the labor market. It has been estimated that mental illness in the United States costs about $3,000,000,000 per year.[30] Such indices only approximately represent other, less readily countable, costs, levied on society via the contribution of mental illness to crime, delinquency, accident, family disorganization, and relative inefficiency in innumerable tasks.

Costs of mental illness are observable in nonindustrial societies. Tooth, evaluating the "sociological" impact of *Trypanosomiasis* in West Africa, makes the following trenchant commentary:

In endemic districts the frequency of the disease may have a profound influence on the lives of the population; the effects may be clearly seen by correlating the vital statistics and the movements of the population with the incidence of infection. But the disorganizing effects on smaller units of the community are not so generally appreciated. Apart from the reduction of efficiency and reproductive capacity due to the physical factors, psychological changes have their repercussions in the home, the schools and the Courts. In social organisation where divorce is relatively easy, the change of character of one of the partners of a marriage frequently leads to the break-up of the home or, at least, to the formation of a most unfavourable atmosphere for the upbringing of the children. Misbehavior and backwardness in school, unless it is recognized as a symptom of illness, can not only cause unhappiness to the children themselves but is also a waste of valuable time and public money; the demand for education is so great that the failure of a pupil to complete the course is a serious matter. There is little doubt that Tryps. is a not uncommon cause of delinquency in children and crime in adults; the police and administrative authorities are aware of this but, in the absence of any gross pathological changes, it may be very difficult for a medical officer unfamiliar with the clinical variations, to express a convincing opinion that disease is the cause of the misconduct. Another not inconsiderable social factor is the existence of advanced and incurable Tryps. dements living as beggars in the

30. Fein, *Economics of Mental Illness.*

towns and taking up space in mental institutions which could be better used for the treatment of recoverable causes of mental illness.[31]

There is no reason to suppose that similar observations could not be made about the consequences of any prevalent mental disorder in any society, primitive or civilized. One also may draw attention to the fact that mental disorders, when they exist in persons who, for one reason or another, occupy strategic decision-making positions in the political structure, may bring about trains of consequences so catastrophic as to magnify the costs of illness to a level that threatens the survival of whole societies.

We have already spoken of the measures that societies take to treat or prevent mental disorder. When such measures fail, and the disorder is too costly to be tolerated, all societies have recourse to a more primitive device: the extrusion of the mentally sick person from the community in order to protect the community. This may, of course, be accomplished by killing him, after defining him as an enemy or criminal; but, more commonly, the victim is forcibly restrained from social participation while he is maintained alive. In our own society, when a person is declared to be legally insane (that is, a potential danger to himself and/or others), he is incarcerated in a mental hospital where he may, or may not, be given treatment. In the absence of hospitals, the socially disruptive person is physically restrained by any convenient device: by being chained to a heavy log; by being confined in a cage; by being tied with ropes, and so on. Such restraint is removed when the sick person ceases to exhibit his threatening symptoms.

The more subtle "cost," however, of mental illness, probably resides in the gradual warping of cultures as they undergo changes whose function (not necessarily intention) is to minimize socially disruptive symptomatology (such as physical aggression, suicide, incest, and so on). Such warping is difficult to recognize and evaluate (since it invokes the problem of the cultural relativity of conceptions of what a "good" culture is).

31. *Studies in Mental Illness in the Gold Coast,* pp. 1–2.

To the aggressively intellectual and materialistic scientist, religious customs that function to minimize mental disorders by institutionalizing them in innocuous "symptoms" appear to be too high a price to pay. To the more humanistic, and less ethnocentric, scientist, this warping hardly seems to be as high a price as such heroic measures as the compulsory sterilization of "defectives" recommended by genetically minded demagogues, or the assumption of responsibility for mental health by social control and education agencies. Whatever the optimum strategy for minimizing the cost of mental illness may be for any particular society, however, the problem is a universal one and a solution is devised by every culture.

CONCLUSION

The foregoing pages have critically reviewed a number of concepts and theories that have been important in the development of the anthropological subdiscipline of culture-and-personality. It has been argued here that the true function of the culture-and-personality approach in anthropology lies not in its ability to provide such descriptions of the psychological correlates of culture—"ethos," "modal personality," "values," "world view," and so on—as will make a kind of humanistic frosting on the scientific cake. Rather, it is suggested that culture-and-personality recognizes that culture is an open system and that without culture-and-personality to connect it to the rest of science, culturology can only blunder into one of those sterile wastelands where all closed-system theories eventually end their days. Culture-and-personality takes the documented facts of cultural evolution, culture change, and cultural diversity as the phenomena to be explained; but in explanation it is—as all scientific explanations must be—unashamedly reductionistic. It seeks to describe in individuals the classes of micro-phenomena that are the parameters of the classes of macro-phenomena, which the pure culturologist describes for groups. In so doing, its traditional concentration on psychoanalytically based theory is being increasingly combined with attention to biological and social variables. For "human nature" is far from being a constant parameter of cultural events; indeed, the biological mechanism upon which culture depends is exquisitely variable in response to genetic and ecological processes that, in part, are radically independent of culture per se. And the culture-and-personality viewpoint is also being broadened to encompass more than the study of affect and motivation and their determinants; greater importance is being given to cognitive, even "rational," processes (which are, incidentally, also receiving increasing attention from contemporary psychology).

REFERENCES

Aberle, David F., Cohen, A., David, A., Levy, M., and Sutton, F. "The Functional Prerequisites of a Society," *Ethics,* 60 (1950), 100–111.

Alland, Alexander, Jr. "Medical Anthropology and the Study of Biological and Cultural Adaptation," *American Anthropologist,* 68 (1966), 40–56.

American Psychiatric Association. *Diagnostic and Statistical Manual: Mental Disorders,* Washington: 1952, 1968.

Ames, Michael M. "Reaction to Stress: A Comparative Study of Nativism," *Davidson Journal of Anthropology,* 3 (1957), 17–30.

Angel, J. Lawrence. "Physical and Psychological Factors in Culture Growth," in Anthony F. C. Wallace (ed.). *Selected Papers of the Fifth International Congress of Anthropological and Ethnological Sciences.* Philadelphia: University of Pennsylvania Press, 1960.

Ardrey, Robert. *African Genesis.* New York: Delta Books, 1961.

_____. *The Territorial Imperative.* New York: Athenaeum, 1966.

Barnett, H. G. *Innovation: The Basis of Cultural Change.* New York: McGraw-Hill, 1953.

Barnouw, Victor. *Culture and Personality.* Homewood, Ill.: Dorsey Press, 1963.

Bateson, Gregory, Don D. Jackson, Jay Haley, and John Weakland. "Toward a Theory of Schizophrenia," *Behavioral Science,* 1 (1956), 251–264.

Beaglehole, Ernest. "Cultural Complexity and Psychological Problems," in Patrick Mullahy (ed.). *A Study of Interpersonal Relations.* New York: Hermitage House, 1949.

Bellak, Leopold. *Schizophrenia: A Review of the Syndrome.* New York: Logos Press, 1958.

Belo, Jane. "The Balinese Temper," *Character and Personality,* 4 (1935), 120–146.

Benedict, Paul K., and Irving Jacks. "Mental Illness in Primitive Societies," *Psychiatry,* 17 (1954), 377–389.

247

Benedict, Ruth. *Patterns of Culture*. Boston: Houghton Mifflin, 1934.

————. "Continuities and Discontinuities in Cultural Conditioning," *Psychiatry*, 1 (1938), 161–167.

Berlin, Brent, and Paul Kay. "Universality and Evolution of Basic Color Terms." Berkeley: Laboratory for Language-Behavior Research, Working Paper No. 1, n.d.

Bidney, David. *Theoretical Anthropology*. New York: Columbia University Press, 1953.

Birdwhistell, Raymond N. "Body Motion Research and Interviewing," *Human Organization*, 11 (1952), 37–38.

Boszormenyi-Nagy, Ivan, and James L. Framo (eds.). *Intensive Family Therapy*. New York: Harper & Row, 1965.

Boulding, Kenneth E. *The Image*. Ann Arbor: University of Michigan Press, 1956.

Bruner, Edward M. "Cultural Transmission and Cultural Change," *Southwestern Journal of Anthropology*, 12 (1956), 191–199. (a)

————. "Primary Group Experience and the Processes of Acculturation," *American Anthropologist*, 58 (1956), 605–623. (b)

Bruner, Jerome, J. J. Goodnow, and G. A. Austin. *A Study of Thinking*. New York: Wiley, 1956.

Burridge, Kenelm. *Mambu: A Melanesian Millenium*. New York: Humanities Press, 1960.

Bury, J. B. *The Idea of Progress*. London: Macmillan, 1921.

Bush, Robert R. "An Algebraic Treatment of Rules of Marriage and Descent," in Harrison C. White. *An Anatomy of Kinship*. Englewood Cliffs, N. J.: Prentice-Hall, 1963, 159–172.

Cassirer, Ernst. *Language and Myth*. New York: Dover, 1946.

Chomsky, Noam. Review of *Verbal Behavior* by B. F. Skinner, *Language*, 35 (1959), 26–58.

————. *Syntactic Structures*. S-Gravenhage: Mouton, 1963.

————. *Language and Mind*. New York: Harcourt, Brace & World, 1968.

Colby, B. N. "Ethnographic Semantics: A Preliminary Survey," *Current Anthropology*, 7 (1966), 3–32.

Conant, James B. *On Understanding Science*. New York: New American Library, 1951.

Coon, Carleton S. *A Reader in General Anthropology*. New York: Holt, Rinehart and Winston, 1948.

_____. "Human Races in Relation to Environment and Culture with Special Reference to the Influence of Culture upon Genetic Changes in the Human Population," in *Origin and Evolution of Man*. Cold Spring Harbor, N. Y.: Symposia on Quantitative Biology, Vol. 15, 1950.

Count, Earl W. "The Biological Basis of Human Sociality," *American Anthropologist*, 60 (1958), 1049–1085.

Darwin, Charles. *The Descent of Man and Selection in Relation to Sex*. 2nd ed. New York and London: D. Appleton and Co., 1924.

Devereux, George. "Normal and Abnormal: The Key Problem of Psychiatric Anthropology," in *Some Uses of Anthropology, Theoretical and Applied*. Washington: Anthropological Society of Washington, 1956.

DeVore, Irven (ed.). *Primate Behavior: Field Studies of Monkeys and Apes*. New York: Holt, Rinehart and Winston, 1965.

De Vos, George. "Achievement and Innovation in Culture and Personality," in Norbeck, 1968, pp. 348–370.

Dobzhansky, Theodosius. *Evolution, Genetics, and Man*. New York: Wiley, 1955.

Dobzhansky, Theodosius, and Gordon Allen. "Does Natural Selection Continue to Operate in Modern Mankind?" *American Anthropologist*, 58 (1956), 591–604.

DuBois, Cora. *The People of Alor*. Minneapolis: University of Minnesota Press, 1944.

Durkheim, Emile. *The Elementary Forms of the Religious Life*. London: Allen & Unwin, n.d.

Eaton, J. W., and R. J. Weil. *Culture and Mental Disorders*. Glencoe, Ill.: Fress Press, 1955.

Edinger, Tilly. *Evolution of the Horse Brain*. New York: Geological Society of America, Memoir 25, 1948.

Eiseley, Loren C. *Darwin's Century: Evolution and the Men Who Discovered It*. New York: Doubleday, 1958.

Ekman, P., E. R. Sorenson, and W. V. Friesen. "Pan Cultural Elements in Facial Displays of Emotion," *Science*, 164 (1969), 86–88.

Endleman, Robert (ed.). *Personality and Social Life*. New York: Random House, 1967.

Etkin, William. "Social Behavior and the Evolution of Man's Mental Faculties," *American Naturalist*, 88 (1954), 129–142.

Fein, Rashi. *Economics of Mental Illness*. New York: Basic Books, 1958.

Festinger, Leon. *A Theory of Cognitive Dissonance*. Evanston, Ill.: Row, Peterson, 1957.

Fischer, J. L. "Art Styles as Cultural Cognitive Maps," *American Anthropologist*, 63 (1961), 79–93.

Fogelson, Raymond. "Psychological Theories of Windigo 'Psychosis' and a Preliminary Application of a Models Approach," in Melford E. Spiro (ed.). *Context and Meaning in Cultural Anthropology*. New York: Free Press, 1965.

Foster, George M. "Peasant Society and the Image of Limited Good," *American Anthropologist*, 67 (1965), 293–315.

Fowler, William. "Cognitive Learning in Infancy and Early Childhood," *Psychological Bulletin*, 59 (1962), 116–152.

Garvin, Paul (ed.). *Cognition: A Multiple Approach*. In press.

Gerlach, Luther P., and Virginia H. Hine. "Five Factors Crucial to the Growth and Spread of a Modern Religious Movement," *Journal for the Scientific Study of Religion*, 7 (1968), 23–40.

Gerard, Ralph, Clyde Kluckhohn, and Anatol Rapoport. "Biological and Cultural Evolution: Some Analogies and Explorations," *Behavioral Science*, 1 (1956), 6–34.

Gladwin, Thomas. "Canoe Travel in the Truk Area: Technology and Its Psychological Correlates," *American Anthropologist*, 60 (1958), 893–899.

Goldhamer, H., and A. Marshall. *Psychosis and Civilization*. Glencoe, Ill.: Free Press, 1953.

Goodenough, Ward H. "Componential Analysis and the Study of Meaning," *Language*, 32 (1956), 195–216.

————. *Cooperation in Change*. New York: Russell Sage, 1963. (a)

————. "Some Applications of Guttman Scale Analysis to Ethnography and Culture Theory," *Southwestern Journal of Anthropology*, 19 (1963), 235–250. (b)

————. "Rethinking Status and Role: Toward a General Model of the Cultural Organization of Social Relationships," in Michael

Banton (ed.). *The Relevance of Models for Social Anthropology.* London: Tavistock Publications, 1965.

Gorer, Geoffrey and J. Rickman. *The People of Great Russia.* London: Cresset Press, 1949.

Hallowell, A. Irving. "Personality Structure and the Evolution of Man," *American Anthropologist,* 52 (1950), 159–174.

————. "Psychology and Anthropology," in John Gillin (ed.). *For a Science of Social Man.* New York: Macmillan, 1954.

————. *Culture and Experience.* Philadelphia: University of Pennsylvania Press, 1955.

————. "The Structural and Functional Dimensions of a Human Existence," *Quarterly Review of Biology,* 31 (1956), 88–101.

————. "Behavioral Evolution and the Emergence of the Self," in *Evolution and Anthropology: A Centennial Appraisal.* Washington, D. C.: The Anthropological Society of Washington, 1959.

Haring, Douglas (ed.). *Personal Character and Cultural Milieu: A Collection of Readings.* 3rd ed. New York: Syracuse University Press, 1956.

Harper, Robert J. D., Anderson, D. C., Christensen, C. M., and Hunka, S. M., (eds.). *The Cognitive Processes: Readings.* Englewood Cliffs, N. J.: Prentice-Hall, 1964.

Hayes, Keith J., and Catharine Hayes. "The Cultural Capacity of Chimpanzees," in James A. Gavan (ed.). *The Non-Human Primates and Human Evolution.* Detroit: Wayne University Press, 1955.

Henry, Jules. "The Formal Social Structure of a Psychiatric Hospital," *Psychiatry,* 17 (1954), 139–151.

————. "Culture, Personality, and Evolution," *American Anthropologist,* 61 (1959), 221–226.

————. *Culture Against Man.* New York: Random House, 1963.

Henry, Jules, and Melford E. Spiro. "Psychological Techniques: Projective Tests in Field Work," in A. L. Kroeber (ed.). *Anthropology Today.* Chicago: University of Chicago Press, 1953.

Herskovits, Melville. *Man and His Works.* New York: Knopf, 1948.

Hess, E. H. "Imprinting," *Science,* 130 (1959), 133–141.

Hodgen, Margaret T. *Change and History.* New York: Wenner-Gren Foundation, 1952.

Hollender, Marc H., and S. J. Hirsch. "Hysterical Psychosis," *American Journal of Psychiatry*, 120 (1964), 1066-1074.

Hollingshead, August B., and Frederick C. Redlich. *Social Class and Mental Illness*. New York: Wiley, 1958.

Holloway, Ralph L., Jr. "Cranial Capacity, Neural Reorganization, and Hominid Evolution: A Search for More Suitable Parameters," *American Anthropologist*, 68 (1966), 103–121.

Honigmann, John J. *Culture and Personality*. New York: Harper & Row, 1954.

_____. *Personality in Culture*. New York: Harper & Row, 1967.

Howell, F. Clark, and Francois Bourliere (eds.). *African Ecology and Human Evolution*. Viking Fund Publications in Anthropology, No. 36. New York: Wenner-Gren Foundation, 1963.

Hsu, Francis L. K. "Anthropology or Psychiatry: A Definition of Objectives and Their Implications," *Southwestern Journal of Anthropology*, 8 (1952), 227–250.

_____ (ed.). *Aspects of Culture and Personality: A Symposium*. New York: Abelard-Schuman, 1954.

_____ (ed.). *Psychological Anthropology: Approaches to Culture and Personality*. Homewood, Ill.: Dorsey Press, 1961.

_____. *Caste, Clan, and Club*. New York: Van Nostrand, 1963.

_____. "The Effect of Dominant Kinship Relationships on Kin and Non-Kin Behavior: A Hypothesis." *American Anthropologist*, 67 (1965), 638–661.

Hughes, Charles, Tremblay, M. A., Rapoport, R. N., and Leighton, A. H. *People of Cove and Woodlot*. New York: Basic Books, 1960.

Hunt, Robert (ed.). *Personalities in Cultures: Readings in Psychological Anthropology*. New York: Natural History Press, 1967.

Huxley, Julian. *Man Stands Alone*. New York: Harper, 1941.

_____. "Evolution, Cultural and Biological," in William L. Thomas, Jr. (ed.), *Current Anthropology: A Supplement to Anthropology Today*. Chicago: University of Chicago Press, 1955.

Inkeles, Alex. "National Character: The Study of Modal Personality and Socio-cultural Systems," in G. Lindzey (ed.). *Handbook of Social Psychology*. Vol. 2. Cambridge, Mass.: Addison-Wesley, 1954.

Jahoda, Marie. *Current Concepts of Positive Mental Health.* New York: Basic Books, 1958.

Jerison, Harry J. "Brain to Body Ratios and the Evolution of Intelligence," *Science,* 121 (1955) , 447–449.

John, Vera P. "The Intellectual Development of Slum Children: Some Preliminary ·Findings," *American Journal of Orthopsychiatry,* 33 (1963), 813–822.

Kallman, Franz J. *The Genetics of Schizophrenia.* New York: J. J. Augustin, 1938.

Kaplan, Bert. "Personality and Social Structure," in J. B. Gittler (ed.). *Review of Sociology: Analysis of a Decade.* New York: Wiley, 1957.

———. (ed.). *Studying Personality Cross-Culturally.* Evanston, Ill.: Row, Peterson, 1961.

Kardiner, Abram. *The Individual and His Society.* New York: Columbia University Press, 1939.

———. *The Psychological Frontiers of Society.* New York: Columbia University Press, 1945.

Kardiner, Abram, and Lionel Ovesey. *The Mark of Oppression.* New York: Norton, 1951.

Kelleher, Roger T. "Concept Formation in Chimpanzees," *Science,* 128 (1958) , 777–778.

Kellogg, W. N. "Communication and Language in the Home-Raised Chimpanzee," *Science,* 162 (October 25, 1968) , 423–427.

Kemeny, John G., J. L. Snell, and Gerald L. Thompson. *Introduction to Finite Mathematics.* Englewood Cliffs, N. J.: Prentice-Hall, 1956.

Kety, S. S. "Biochemical Theories of Schizophrenia," *Science,* 129 (1959), 1528–1532, 1590–1596.

Kiev, Ari (ed.) . *Magic, Faith and Healing.* London: Free Press, 1964.

Klineberg, Otto. "Emotional Expression in Chinese Literature," *Journal of Abnormal and Social Psychology,* 33 (1938), 517–520.

Kluckhohn, Clyde. "The Influence of Psychiatry on Anthropology in America During the Past One Hundred Years," in J. K. Hall, G. Zilboorg, and H. A. Bunker (eds.). *One Hundred Years of American Psychiatry.* New York: Columbia University Press, 1944.

———. "Culture and Behavior," in G. Lindzey (ed.), *Handbook of Social Psychology.* Vol. 2. Cambridge, Mass.: Addison-Wesley, 1954.

Kluckhohn, Clyde, Henry A. Murray, and David M. Schneider (eds.). *Personality in Nature, Society, and Culture.* 2nd ed. New York: Knopf, 1953.

Koch, Sigmund (ed.). *Psychology: A Study of a Science.* 6 vols. New York: McGraw-Hill, 1963.

Kroeber, A. L. "The Superorganic," *American Anthropologist,* Vol. 19, No. 2 (1917).

―――――. *Cultural and Natural Areas of Native North America.* Berkeley and Los Angeles: University of California Press, 1939.

―――――. *Configurations of Culture Growth.* Berkeley and Los Angeles: University of California Press, 1944.

―――――. *Anthropology.* New York: Harcourt, Brace & World, 1948.

Kuhn, Thomas S. *The Structure of Scientific Revolutions.* Chicago: University of Chicago Press, 1962.

La Barre, Weston. *The Human Animal.* Chicago: University of Chicago Press, 1955.

―――――. "The Influence of Freud on Anthropology," *American Imago,* 15 (1958), 275–328.

Leighton, A. H., Lambo, A. T., Hughes, C. C., Leighton, D. C., Murphy, J. M., and Macklin, D. B. *Psychiatric Disorder Among the Yoruba.* Ithaca: Cornell University Press, 1963.

Leighton, A. H. "Poverty and Social Change," *Scientific American,* 212, No. 5 (1965), 21–27.

Lessa, William A., and Marvin Spiegelman. *Ulithian Personality as Seen Through Ethnological Materials and Thematic Test Analysis.* Berkeley: University of California Press, 1954.

LeVine, Robert A. *Dreams and Deeds: Achievement Motivation in Nigeria.* Chicago: University of Chicago Press, 1966.

Lévi-Strauss, Claude. "The Structural Study of Myth," *Journal of American Folklore,* 68 (1955), 428–444.

―――――. *Totemism.* Rodney Needham (tr.). Boston: Beacon Press, 1963.

―――――. *The Savage Mind.* Chicago: University of Chicago Press, 1966.

Lewis, Oscar. *The Children of Sanchez.* New York: Random House, 1961.

Lindesmith, Alfred R., and Anselm L. Strauss. "A Critique of Culture-Personality Writings," *American Sociological Review*, 15 (1950), 587–600.

Lindzey, Gardner. *Projective Techniques in Cross-Cultural Research*. New York: Appleton-Century-Crofts, 1961.

—————. (ed.). *Handbook of Social Psychology*. 2nd ed. Reading, Mass.: Wesley, 1968.

Linton, Ralph. *The Study of Man*. New York: Appleton-Century-Crofts, 1936.

—————. *The Cultural Background of Personality*. New York: Appleton-Century-Crofts, 1945.

—————. "The Change from Dry to Wet Rice Culture in Tanala-Betsileo," in T. M. Newcomb and E. L. Hartley (eds.). *Readings in Social Psychology*. New York: Holt, Rinehart and Winston, 1947.

—————. *Culture and Mental Disorders*. Springfield, Ill.: Thomas, 1956.

Lorenz, Konrad. *On Aggression*. New York: Harcourt, Brace & World, 1963.

Lounsbury, Floyd G. "A Semantic Analysis of the Pawnee Kinship Usage," *Language*, 32 (1956), 158–194.

Löwith, Karl. *Meaning in History*. Chicago: University of Chicago Press, 1949.

MacAndrew, Craig and Robert B. Edgerton. *Drunken Comportment: A Social Explanation*, Chicago: Aldine, 1969.

Malzberg, Benjamin, and E. S. Lee. *Migration and Mental Disease*. New York: Social Science Research Council, 1956.

Mandelbaum, David G. (ed.). *Selected Writings of Edward Sapir*. Berkeley: University of California Press, 1949.

Mannheim, Karl. *Ideology and Utopia*. New York: Harcourt, Brace & World, 1936.

McClelland, David C. *The Achieving Society*. New York: Free Press, 1961; reprinted 1967.

Mead, George H. *Mind, Self, and Society*. Chicago: University of Chicago Press, 1934.

Mead, Margaret. "The Concept of Culture and the Psychosomatic Approach," *Psychiatry*, 10 (1947), 57–76. (a)

————. "The Implications of Culture Change for Personality Development," *American Journal of Orthopsychiatry*, 17 (1947), 633–646. (b)

————. "National Character," in A. L. Kroeber (ed.), *Anthropology Today*. Chicago: University of Chicago Press, 1953.

————. *Cultural Patterns and Technical Change*. New York: New American Library, 1955.

————. *New Lives for Old*. New York: Morrow, 1956.

Mead, Margaret, and Rhoda Metraux (eds.). *The Study of Culture at a Distance*. Chicago: University of Chicago Press, 1953.

Miller, George. "The Magical Number Seven, Plus or Minus Two: Some Limits on Our Capacity for Processing Information," *Psychological Review*, 63 (1956), 81–97.

Miller, George, E. Galanter, and K. Pribram. *Plans and the Structure of Behavior*. New York: Holt, Rinehart and Winston, 1960.

Montagu, M. F. Ashley, and Theodosius Dobzhansky. "Natural Selection and the Mental Capacities of Mankind," *Science*, 105 (1947), 587–590.

Moore, Omar Khayyam. "Divination—A New Perspective," *American Anthropologist*, 59 (1957), 69–74.

Morris, Desmond (ed.). *Primate Ethology*. Chicago: Aldine, 1967.

Murdock, George P. *Social Structure*. New York: Macmillan, 1947.

Murphy, Jane, and A. N. Leighton. *Approaches to Cross-Cultural Psychiatry*. Ithaca, N.Y.: Cornell University Press, 1965.

Norbeck, Edward, Douglass Price-Williams, and William M. McCord (eds.). *The Study of Personality: An Interdisciplinary Appraisal*. New York: Holt, Rinehart and Winston, 1968.

Oakley, Kenneth. "Fire as Paleolithic Tool and Weapon," *Proceedings of the Prehistoric Society*, 21 (1955), 36–48.

Opler, Marvin. *Culture, Psychiatry, and Human Values*. Springfield, Ill.: Thomas, 1956.

Opler, Marvin, and J. L. Singer. "Contrasting Patterns of Fantasy and Mobility in Irish and Italian Schizophrenics," *Journal of Abnormal and Social Psychology*, 53 (1956), 42–47.

Opler, Morris. "Themes as Dynamic Forces in Culture," *American Journal of Sociology*, 51 (1945), 198–206.

Orlansky, Harold. "Infant Care and Personality," *Psychological Bulletin*, 46 (1949), 1–48.

Osgood, Charles E., George J. Suchi, and Percy H. Tannenbaum. *The Measurement of Meaning*. Urbana: University of Illinois Press, 1957.

Parsons, Talcott, and Edward Shils (eds.). *Toward a General Theory of Action*. Cambridge, Mass.: Harvard University Press, 1952.

Paul, Benjamin D. (ed.). *Health, Culture, and Community: Case Studies of Public Reactions to Health Programs*. New York: Russell Sage Foundation, 1955.

Paul, Gordon L. "Chronic Mental Patient: Current Status—Future Directions," *Psychological Bulletin,* 71 (1969), 81–94.

Pettitt, George A. *Primitive Education in North America*. Berkeley and Los Angeles: University of California Press, 1946.

Pitts, Ferris N., Jr. "The Biochemistry of Anxiety," *Scientific American,* 220 (February 1969), 69–76.

Plog, Stanley C., and Robert B. Edgerton (eds.). *Changing Perspectives in Mental Illness*. New York: Holt, Rinehart and Winston, 1969.

Potter, Van R. *Biological Disorder and the Uncertainty of Man's Future*. Englewood Cliffs, N. J.: Prentice-Hall (in press).

Rapoport, Robert N. *Changing Navaho Religious Values*. Cambridge, Mass.: Peabody Museum of American Archaeology and Ethnology, Harvard University, 1954.

Rashkis, Harold A. "A General Theory of Treatment in Psychiatry." *A.M.A. Archives of Neurology and Psychiatry,* 78 (1957), 491–499.

Redfield, Robert. "The Primitive World View," *Proceedings of the American Philosophical Society,* 96 (1952), 30–36.

————. *The Primitive World and Its Transformations*. Ithaca, N. Y.: Cornell University Press, 1953.

Reich, Wilhelm. *Selected Writings: An Introduction to Orgonomy*. New York: Farrar, Straus and Cudahy, 1960.

Reina, Ruben. "Political Crisis and Revitalization: The Guatemalan Case," *Human Organization,* 17 (1958), 14–18.

Riesman, David. *The Lonely Crowd: A Study of the Changing American Character*. New Haven, Conn.: Yale University Press, 1950.

Roheim, Geza. *The Origin and Function of Culture*. New York: Nervous and Mental Disease Monographs, No. 69, 1943.

Rubel, Arthur J. "The Epidemiology of a Folk Illness: Susto in Hispanic America," *Ethnology,* 3 (1964), 268–283.

Sabloff, Jeremy, and Robert E. Smith. "Ceramic Wares in the Maya Area: A Clarification of an Aspect of the Type-Variety System and Presentation of a Formal Model for Comparative Use." In press.

Sapir, Edward. See Mandelbaum, David G.

Sahlins, Marshall D., and Elman R. Service (eds.). *Evolution and Culture*. Ann Arbor: University of Michigan Press, 1960.

Sarason, Seymour B., and Thomas Gladwin. *Psychological and Cultural Problems in Mental Subnormality: A Review of Research*. Genetic Psychology Monographs, No. 57, 1958.

————. *Psychological Problems in Mental Deficiency*. 3rd ed. New York: Harper, 1959.

Sargant, S. Stansfeld, and Marian W. Smith (eds.). *Culture and Personality*. New York: Viking Fund, 1949.

Sargant, William. *Battle for the Mind*. New York: Doubleday, 1957.

Schaller, George B. *The Mountain Gorilla: Ecology and Behavior*. Chicago: University of Chicago Press, 1963.

Scheerer, Martin. "Cognitive Theory," in G. Lindzey (ed.), *Handbook of Social Psychology*. Vol. 1. Cambridge, Mass.: Addison-Wesley, 1954.

Schilder, Paul. *The Image and Appearance of the Human Body*. London: Kegan Paul and Trench, Trubner, 1935.

Schultz, Adolph H. "The Specializations of Man and His Place Among the Catarrhine Primates," in *Origin and Evolution of Man*. Cold Spring Harbor, N. Y.: Symposia on Quantitative Biology, Vol. 15, 1950.

Sears, R., E. Macoby, and N. Levin. *Patterns of Child Rearing*. Evanston, Ill.: Row, Peterson, 1957.

Sewell, William H. "Infant-Training and the Personality of the Child," *American Journal of Sociology*, 58 (1952), 150–159.

Simpson, George G. *The Meaning of Evolution*. New Haven, Conn.: Yale University Press, 1949.

Spicer, Edward H. *Human Problems in Technological Change*. New York: Russell Sage Foundation, 1952.

Spindler, George D. *Sociocultural and Psychological Processes in Menominee Acculturation*. Berkeley and Los Angeles: University of California Press, 1955.

Spiro, Melford E. "Culture and Personality: The Natural History of a False Dichotomy," *Psychiatry*, 14 (1951), 19–46.

————. "Ghosts, Ifaluk, and Teleological Functionalism," *American Anthropologist*, 54 (1952), 497–503.

————. "Human Nature in Its Psychological Dimensions," *American Anthropologist*, 56 (1954), 19–30.

Spuhler, J. N. (ed.). *The Evolution of Man's Capacity for Culture.* Detroit: Wayne State University Press, 1959.

Stein, Maurice, A. J. Vidich, and D. M. White (eds.). *Identity and Anxiety.* Glencoe, Ill.: Free Press, 1960.

Szasz, Thomas S. "The Myth of Mental Illness," *American Psychologist*, 15 (1960), 113–118.

Tappen, Neil C. "A Mechanistic Theory of Human Evolution," *American Anthropologist*, 55 (1953), 605–607.

Tiger, Lionel. *Men in Groups.* New York: Random House, 1969.

Tolman, E. D. "Cognitive Maps in Rats and Men," *Psychological Review*, 55 (1948), 189–208.

Tooth, Geoffrey. *Studies in Mental Illness in the Gold Coast.* London: H. M. Stationery Office, 1950.

Turner, Victor. "Myth and Symbol," *International Encyclopedia of the Social Sciences.* 1967.

————. *The Ritual Process: Structure and Anti-Structure.* Chicago: Aldine, 1969.

Tyler, Stephen A. *Cognitive Anthropology.* New York: Holt, Rinehart and Winston, 1969.

Tylor, Edward B. *Primitive Culture: Researches into the Development of Mythology, Philosophy, Religion, Language, Art and Custom.* 2 vols. New York, 1874.

————. *Anthropology.* New York: Appleton-Century-Crofts, 1900.

Vogt, Evon, and E. M. Albert (eds.). *People of Rimrock: A Study of Values in Five Cultures.* Cambridge, Mass.: Harvard University Press, 1966.

Von Mering, Otto and Leonard Kasdan (eds.). *Anthropology and the Behavioral and Health Sciences.* Pittsburgh: University of Pittsburgh Press, 1970.

Wallace, Anthony F. C. "Some Psychological Determinants of Culture Change in an Iroquoian Community," in W. N. Fenton (ed.). *Symposium on Local Diversity in Iroquois Culture.* Washington: Bulletin 149, Bureau of American Ethnology, 1951.

————. *The Modal Personality Structure of the Tuscarora Indians, As Revealed by the Rorschach Test*. Washington: Bulletin 150, Bureau of American Ethnology, 1952. (a)

————. "Individual Differences and Cultural Uniformities," *American Sociological Review*, 17 (1952), 747–750.

————. "Mazeway Resynthesis: A Bio-Cultural Theory of Religious Inspiration," *Transactions of the New York Academy of Sciences*, 18 (1956), 626–638. (a)

————. "Stress and Rapid Personality Changes," *International Record of Medicine*, 169 (1956), 761–774.

————. "Revitalization Movements," *American Anthropologist*, 58 (1956), 264–281.

————. *Tornado in Worcester: An Exploratory Study of Individual and Community Behavior in an Extreme Situation*. Washington: National Academy of Sciences—National Research Council, 1956. (d)

————. "Mazeway Disintegration: The Individual's Perception of Socio-Cultural Disorganization," *Human Organization*, 16 (1957), 23–27.

————. "Dreams and the Wishes of the Soul: A Type of Psychoanalytic Theory Among the Seventeenth Century Iroquois," *American Anthropologist*, 60 (1958), 234–248.

————. "Cultural Determinants of Response to Hallucinatory Experience," *A.M.A. Archives of General Psychiatry*, 1 (1959), 58–69.

————. "The Institutionalization of Cathartic and Control Strategies in Iroquois Religious Psychotherapy," in Marvin Opler (ed.). *Culture and Mental Health*. New York: Macmillan, 1960. (a)

————. "The Bio-Cultural Theory of Schizophrenia," *International Record of Medicine*, 173 (1960), 700–714.

————. "The Psychic Unity of Human Groups," in Bert Kaplan (ed.). *Studying Personality Cross-Culturally*. Evanston, Ill.: Row, Peterson, 1961. (a)

————. "On Being Just Complicated Enough," *Proceedings of the National Academy of Sciences*, 47 (1961), 458–464. (b)

————. "Culture and Cognition," *Science*, 135 (1962), 351–357.

————. "Driving to Work," in Melford E. Spiro (ed.). *Context and Meaning in Cultural Anthropology*. New York: Free Press, 1965.

_____. *Religion: An Anthropological View.* New York: Random House, 1966.

_____. "Identity Processes in Personality and in Culture," in Richard Jessor and Seymour Feshback (eds.). *Cognition, Personality, and Clinical Psychology.* San Francisco: Jossey-Bass, 1967.

_____. "Anthropological Contributions to the Theory of Personality," in Edward Norbeck, Douglass Price-Williams, and William M. McCord (eds.). *The Study of Personality: An Interdisciplinary Appraisal.* New York: Holt, Rinehart and Winston, 1968.

_____. *The Death and Rebirth of the Seneca.* New York: Knopf, 1970.

_____. "A Relational Analysis of American Kinship Terminology," *American Anthropologist* (1970).

_____, and John Atkins. "The Meaning of Kinship Terms," *American Anthropologist,* 62 (1960), 58–80.

_____, and H. A. Rashkis. "The Relation Between Staff Consensus and Patient Disturbance on Mental Hospital Wards," *American Sociological Review,* 24 (1959), 829–835.

Wallis, Wilson D. *Culture and Progress.* New York: McGraw-Hill, 1930.

Washburn, S. L., and F. C. Howell. "Human Evolution and Culture," in Sol Tax (ed.). *The Evolution of Man.* Vol. 2 of *Evolution After Darwin.* Chicago: University of Chicago Press, 1960.

Weber, Max. *The Protestant Ethic and the Spirit of Capitalism.* New York: Scribner, 1930.

Wechsler, David. "The Range of Human Capacities," *Scientific Monthly,* 31 (1930), 35–39.

Wegrocki, Henry J. "A Critique of Cultural and Statistical Concepts of Abnormality," *Journal of Abnormal and Social Psychology,* 1934 (1939), 166–178.

Weil, Andre. "On the Algebraic Study of Certain Types of Marriage Law (Murngin's System)," in Harrison C. White. *An Anatomy of Kinship.* Englewood Cliffs, N. J.: Prentice-Hall, 1963, 151–157.

White, Harrison. *An Anatomy of Kinship.* Englewood Cliffs, N. J.: Prentice-Hall, 1963.

White, Leslie. *The Science of Culture.* New York: Farrar, Strauss, 1949.

_____. "The Concept of Culture," *American Anthropologist,* 61 (1959), 227–251.

Whiting, Beatrice. *Six Cultures: Studies of Child Rearing.* New York: Wiley, 1963.

Whiting, John W. M. *Becoming a Kwoma.* New Haven, Conn.: Yale University Press, 1941.

Whiting, John W. M., and Irving Child. *Child Training and Personality.* New Haven, Conn.: Yale University Press, 1953.

Whiting, John W. M., I. L. Child, and W. W. Lambert. *Field Guide for a Study of Socialization.* Vol. 1 of the Six Cultures Series. New York: Wiley, 1966.

Whorf, Benjamin Lee. *Language, Thought, and Reality.* New York: Wiley, 1956.

Wolfenstein, Martha. *Disaster: A Psychological Essay.* Glencoe, Ill.: Free Press, 1957.

Wright, Sewall. "Evolution in Mendelian Populations," *Genetics,* 16 (1931), 97–159.

Index

265

ABOUT THE AUTHOR

ANTHONY F. C. WALLACE is Professor of Anthropology at the University of Pennsylvania, where he has taught since 1955. He has served as Director of Clinical Research at the Eastern Pennsylvania Psychiatric Institute and as a consultant for numerous governmental agencies. His other books include *Religion: An Anthropological View* and *The Death and Rebirth of the Seneca*.